PARALLELS:

MESOAMERICAN AND ANCIENT MIDDLE EASTERN TRADITIONS

By

Diane E. Wirth

Stonecliff Publishing

Dedicated to the Maya

Cover:
 Left: Incense burner with bearded dignitary
  from Iximché, Guatemala (photograph courtesy
  of Musée de l'Homme, Paris).
 Right: Maya king, K'inich Ahkal Mo' Naab',
  Tablet of the Slaves, Palenque, Chiapas, Mexico
  (photograph by Arpad Elfer).

© 2003 Diane E. Wirth

Illustrations by Diane E. Wirth unless otherwise specified.

ISBN 0-9602096-0-3 (softbound)

Library of Congress Control Number: 2003090603

First Edition

Printed in the United States of America

ACKNOWLEDGMENTS

The findings of archaeologists, anthropologists, theologians, linguists, folklorists, epigraphers, iconographers, and other scholars are cited in this book to piece together symbols and their related traditions that link ancient cultures of the Middle East and Mesoamerica together in an unprecedented manner. To the authors of these innumerable articles and books, I owe more than a listing in a bibliography. The majority of these scholars do not advocate the theory proposed in this work that ancient voyages were made to the western hemisphere. However, by combining the details of ethnic traditions, one finds an amazing number of cultural similarities between the regions considered. The analyses and investigations of individuals cited in this book are used to support the plausibility of this hypothesis by stressing the many parallels that are common to both Near Eastern and Mesoamerican cultures.

In addition to my gratitude for the vast amount of research accomplished by those cited, my thanks go to Linda Schele, Michael Coe, Garth Norman, and Tom Weller for use of their drawings, and to Harvard's Peabody Museum and the Musée de l'Homme for permission to use photographs. In order of their reading the manuscript, a special thank you to Brian Stross, Stephanie Sher, Allen Christenson, John Tvedtnes and John Gee who reviewed the text and offered comments and valuable suggestions. Larry Brady of Impact Manuscripts, Inc., was instrumental in editing most of the text. My thanks also to Merle Greene-Robertson, David Stuart, and Michael Coe for reviewing working papers in their early stages, which later developed into individual chapters. John Welch suggested guidelines on format which are greatly appreciated.

"Within orthodox academics there are a lot of people who simply dismiss the argument out of hand on the ground that the mechanics of overseas diffusion themselves are too difficult. But there are others—and I put myself in that group—who don't doubt there's been contact. I don't think that the transport problems are such that they prevented people from moving between continents."

Arthur Demarest of Vanderbilt University
quoted by Mark K. Stengel, "The Diffusionists Have Landed,"
The Atlantic Monthly 285/1 (2000), 47.

"It is true that books on archaeology of Jerusalem, including my own, now contain a lot of misinformation. More bluntly, they are wrong. The lesson: The archaeological story is never finished."

Hershel Shanks, "Everything You Ever Knew About Jerusalem is Wrong,"
Biblical Archaeology Review 25/6 (1999), 20.

CONTENTS

INTRODUCTION

There are two major schools of thought as to how the Americas were populated. Traditionally in modern academia there is the theory of isolationism, which holds to the tenet that Asians crossed the Bering Land Bridge thousands of years ago, eventually filtering down through North, Middle, and South America. An alternative hypothesis is the theory of diffusionism, which is based on the concept of a mixing of indigenous cultures with small groups of foreigners who arrived as a result of early voyages to the Americas long before Columbus made the claim of being the first. This inter-hemispheric proposition is not widely accepted, although mounting evidence is impressive.[1]

The Controversy

Most laymen are unaware of the ongoing controversy between the archaeological establishment and the diffusionists, which takes the form of verbal and written attacks on each other's research. In medieval times scientists were burned at the stake or imprisoned for their outlandish theories that were unacceptable to their peers. Today such things are often replaced with ostracism, and until traditional pre-Columbianists accept the challenge of new findings with their relevancy to this field of study, the heated debate will no doubt continue.

The Isolationists

On occasion, mainstream isolationists write articles and books filled with remarks that are most unprofessional. For example, in March 1979 *American Anthropologist* published "Biological Analogy, Diffusionism, and Archaeology," by Godfrey and Cole.[2] Negative expressions used in this article regarding diffusionist research include: "faulty analogy," "questionable," "unorthodox," "popular infatuation," "discredited ideas," and so on. This cynical condemnation has been going on for years and continues to be popular today. A case in point is an article by Frost entitled "Voyages of the Imagination," appearing in *Archaeology,* March/April 1993.[3] Cartoon illustrations used in this piece set the tone for Frost's scathing remarks against diffusionists. Some of the phrases he uses are "lunatic logic," "feverish speculation," "runaway branch of the theory of diffusionism," and "radical diffusionist sympathies."

In addition to these comments, diffusionists have been called racists. Today this popular notion is communicated on the Internet in archaeology oriented lists and newsgroups. Scholars who express such views believe that diffusionists (referred to as hyperdiffusionists or neodiffusionists), give sole credit to Old World peoples for the building of New World civilizations. Some diffusionists hold to this groundless theory, yet most serious diffusionists acknowledge early crossings over the Bering Land Bridge to the Americas. They recognize achievements of the indigenous cultures for their civilization as well as an occasional foreign infiltration. The concept of diffusionism is not intended to be racist. Europeans experienced the influence of foreigners (Romans, Huns, Moors, Arabs, etc.), who had occasion to live in their lands. Many foreign cultures left their traditions in Europe. To accept and admit this historical verity is not considered an insult nor a racist attitude.

A Hypothesis

An example of diffusion to the Americas may have involved a boatload of people—let us say anywhere from a small crew up to one hundred individuals. Hypothetically speaking, if this seagoing vessel were Phoenician, its crew may have been composed of Egyptians, Africans, Greeks and, of course, Phoenicians as well and possibly other Mediterranean peoples. Such a group arriving on the shores of the western hemisphere may have shared with the natives various traditions that would eventually be assimilated with those existing in the New World. These seafaring voyagers certainly would not remodel any civilizations that already prevailed prior to their arrival. Native cultures in the process of developing their own civilizations would accept or reject foreign imports as needed. Therefore, the outcome of early transoceanic voyages may have resulted in a foreign cultural influence, not a complete makeover of cultural mores, religion, art, and architecture. In other words, the diffusionist proposes a merging with the indigenous system and does not negate the concept of native independent invention—one of the major criticisms of isolationists against diffusionists.

The above hypothetical scenario cannot be compared to the arrival of Spaniards and the culturally disruptive effect of the Spanish Conquest. The Spanish brought powerful weapons of war, and a continuous stream of people arrived from their homeland having the intent of colonizing and taking the new land for their own purposes. If the original landing of some 200 conquistadors had been the only contact (without rifles, military reenforcements, women, and fortune seekers), a profound difference in Latin America during the sixteenth century would be seen from what is recorded in our history books.

The Diffusionists

In all fairness, those who support the theory of diffusionism are not exempt from attacking conservative scholars who promote the more popular theory of isolationism. Diffusionists use words such as "academic snobbery," "block-headed attitudes," and "narrow-mindedness," to describe the world of their traditional opponents. More would be accomplished if both sides would engage in constructive discussions, examine the data, and attempt to understand each other's point of view. Such a symposium and debate was sponsored in Georgia by the Institute for the Study of American Cultures at the Columbus Museum in April 1993, in hope of having more mature and comprehensive discussions of this complex subject in the future.

Dr. Michael Coe is an esteemed Mesoamericanist and Curator of Anthropology in the Peabody Museum at Yale University. He is not a full-blown diffusionist, yet he admits a leaning towards the plausibility of Mesoamerican connections with the Far East and Southeast Asia and remains receptive to a broad range of interpretations. According to the January/February 1996 issue of *America Magazine*,[4] Coe speaks of parallels he notes between Indonesian and Mesoamerican cosmology systems, calendrics, and jade usage. In Coe's recentbook, *The Art of the Maya Scribe*, he notes that Chinese, Japanese, Egyptian, and Maya calligraphic traditions contain similarities.[5] Explaining the difficulty of keeping an open mind in his field of expertise, Coe remarks in the *America Magazine's* interview, "There used to be more freedom of thought and expression, less worry about what peers said. Today there's sort of an academic mafia that runs things."[6]

This, too, is the plight of most diffusionist researchers. Jett, a diffusionist who teaches at the University of California at Davis, also makes a good point: "Perhaps most scholars of the present generation will never accept the occurrence of meaningful transoceanic contacts, no matter how convincing the circumstantial evidence—not for intellectual reasons, but for psychological and cultural ones."[7]

Those who adhere to the theory of diffusionism collect data that they believe contributes to the plausibility of pre-Columbian voyages. Perhaps significantly, most diffusionists do not exclude the Bering Land Bridge as a route to the Americas but maintain that, in addition to this early group of travelers to the Americas, people from other cultures came across the seas. Most of the evidence is tangible such as flora and fauna with genetically linked counterparts in the Old World. Also, included in this category, are inscriptions and artifacts. Parallel traditions too are of great importance, but their study is less pursued or assessed in quantifiable terms.

Scholarly Solutions

The academic establishment postulates various solutions to the diffusionist issue; e.g., (1) evidence used to support diffusionist ideas are the result of deception; (2) observational logic leads people to similar independent conclusions; or (3) if the evidence is valid, parallel developments are merely coincidental and may be a result of the human psyche. The latter hypothesis was developed by the famous psychologist Carl Jung, who referred to the cause of culturally parallel phenomena as the collective unconscious. In other words, cultural preferences common to both the Old and New Worlds are due to certain innate qualities that are part of human nature. That being the case, these parallels may occur anywhere in the world in complete isolation. In part, this may be true, but it certainly is not an all-encompassing answer to similar conceptions, especially when these traits are specific and part of a complex of ideas or motifs handled in identical or nearly identical ways.

Researchers, such as Frazer, Eliade, and Campbell examine Old World societies with one another, yet only briefly mention the grand civilizations of the Americas. Studies of the western world are relatively new compared with cultures of the Old World. The latter hold well-established theories regarding traditions as a result of hundreds of years of research.

The Various Disciplines

The region of Mesoamerica is of particular interest in this book and covers an area wherein high cultures existed in pre-Columbian times, stretching from north-central Mexico to Costa Rica. Fortunately, Mesoamerican studies are increasing at a rapid pace. In-depth studies are now widespread and are no longer carried out solely by archaeologists as in years past. Scientific advancements, and especially breakthroughs in hieroglyphic and iconographic decipherment, serve as the catalyst.[8] Epigraphy and art history are now two disciplines crucial to the understanding of Mesoamerican cultures.

Anthropology and Genetics

Anthropology is also an important discipline in Mesoamerican studies. Although much needs to be accomplished in this area, there are researchers who draw some interesting conclusions regarding the physical attributes of Native Americans. Geneticists are making progress to determine the origin of the Native American. A DNA study reported by Morell indicates that a minimum of eleven biological lines existed in pre-Columbian America.[9] Douglas C. Wallace and his colleagues at Emory University in Atlanta found that some Native Americans may have ancestors from Polynesia. This is based on results of DNA studies and how prehistoric migrations relate to each other. This researcher suggests that groups of ancient mariners came to the Americas from Southeast Asia, not solely over the Bering Land Bridge, as anthropologists have long held to be the case. A news item on this subject by Bishop appeared on the front page of *The Wall Street Journal*, November 10, 1993. In his concluding remarks Bishop writes, "mtDNA is turning into a kind of biological Rosetta Stone for decoding human origins."[10]

Recent news breaking research in genetic studies also comes to us from Morell, who states:

Now a new genetic study may link Native Americans and people of Europe and the Middle East, offering tantalizing support to a controversial theory that a band of people who originally lived in Europe or Asia Minor were among this continent's first settlers. The new data comes from studies of a genetic marker called Lineage X, which has been found both in living Native Americans and in certain groups in Europe and Asia Minor, including Italians, Finns, and certain Israelis—but not in any Asian population.[11]

Continued efforts in this field should prove to be most interesting, although tests must be performed on a wide range of pre-Columbian remains to make an equitable determination. Nevertheless, there will always exist two sides of a coin, and scientists may agree or disagree according to their methods of research.

Seafaring

The Bering Land Bridge represents one avenue by which the Americas became populated—but only one. In a book published by the University of New Mexico, James Dixon demonstrates from onsite research that Beringia could not have been the route responsible for the earliest migrations to the Americas. He even considers the plausibility of watercraft as a means of early voyages to the western hemisphere.[12] In fact, without the land bridge, this is his only alternative hypothesis. Seafaring vessels of the ancient world should not be disregarded or underestimated.

Both the Egyptians and the Phoenicians constructed vessels capable of reaching the New World (Figs. 1 and 2); in fact, the Phoenician ships of Tarshish, according to Middle Eastern specialist Gordon, were far more seaworthy than Heyerdahl's "extravaganzas."[13] Except for Patai's excellent work on Jewish navigation in ancient times, little is written on this subject about the Hebrews' seafaring capability.[14] Barely acknowledged is the fact that the Hebrews built ships. Many researchers assumed they were strictly a landlocked people. Hoever, Patai conclusively demonstrates this certainly was not the case (Fig. 3).

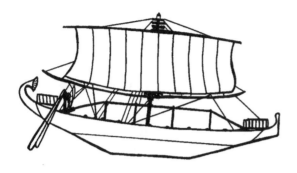

Fig. 1   Egyptian seagoing vessel, 15th century B.C. (redrawn after Gordon 1974: Plate 2).

Fig. 2   Phoenician merchant ship, 1500 to 300 B.C. (redrawn after G. Thompson 1992: 140).

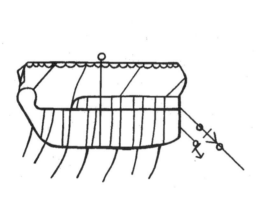

a.

b.

Fig. 3   Ships from Israel: a. Drawing 3rd century B.C., Mareshah, southwest of Jerusalem; b. Sketch on wall in the Beth-Shearim catacombs near Haifa (redrawn after Patai 1998: 31 and 24 respectively).

The Hebrews had a long naval history. In fact, three of the twelve tribes of Israel are referred to in the Bible as having maritime capabilities. Southwest Asia also had very competent water craft and, although small in size, were actually more seaworthy than larger vessels.[15] Anyone familiar with ocean currents should consider the possibility of transoceanic excursions (Fig. 4).

R. H. Francé writes: "The sea taught man how to conquer distance and opened before him a road around the globe."[16] How far these ancient ships traveled from their ports is a question we must consider. Patai remarks, "Large and dangerous as the Mediterranean was for ancient seafarers, they nevertheless, willy-nilly, ventured beyond it into the unknown waters of the faraway Atlantic Ocean."[17] Yet many scholars remain reluctant to accept the idea of ancient crossings.

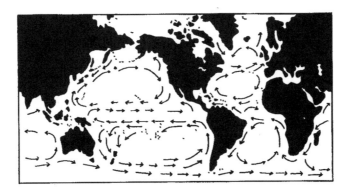

Fig. 4   Ocean currents (redrawn after Jett 1978).

Parallel Traditions

Although the great religious historian, Eliade, never proposed cultural diffusion from the Middle East to the western hemisphere to explain parallel traditions, he did state the following:

> . . . certain myths and symbols have circulated throughout the world . . . this means that those myths and symbols are not, as such, spontaneous discoveries of archaic man, but creations of a well defined cultural complex, elaborated and carried on in certain human societies: such creations have been diffused very far from their original home and have been assimilated by peoples who would not otherwise have known them.[18]

For an excellent bibliography of books, articles, and papers that support pre-Columbian voyages to the Americas, the reader is referred to *Pre-Columbian Contact with the Americas Across the Ocean: An Annotated Bibliography* by Sorenson and Raish.[19] This bibliography contains more than 5,000 references on the subject of diffusionism and is a veritable mine of source material on similarities between pre-Columbian America and ancient cultures across the sea.

The many similarities in symbols and traditions of all ancient cultures call for serious investigation. Those that prove to be exactly the same—oceans apart—cannot always be attributed to coincidence, isolation, or human psychological unity. In his chapter on Hebrew Installation Rites, Patai explains how the study of ritual conventions relating to kingship found in the Nilotic Sudan and West Africa tribes, led him to understand that these traditions originated in the ancient Near East.[20] Some of the key features listed by Patai that correspond to rites in the Near East confirm that there were ceremonies symbolizing the king's death and rebirth; the king received a new name at the time of his accession to the throne; ritual fights were performed for the public; the king planted his life tree; the king received certain regalia; fires were extinguished and rekindled as the king took his throne; and human sacrifices substituted for the king's symbolic death.[21] These ritual practices may also be found in Mesoamerica.

The following chapters take a wider view than most books on diffusionism and correlate traditions of both the east and the west with a concentration on Mesoamerican and Middle Eastern art, festivals, and religion. We notice, however, that not all belief systems among the various cultures of Mexico and Central America were pan-Mesoamerican in nature. Each locale and group of people had its own perspective on cosmology, religion, warfare, and politics; yet, there are certain traditions that held sway throughout Mesoamerica. These include the concept of a World Tree, ancestral worship, and the ballgame rite. Buying, selling, and exchanging marketable goods by merchants on long-distancetrade routes were key methods by which ideologies were spread from one geographical area to another in ancient Mesoamerica. Each culture, in its own right, was well defined.

This same type of relevancy also holds true for the surrounding areas of the Middle East. For example, Witt writes: "Our Western World's Graeco-Roman and Christian civilization emerged and taken shape out of the cultural melting pot of the Near East. Historians, however, have not always acknowledged how potent a factor in this process was the religion of Egypt."[22] This is particularly true of Mediterranean traditions occasionally mentioned in following chapters that were strongly influenced by Egypt. In fact, most of the cultural connections in this book are between Mesoamerica and Egypt, while others from the Middle East and the Mediterranean are worthy of note and are included in this study.

Admittedly, it proves to be more difficult to coordinate Middle Eastern traditions or myths that are recorded in texts or alluded to in artistic renditions, which do not appear to be close to the time frame of some of their counterparts in the New World. The first occurrence in a historical or religious context cannot be determined as to when the concept or tradition originated. We must acknowledge that Mesoamerican oral traditions preceded their iconography and epigraphy. Texts, especially, bring us closer to a date commensurate with data from the Near East.

The mounting number of parallels, down to the minutest detail in some cases, may persuade some members of the archaeological establishment to consider an alternative to the origin (or at least an outside influence) of some Native American traditions.

NOTES - Introduction

1. See, for example, John L. Sorenson and Martin H. Raish, *Pre-Columbian Contacts with the Americas Across the Ocean: An Annotated Bibliography*, 2 volumes (Provo, Utah: F.A.R.M.S, 1996).

2. Laurie R. Godfrey and John Cole, "Biological Analogy, Diffusionism, and Archaeology," in *American Anthropologist* 81/3 (1979), 37-42.

3. Frank J. Frost, "Voyages of the Imagination," in *Archaeology* 46/2 (1993), 41-51.

4. Caleb Bach, "Michael Coe: A Question for every Answer," in *America Magazine* 48/1 (1996), 14-21.

5. Michael D. Coe and Justin Kerr, *The Art of the Maya Scribe* (New York: Harry N. Abrams, Inc., 1998), 146-47, 171, 173.

6. Bach, 21.

7. Stephen C. Jett, "Comments on Covey's 'The Egypto-Libyan Presence in PreColumbian America,'" in *Midwestern Epigraphic Journal* 10/1 (1996), 38.

8. Michael D. Coe, *Breaking the Maya Code* (New York: Thames and Hudson, 1992).

9. Virginia Morell, "Research News: Confusion in Earliest America," in *Science* 248 (27 April 1990), 439- 41.

10. Jerry E. Bishop, "Strands of Time: A Geneticist's Work on DNA Bears Fruit for Anthropologists," in *Wall Street Journal* CCXXII/93, November 10.

11. Virginia Morell, "Genes May Link Ancient Eurasians, Native Americas," in *The American Association for the Advancement of Science* 280/5363 (1998), 520.

12. E. James Dixon, *Quest for the Origins of the First Americans* (Albuquerque: University of New Mexico, 1993), 120.

13. Cyrus H. Gordon, "A Hebrew Inscription Authenticated," in *By Study and Also by Faith*, vol. 1, John M. Lundquist and Stephen D., Ricks, eds. (Salt Lake City: Deseret Book Company, and Provo, Utah: FARMS, 1990), 75.

14. Raphael Patai, *The Children of Noah: Jewish Seafaring in Ancient Times* (Princeton: Princeton University Press, 1998).

15. Stephen C. Jett, "Pre-Columbian Transoceanic Contacts," in *Ancient Native Americans*, Jesse D. Jennings, ed. (San Francisco: W. H. Freeman and Company, 1978), 595.

16. Raoul Heinrich Francé, *Das Buch des Lebens* (Berlin, 1924), 146.

17. Patai, *The Children of Noah*, xviii.

18. Mircea Eliade, *Images and Symbols: Studies in Religious Symbolism*, trans. Willard R. Trask (London: Harvill Press, 1961), 34.

19. Sorenson and Raish.

20. Raphael Patai, *On Jewish Folklore* (Detroit: Wayne State University Press, 1983), 110-73.

21. Ibid., 113.

22. R. E. Witt, *Isis in the Ancient World* (Baltimore, Maryland: John Hopkins University, 1997), 11.

CHAPTER I

BEARDED FOREIGNERS?

Seldom seen in Mesoamerican coffee table books or in museum exhibits of Mesoamerican art, are bearded figures, which are apparently a cultural enigma. Except for a scanty growth of facial hair, Native Americans cannot grow a sufficient amount of hair to produce full beards. They can, however, grow sparse facial hairs that, in ancient times, were often plucked.[1] Few comments are made on pre-Columbian art objects that portray men with beards. On occasion these pieces are referred to as elderly or wise individuals—because of their beards. Even so, there is little basis for such statements. Men who grow beards in their later years can certainly grow them in their prime.

Beards Not Typical

Although portraits of bearded men are in the minority, hundreds were found in the ancient ruins of Mesoamerica. Either some natives just happened to look non-Native American, or a foreign element came into this part of the world. A number of bearded individuals from Mesoamerica are shown in this chapter to strengthen the supposition that foreigners were present. These pieces of art portraying bearded men are found in a variety of media including terracotta, stone, and screen-folded picture books called codices.

There is quite a diversity of physiognomic types among Mesoamericans, as is demonstrated in their artistic record. Each geographical area exhibited a special look, or visage, that was predominant. Many ancient Maya Indians, for example, deformed the heads of infants causing a sloping forehead. The Maya also had large but soft curving noses, and nearly hairless chins (Fig. I.1). However, an early Maya ruler of Palenque, Chiapas, Mexico, does not fit this physical type (Fig. I.2). This full-bearded dignitary is often referred to as Casper, due to the visual similarity of a glyph associated with this ruler to Casper the Friendly Ghost (see insert, Fig. I.2).[2] The date of Casper's accession to the throne is 435 A.D., making him the second known ruler of Palenque.[3] Casper does not appear to be of typical Maya lineage.

Fig. I.1 K'inich Ahkal Mo' Naab, Tablet of the Slaves, Palenque, Chiapas, Mexico (drawn after photograph).

Fig. I.2 Maya ruler on onyx bowl (drawn after photograph, Bliss Collection, Dumbarton Oaks, Washington, D.C.).

Commenting on a bearded figure from Tepatlazco, Veracruz (Fig. I.3), Burland writes: "Most of the bearded figures in older Mexican art are found in Olmec and Totonac material, near the Gulf Coast. They may represent some tradition, or even a physical inheritance, from a few drift voyages from the Old World."[4]

Giving careful consideration to the bearded figure on a ballgame yoke (Fig. I.4), Berjonneau and Sonnery surmise: "On this yoke fragment, strange profiles appear that do not seem to be native ones. In Mesoamerican art it is not unusual to find faces with somewhat 'Negroid,' 'Semitic' or 'Chinese' features. Is this the result of particular stylizations or could it suggest intercontinental contacts?"[5]

The Museum of Primitive Art in New York saw an enigmatic dilemma in the genetic makeup of a man depicted in a beautiful wood carving (Fig. I.5). They find the piece raises a difficult problem, "for although beards were often depicted in Mesoamerican art, representations of mustaches are not common. . . . It raises the often argued question whether the Mongoloid Native American had sufficient facial hair to grow a heavy beard—or mustache such as this."[6] Another important factor concerning this particular sculpture is the man's bald head. The propensity for baldness is from a gene carried on the mother's X chromosome which she receives from her father. Native Americans do not become bald, yet this sculpture and others such as that of Yax Pas of Copan, are (Fig. I.6).

Fig. I.3 Ballplayer with false beard on stela from Tepatlaxco, Veracruz, Mexico (drawn after photograph).

Fig. I.4 Bearded man on end of yoke fragment, Veracruz, Mexico (redrawn after Berjoneau & Sonnery 1985: 64).

Fig. I.5 Wood sculpture, Maya bald-headed lord with mustache, Tabasco, Mexico (drawn after photograph in M. Coe 1987: 86).

Fig. I.6 Stela 11, Yax Pas, a ruler of Copan, Honduras (redrawn after B. Fash in Baudez 1994: Fig. 98).

False Beards

The portraits shown in this chapter are from various cultures throughout Mesoamerica. A few clearly wear false beards as was the custom among rulers in Egypt and China.[7] Perhaps some Mesoamericans wore false beards to emulate lineages for whom facial hair was a natural phenomena. False beards were ubiquitous in the art of the Mixtec of Oaxaca, Mexico, whose history is documented as early as 692 A.D. One of their accordion-like picture books called the *Codex Nuttall* is filled with such portraits (Fig. I.7). Nevertheless, a great many of the men sporting beards in Mesoamerica do not wear false beards.

Fig. I.7 Bearded Mixtec warrior (redrawn after
Codex Nuttall).

What Happened?

Some bearded figures appear among the early Olmec culture (1500–400 B.C., see for example Fig. I.11); however, a study by Magelby shows there was a preponderance of bearded figures in the Classic Period (300–900 A.D.) of Mesoamerica, with a diminishing number after that time.[8] Apparently not many men were capable of growing full beards by the time of the Spanish Conquest in 1521.

A few Aztec rulers are shown with beards but, for the most part, by the time of the Conquest any foreigners from earlier voyages would have integrated with the natives through marriage. They may even have been annihilated through sacrifice, war, famine, disease, or other unknown factors. In fact, there are a few statements, independent of one another, that note those men with a white skin were sacrificed in Mexico. The first is from Father Sahagún, a sixteenth century ethnographer who writes of a ritual sacrifice performed at the eclipse of the sun in which he states: "When the sun is eclipsed—they then raise a tumult. . . . And then they hunt out men of fair hair and white faces; and they sacrifice them to the sun."[9] Another source is recorded in Lord Kingsborough's work regarding the sixteenth century native historian, Ixtlilxochitl, in his discourse on "The Tultec Kings and their Destruction." He indicates this tradition: "There was a law that wherever a child was born that was very white and blond, when it was five years of age it was right away sacrificed. This law lasted until the coming of the Spaniards."[10]

Chavero comments in his 1891–1892 work, *Obras Históricas de Ixtlilxochitl,* that, Tezozómoc, another native historian, made frequent reference to the sacrifice of white children at the center of Lake Pantitlan, which practice may have originated with the Toltec.[11] Were those determined as being fair or white also those who were capable of growing beards? One cannot say, but the remarks of these historians are noted. Whatever the demise of these bearded foreigners, some of their customs may have become infused with those of indigenous Mesoamerican cultures, and this will be the focus of our study in this book.

Middle Eastern Types

Referring to the Pre-Classic Period in Mesoamerica (B.C. 2000–250 A.D.), Kidder, Jennings, and Shook maintain that these civilizations were "approximately on the level with, and in general extraordinarily like those of our own cultural ancestors of the ancient Near East";[12] and von Wuthenau, a Mesoamerican art historian, writes: "In recent years a considerable amount of terracottas which show characteristic Semitic traits have been found at archaeological sites."[13]

Figures I.8 through I.10 render a very strong Near-Eastern appearance in both physical and headgear fashions. These Near Eastern types are found with and without beards. Von Wuthenau further remarks: "What is considered to be genuine Indian only developed, so far as I am able to judge on the strength of these terracotta representations, in early and Middle-Classic times, and probably derived from earlier types."[14]

Although not a diffusionist, Nicholson expresses her wonderment at the obvious parallels peculiar to Mesoamerica and the Old World. She writes in her book, *Mexican and Central American Mythology*, the following:

> One unexplained mystery befuddles modern scholars: How is it that the New World before the arrival of the Spaniards contained ethnic types of such a wide diversity that there have been clay and stone portraits discovered representing practically every known human race? . . . The legends we shall study have traces of oriental influence, and possibly even of Judaism and Mediterranean cultures.[15]

A specific answer cannot be given regarding that part of the world from where these bearded men came. However, an analysis of cultural traditions leaves a string of clues. One area that would qualify is the Middle East. Even so, this area of the world should not be considered the one and only locale to qualify for this physical model. Figures I.11 through I.26 are bearded figures who certainly do not appear to fit the paradigm of expected Native Americans, nor would be their forebears.

a.

b.

Fig. I.8 Similar Semitic-type bearded men: a. Canaanite in an Egyptian wall painting (redrawn after Gonen 1992: 249, Fig. 7.26). b. Bearded man carved on stone disk, Veracruz, Mexico, housed at American Museum of Natural History, New York (drawn after photograph).

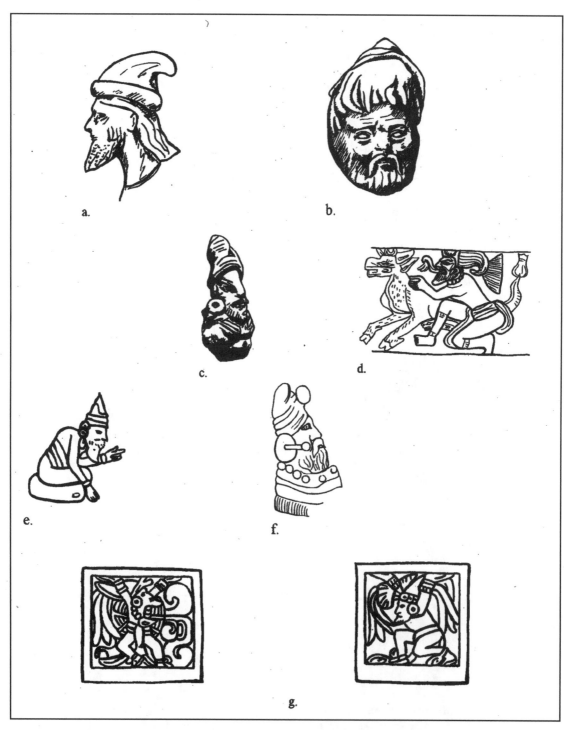

Fig. I.9 Stocking capped bearded figures from the Middle East and Mesoamerica: a. Israelite King
Jehu (845 to 818 B.C.) from Obelisk of Shalamaneser III (drawn after photgraph). b. Man
from Tecáxic-Calixtlahuaca, Mexico (drawn after photograph in Hristov and Genovés 1998:
51). c. Figure from Guerrero, Mexico (drawn from photograph in von Wuthenau 1965: 54).
d. Man with deer on Maya vase, housed at Princeton Art Museum (drawn after photograph
in Kerr 1994: File No. 4599). e. Detail from Stela 5, Izapa, Chiapas, Mexico (drawn after
photograph). f. Dwarf from Los Duendes, Guatemala (drawn after photograph in Van Kirk
and Basset-Van Kirk 1996: 141). g. Sky-bearers, Chichen Itza, Yucatan, Mexico (drawn after
Spinden 1975: Fig. 11).

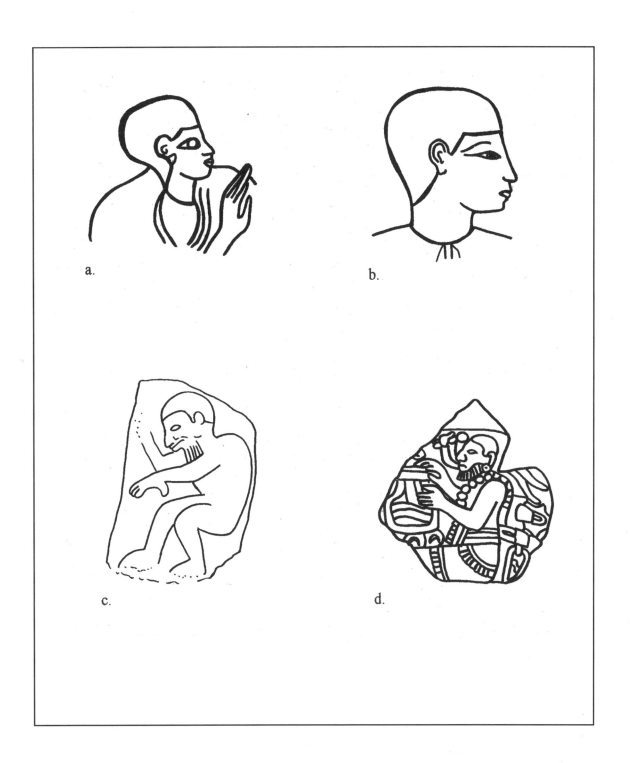

Fig. I.10   Hair cloaks worn by men from Middle East and Mesoamerica: a. Canaanite dignitary
from Hazor, Canaan (redrawn after Kempinski 1992: 200, Fig. 6.33). b. Egyptian, tomb
of vizier Ramosa, 18th Dynasty (drawn after photograph in Hornung 1990: 174).
c. Stone slab of bearded man 500 B.C., Monte Alban, Oaxaca, Mexico (drawn after
photograph). d. Bearded man on carved ceramic piece, Mitla, Oaxaca, Mexico, Museo
Frissel (redrawn after Urcid 1993: 162).

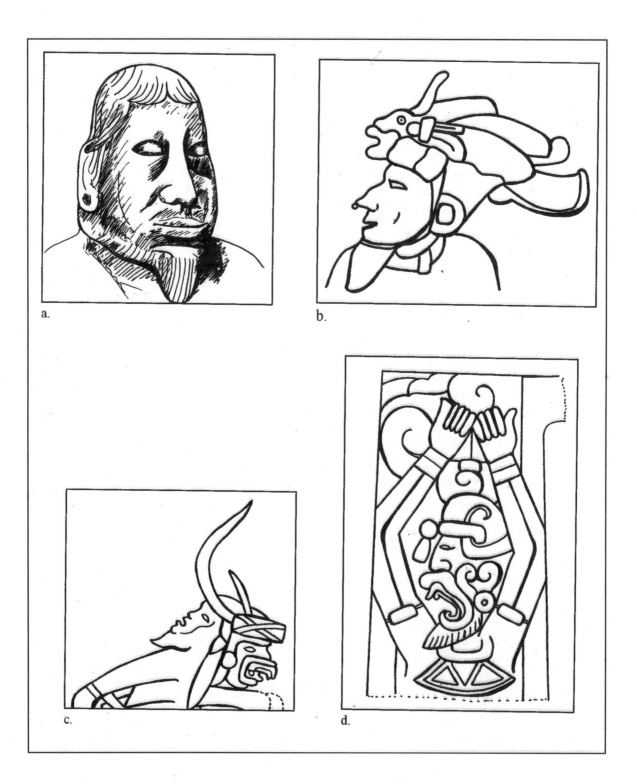

Fig. I.11   Bearded Olmec men (before 400 B.C.): a. Figure carved in serpentine, Puebla, Mexico
(private collection, drawn after photograph in Benson and de la Fuente 1996: Plate
67). b. Portion of Stela 3, La Venta, Tabasco, Mexico (drawn after photograph).
c. Portion of Olmec Relief 2, Chalcatzingo, Morelas, Mexico (redrawn after Covarrubias 1971: Fig. 24). d. Coined as "Slim," figure on greenstone yoke (redrawn after
Covarrubias 1971: Fig. 175).

Fig. I.12 Bearded Shaman standing on end of a
drum, Colima, Mexico (drawn after
photograph in P. Furst 1998: Fig. 24).

Fig. I.13 Bearded figure from Las Bocas,
Puebla, Mexico (drawn after photograph in Wuthenau 1975: Fig. 12b).

a.

b.

Fig. I.14   Bearded Toltecs with nose bar: a. Portion of stone carving of masked and bearded
Toltec from Tula Hidalgo, Hidalgo, Mexico (redrawn after Piña Chan 1960: Fig. 25).
b. Hollow terracotta of a full figure, housed at the Los Angeles County Museum of
Natural History (drawn after photograph).

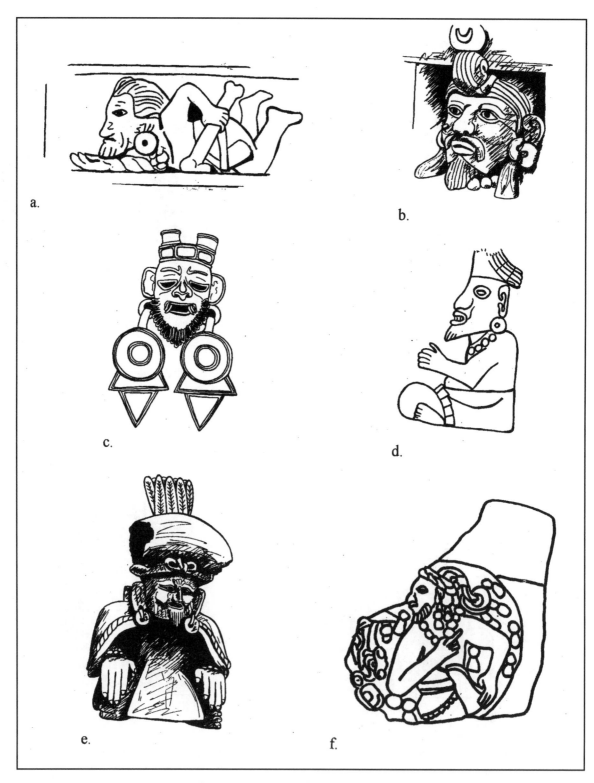

Fig. I.15 Bearded men from Oaxaca, Mexico: a. Man holding femur bone of ancestor, Lambityeco, (drawn after photograph in Wuthenau 1975: 55c). b. Stucco head in niche, Zapotec culture, Lambityeco (drawn after photograph in Gordon 1974: 150). c. Gold pendant, Mixteca Alta, Coixtlahuaca (redrawn after Fox 1976: 156). d. Zapotec man at his wedding ceremony (redrawn after Marcus 1992b: 239, Fig. 8.11). e. Funerary urn, Macuilxochitl (drawn after photograph in Covarrubias 1971: Plate XXXV). f. Carved ceramic piece, Mitla, housed at Museo Frissel (redrawn after Urcid 1993: 162).

a.

b.

Fig. I.16   Bearded men from Guerrero, Mexico: a. From Pacific coast of Guerrero (drawn after
photograph in Wuthenau 1975: Fig. 12d); b. Terracotta head of man with enormous
beard, Balsas River area, housed at American Museum of Natural History, New York
(drawn after photograph).

Fig. I.17 Bearded men from Veracruz, Mexico: a. Flute with bearded head (drawn after photograph in Franco 1971: Plate 79). b. Terracotta flute headpiece (drawn after photograph in Wuthenau 1965: 34). c. Terra cotta head (drawn after photograph in Wuthenau 1975: 114). d. Terracotta figure (drawn after photograph in Leyenaar, van Bussel, and Weber 1992). e. Hankins Collection, Mexico City (drawn after photograph in Wuthenau 1965: 135). f. Sculptured pendant (drawn after photograph in Wuthenau 1975:114).

Fig. I.18   Bearded men from Guatemala: a. Terracotta figurine (drawn after photograph in
Spinden 1975: Plate 17). b. Vase from Quirigua, housed at St. Louis Art Museum
(drawn after photograph). c. Detail from mold-made vase, Peten (redrawn after Coe
and Kerr 1982: 119: Fig. 62). d. Plumbate ware, Pacific Coast (drawn after photo
graph in Couch 1988: 50).

Fig. I.19 Bearded men from Guatemala: a. Carved from volcanic tuff, housed at Musée de
l'Homme, Paris (drawn after photograph in d'Harcourt 1950: 53). b. Stela 1, Seibal
(drawn after photograph). c. Terracotta incense burner, Iximché, housed at Musée de
l'Homme, Paris (drawn after photograph). d. Man holding jaguar cub, housed at
National Museum of Guatemala (drawn after photograph).

Fig. I.20   Bearded men from Guatemala: a. Bearded captive on Stela 39, Tikal (redrawn after
Schele and Freidel 1990: 145). b. Detail from Monument 38, Bilbao (redrawn after
Parson 1969: Frontpiece). c. Detail from Stela 10, Kaminaljuyu, housed at Museo
Nacional, Guatemala (redrawn after Girard 1966: Pl. 194). d. Detail from molded-
carved bowl, Altar de Sacrificios, Peten (redrawn after Adams: Fig. 68a).

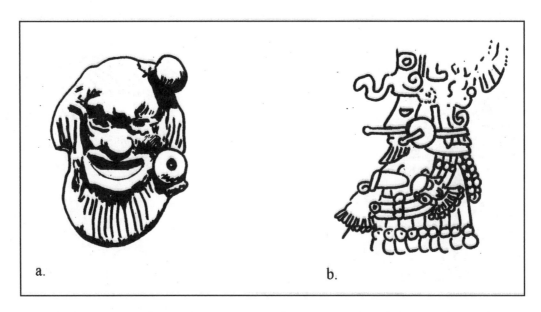

Fig. I.21   Bearded men from Chiapas, Mexico: a. Terracotta pendant, Labartero (drawn after photograph in Ekholm 1985: 212). b. Stela 27 (redrawn after Tate 1992: 65, Fig. 26b).

Fig. I.22   Bearded men from Campeche, Mexico: a. Stela 16, Edzna (redrawn after Taube 1992b: 139, Fig. 76a). b. Stela with possible Star of David earflare, housed at National Museum of Mexico (drawn after photograph).

Fig. I.23   Bearded men from Chichen Itza, Yucatan, Mexico: a. Door jamb from on top of
Castillo (drawn after photograph). b. Stone bas-relief (drawn after photograph).
c. Jade piece from Cenote (redrawn after Proskouriakoff 1974: Pl. 43:9). d. Detail
of warrior on gold disk from Cenote (redrawn after Lothrop 1952). e. Detail on gold
disk (redrawn after Schele and Freidel 1990: 395).

Fig. I.24 Aztec bearded men: a. Pochteca merchant (redrawn after *Codex Fejervary-Mayer*). b. Stone sculpture, housed at Museum für Völkerkunde, Basel, Switzerland (drawn after photograph).

Fig. I.25 Mexican bearded men: a. Quetzalcoatl on a stone box, housed at Ethnographic Museum of Vienna (redrawn after Covarrubias 1971: Fig. 117). b. Detail of a representation of Quetzalcoatl (redrawn after Covarrubias 1971: Fig. 118).

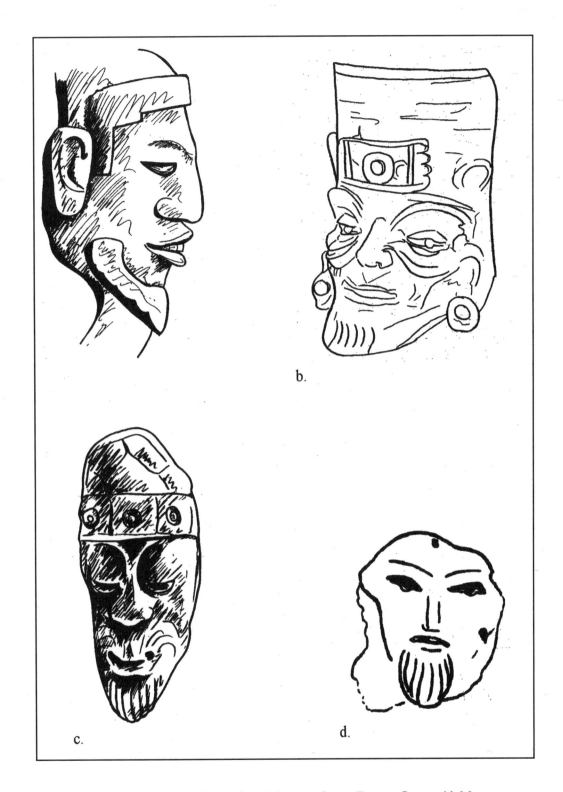

Fig. I.26 Miscellaneous bearded figures from Mesoamerica: a. Totonac figure with Maya features and false beard, Mexico (drawn after photograph in Wuthenau 1975: 41a). b. Bearded effigy head, housed at University Museum, Philadelphia (drawn after photograph). c. Jade head, housed at Musée de l'Homme, Paris (drawn after photograph). d. Pectoral of bearded man, Tabasco, Mexico (redrawn after Wuthenau 1965: 36).

NOTES - CHAPTER I

1. Paul Shellhas, "Comparative Studies in the Field of Maya Antiquities," in *Central American Antiquities, Calendar Systems, and History*, Bulletin 28, trans. Charles P. Bowditch (Washington, D.C.: Smithsonian Institution, 1904), 599.

2. Linda Schele and Peter Mathews, *Notebook for the XVII Maya Hieroglyphic Workshop at Texas* (Austin: University of Texas, 1993), 103.

3. Linda Schele and David Freidel, *A Forest of Kings: The Untold Story of the Ancient Maya* (New York: William Morrow and Company, Inc., 1990), 219.

4. Cottie A. Burland, *The People of the Ancient Americas* (London: Paul Hamlyn, 1970), 55.

5. Gerald Berjonneau and Jean-Louis Sommery, *Rediscovered Masterpieces of Mesoamerica* (Boulogne, France: Edition Arts, 1985), 268.

6. Museum of Primitive Art, *A Maya Sculpture in Wood* (New York: Museum of Primitive Art, 1964), 9.

7. Sue D'Auria, Peter Lacovara, and Catharine H. Roehrig, *Mummies & Magic: The Funerary Arts of Ancient Egypt* (Boston: Museum of Fine Arts, 1988), 164.

8. Kirk A. Magelby, "A Survey of Mesoamerican Bearded Figures," in *F.A.R.M.S. Report*, MAG-79 (Provo, Utah: F.A.R.M.S., 1979).

9. Bernardino de Sahagún, *Florentine Codex: General History of the Things of New Spain*, Arthur J. O. Anderson and Charles E. Dibble, eds. and trans., Monographs of the School of American Research, no. 14, 12 bks., 30 pts. (Santa Fe, New Mexico: School of American Research; and Salt Lake City: University of Utah Press, 1953-82), Bk. 2, Note 8: 36-8.

10. Edward Kingsborough, "The Works of Ixtlilxochitl," in *Antiquities of Mexico,* Vol. IX (London: Henry G. Bohn, Pub., 1848).

11. Alfredo Chavero, ed., *Obras Historicas de Ixtlilxochitl*, vol. 1 (Mexico, 1891), n. 2: 39-40.

12. Alfred V. Kidder, Jesse D. Jennings, and Edwin M. Shook, *Excavations at Kaminaljuyu, Guatemala*, Publication No. 561 (Washington, D.C.: Carnegie Institute of Washington, 1946), 160.

13. Alexander von Wuthenau, *The Art of Terracotta Pottery in Pre-Columbian Central and South America* (New York: Crown Publishers, 1965), 49.

14. Ibid.

15. Irene Nicholson, *Mexican and Central American Mythology* (New York: Paul Hamlyn, 1967), 19.

CHAPTER II

OSIRIS AND HUN HUNAHPU[1]

One of the more important records of early religious thought in Mesoamerica is the *Popol Vuh,* written by the Quiché Maya of Guatemala shortly after the Spanish Conquest in the mid-sixteenth century. The *Popol Vuh* claims to be based on an ancient written text.[2] This account includes a complex creation myth that revolves around supernatural Hero Twins, sons of the dying and resurrecting maize god named Hun Hunahpu. Together the Hero Twins face many challenges in a place called Xibalba, a location comparable to the Underworld or Otherworld in Old World mythologies. As will be demonstrated, a similar scenario to the story of the Mesoamerican *Popol Vuh* Twins may be found in ancient Egypt, particularly in traditions relating to the dying and resurrecting grain god, Osiris, and his son Horus.

No doubt it will be argued that there is a discrepancy in the time period in which the civilization of Egypt existed, which was from approximately 3000 B.C. to the fourth or fifth century A.D.[3] and the Maya of Mesoamerica from roughly 300 B.C. to the time of the Spanish Conquest in the early sixteenth century.[4] This time gap, however, may be bridged to some extent by considering two factors. First, many traditions were slow to change in both these ancient cultures; and second, we do not know how remote in time the concepts of the *Popol Vuh* had their beginnings in Mesoamerica. There are some indications that the myth goes back to the Olmec culture around 1200–400 B.C., which we will consider in this chapter.

It is acknowledged that some aspects of myth are inherently common to diverse cultures throughout the world. However, when identical subtleties are shared within the context of one particular scenario as these are, there may be more to the root of the myth than appears on the surface. Common irregularities support, rather than harm the hypothesis of cultural diffusion, which is the premise of this book.

THE GRAIN GODS OF MESOAMERICA AND EGYPT

Various events in the *Popol Vuh* are portrayed on vases, the picture books called codices, and carvings in stone.[5] Hun-Nal-Ye, the Maya maize god is referred to in hieroglyphic texts,[6] and sometimes nicknamed by Mayanists as First Father. We know from narrative style illustrations on pottery that Hun-Nal-Ye is one and the same with Hun Hunahpu, the father of the *Popol Vuh* Hero Twins.[7] The *Popol Vuh* writers patterned the name of one of the Hero Twins, Hunahpu, after that of his father, Hun Hunahpu. The other twin, Xbalanque, was associated with the Maya's jaguar god representing the night sun of the Underworld.[8]

The Egyptian gods Osiris and his son Horus, as well as their enemy a lord of death, Seth, are more well known and publicized in scholarly circles than are the characters of the *Popol Vuh*. Needless to say, Egyptology is a seasoned science, whereas Mesoamerican archaeology, iconography, and epigraphy are just now coming out of their infancy and quickly growing into adolescence with the recent advancement in translations of Maya hieroglyphics.[9]

Although there are many narratives regarding certain highlights in the life of the grain god, Osiris of Egypt, no complete text has been found. The most useful version is the work of the Greek biographer Plutarch from the second century A.D., which he compiled from older sources.[10]

Creation Myths

Egyptian texts containing stories of Osiris as well as creation myths in the *Popol Vuh,* may be confusing to the first-time reader and very difficult to sort into a logical sequence of events, even after careful study. It must be acknowledged that no two storytellers relate identical narratives, nor do they make use of quite the same elements in the same order. Old components are dropped and new ones added; therefore, we cannot expect these mythologies to be exactly the same throughout the history of a people. Elements common to both accounts will be noted here, and will be used to illustrate a plausible correlation between these two mythological traditions. Our comparison of selected portions of Osiris and Hun Hunahpu myths begins with their respective murders by the Lord or Lords of Death—Hun Hunahpu by decapitation and Osiris by decapitation and total dismemberment.

Off with their Heads

Egyptian priests recited formulae to ensure that the deceased would not be deprived of their heads in the afterlife.[11] This recitation was in direct reference to the decapitation of Osiris by Seth.[12] As Hart notes: "For the Underworld of the private Egyptian, Seth was a terror to be avoided."[13] When Seth murdered Osiris, Seth became a god of death.[14]

The body parts of Osiris were placed in a tree, while the head of Hun Hunahpu was hung in a tree. Silverman writes that "Osiris could be slain but not killed. . . . his resurrection is constantly referred to."[15] The same may be said of Hun Hunahpu as there are examples in art of his decapitated but living head (Fig. II.1), which represents cut and harvested corn that had the innate capability of living again.[16]

The deceased bodies of both Osiris and Hun Hunahpu were able to produce children—the Egyptian god through his sperm (Fig. II.2),[17] and the Maya god through his spittle.[18] It may be significant that in Egypt some gods were conceived through spittle; e.g., Atum's spittle gave birth to Shu and Tefnut.[19]

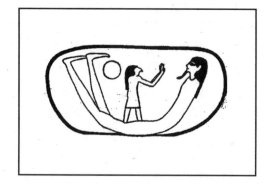

Fig. II.1 Decapitated, living head of Hun Hunahpu on Maya vase housed at Museo Popol Vuh, Universidad Francisco Marroquin, Guatemala (drawn after photograph).

Fig. II.2 The falcon-headed Horus emerges from corpse of Osiris. Burial chamber of Ramesses VI (redrawn after Hornung 1990: 116).

Defeating their Father's Murderer

Horus, the son of the grain god Osiris, participates in a series of tests involving Seth, his father's murderer. In the end Horus is victorious.[20] The *Popol Vuh* Hero Twins also defeat the Lords of Death and Chaos, who were responsible for killing their father, the grain god. One reason they are able to achieve this goal was that they obtained the names of the Lords of Death by enlisting the aid of a wise mosquito. According to D. Tedlock, this knowledge gave the Twins the upper hand.[21]

To better understand the advantage one had as a result of learning the name of a god, a plausible explanation may be found in Egyptian texts. The names of Egyptian gods were held secret and only through trickery were they occasionally discovered.[22] Spencer deduces: "The Egyptians believed that to know someone's name was to have power over them."[23] And Hornung explains: "The name of a god . . . exuded power that could be enlisted in the service of magic."[24] We are reminded that it was by magic that the *Popol Vuh* Hero Twins were able to defeat the lords of the Underworld after they became apprized of their names.

After death, both Egyptian and Maya kings were expected to go through a series of trials in the Underworld with the hope of overcoming death as was accomplished by Horus and the Hero Twins, respectively. In death, the Pharaoh became an Osiris and, like this grain divinity who died and was resurrected, the Pharaoh was confident that he would do likewise. Together with the sun they would be reborn in the east.

In Mesoamerica we find a nearly identical tradition. The Maya king equated himself with the sun of the Underworld, which would rise again.[25] Moreover, the ruler sometimes dressed as First Father, or Hun Hunahpu. Pakal (full name, K'inich Janahb' Pakal), the great ruler of Palenque, became apotheosized as this young maize god in a transitional point between death and rebirth on his sarcophagus (see Fig. VI.26).[26] Though deceased, Pakal was thought to be reborn in the east.

Events in the Underworld

The atmosphere in the Underworld of these two lands was also remarkably similar. For example, both the Mesoamerican and Egyptian Underworlds were dark, contained mountains, a river, and both were divided by gates that led to various compartments. It was there that the deceased faced trials such as avoiding the blades of attacking knives and the threat of monstrous beasts whose aim was to destroy. In addition, the Underworld was the abode of the deceased, somehow under the world but, at the same time, viewed as the night sky where ancestral spirits exist as stars.[27]

The Enemy and the Big Dipper

An obscure yet significant part of this story is the relationship between the Big Dipper and the one who instigated chaos. In Egypt this individual was Seth, whereas among the Quiché Maya of Guatemala, it was a bird deity named Vucub Caquix (in English, Seven Macaw).

Vucub Caquix resided at the north celestial pivot, and as the Big Dipper he was able to swing around instead of traveling the longer route taken by the sun and moon.[28] On a codex-style Classic Maya vase, Hunahpu is portrayed shooting Vucub Caquix, who wanted to be the sun of this world (Fig. II.3). The prideful nature of Vucub Caquix was destroyed when Hunahpu knocked out his jeweled teeth and eyes.

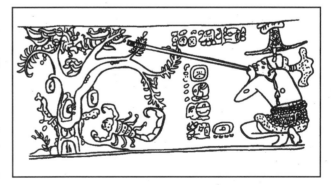

Fig. II.3 Hunahpu shooting Vucub Caquix, from the Maya "blowgunner Pot" (redrawn after Freidel, Schele, and Parker 1993: Fig. 2.7).

According to Eliade, mutilations such as the knocking out of teeth or the amputation of body parts are connected to death.[29] In the end, Vucub Caquix was ultimately defeated by Hunahpu when he was shot out of his tree with a blowgun.

Among the Aztec one encounters a myth concerning the god Tezcatlipoca who was also associated with the Big Dipper. A post-Conquest chronicle called *La Historia De Los Mexicanos Por Sus Pinturas,* informs us that Tezcatlipoca lost his foot while in a conflict with the dying and resurrecting god Quetzalcoatl at the end of the last creation as the world was approaching a renewal.[30] Like Vucub Caquix of the *Popol Vuh,* Tezcatlipoca attempted to rule as the sun of this new world. It is at this point that Tezcatlipoca's vainglorious aspiration to control all things failed as he was pushed through the night sky by Quetzalcoatl and defeated. Dr. Krupp of the Griffith Observatory explained this event: in a twenty-four-hour period the Big Dipper completely circles the pole. It climbs to the top of its arc and then descends back to the horizon.[31] From the viewpoint of Guatemalans in the highlands, the Big Dipper appears to drop below the horizon. This phenomenon also corresponds to the fall of the vanquished Vucub Caquix after he attempted to imitate the glory of the sun.[32]

The Egyptian name for the Big Dipper is Meskhetiu and means bull's leg and haunch. Wilkinson reports that the Papyrus Jumilhac (pl. XVII, 11–13), explicitly mentions this constellation was the leg of Seth, which leg was torn off by Horus and hurled into the heavens (Fig. II.4).[33] This is similar to the story of Tezcatlipoca—both lost body parts in a cosmic struggle. Possessing the same characteristics of the Mexican myth, the leg of Seth appeared to be severed as the Big Dipper dropped beneath the horizon. Seth wanted to be Pharaoh and, according to Quirke, the place of the sun god was filled on earth by the king.[34] Seth temporarily accomplished this when he usurped the throne of Egypt with the death of Osiris. Although Seth became Pharaoh for a short time, Horus was the rightful heir to the throne of Egypt with the death of Osiris. Although Seth became Pharaoh for a short time, Horus was the rightful heir to the throne and eventually succeeded in obtaining it. Horus then became the representative of Ra, the sun god, as did all Pharaohs during their lifetime. There may be no coincidence that both the son of the murdered Osiris and the sons of the murdered Hun Hunahpu defeated the would-be usurpers of the sun's authority, but the stories are surely similar.

Fig. II.4 Seth as the Big Dipper, visualized as the foreleg of an ox (redrawn after Wilkinson 1992:74).

Creation and Order

The creation of this world was associated by the Egyptians with order, renewal, and kingship. Taking this concept a step further, Griffiths' book, *The Conflict of Horus and Seth,* gives one of the most authoritative studies of this myth. Griffiths explains that the conflict between Horus and Seth was symbolic of a clash between order and chaos.[35] In other words, before our present creation, chaos challenged order and order was restored as a result of the defeat of Seth by Horus. This concept works beautifully with the same notion held in Mesoamerica. Once Vucub Caquix was vanquished and order set into place, as it was at the moment of creation, kingship was also stabilized.

The conflict between the Egyptian gods Seth and Horus and the hostilities between the Hero Twins of the *Popol Vuh* and their enemies, worked both ways as they inflicted serious injuries on each other in a series of battles, mind games, and magical tricks. Vucub Caquix tore off the forearm of Hunahpu during a struggle. On Stela 25 at Izapa, Chiapas, Mexico, Hunahpu is portrayed with blood dripping from his severed arm (Fig. II.5).[36] This is extremely important in that stelae at Izapa date back as early as 400 B.C.,[37] which brings us closer to an overlap in time with the Egyptian culture.

Fig. II.5   Vucub Caquix perches on stylized World Tree, while Hunahpu displays his severed, bloody arm on Stela 25, Izapa, Chiapas, Mexico (redrawn after Norman 1976: 133).

THE HEROES AND ORION

The relationship of both Osiris and Hun Hunahpu was signifi-cant to the constellation of Orion, which presents a string of three stars in the center named Alnitak, Alnilam, and Mintaka (see Fig. II.9). From a cross section of the Egyptian Great Pyramid of Cheops (Fig. II.6), two shafts coincide with the north and south passage of two stars that existed in the sky at the time of the pyramid's construction. One of the stars is Alnitak in the belt of Orion. Hadingham suggests that these shafts were never meant to be used to view the stars in that they end before the exterior wall of the pyramid. Hadingham main-tains that these shafts were astronomical alignments designed to express Egyptian beliefs.[38] Krupp agrees with this analysis.[39]

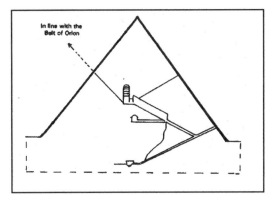

Fig. II.6 The Great Pyramid of Cheops in Egypt and its shaft alignment to the belt of Orion.

Osiris and Orion

Osiris is definitely associated with the constellation of Orion (Fig. II.7). Lines three and four of an Egyptian *Book of Breathings* text (Louvre Papyrus, No. 3284) contains a passage wherein a request was made that Osiris join in the horizon along with his father Ra to make his Ba [soul] appear in glory in heaven in the disk of the moon, and that his body might shine in Orion.[40] Therefore, it was significant that the Pharaoh's burial chamber included a shaft pointing to the place important to the god who dies and is reborn.[41] Krupp corroborated this by writing that the deceased Pharaoh of Egypt rose to the northern undying stars and to Orion, the celestial incarnation of Osiris.[42] Also in the Louvre's Egyptian *Book of Breathings,* Isis writes on behalf of Osiris to ensure that his body would shine in Orion in the womb of Nut. Nut was the night sky, and her womb, of course, was the place from which Osiris was to be reborn.

Fig. II.7 Osiris as Sahu-Orion (redrawn after Sellers 1992: Fig. 1a).

Another related celestial incident may also prove to be pivotal. Krupp explains that Osiris, in his role as Orion, is sometimes shown in a celestial boat.[43] This is similar to the myth of Osiris who was killed by Seth, then put adrift on the Nile in a tree-like coffin. The Nile may have been construed as the earthly symbol of the Milky Way.[44] Although there is no word in Egyptian for the Milky Way, this band of stars may be what is referred to in their writings as The Great Winding Waterway, an area in the Egyptian heavens. Davis, lecturer in Egyptology at Yale University, posits that this name cannot be considered the ecliptic, as some surmise,[45] but is the waterway that is crossed by the sun god, Re, in Coffin Text VI. The sun crosses the Milky Way, not the ecliptic.[46] In Egypt, ferrymen were noted for carrying gods, and/or the deceased who were comparable to Osiris, through the waters of the Underworld (the night sky) to their final destination. In some instances the ferrymen were referred to as collectors of souls.[47] As we will see, this scenario is of interest for several reasons in this study.

Hun Hunahpu and Orion

Returning to Maya myth, we find that Hun Hunahpu, the maize god, is portrayed on a carved bone being ferried down a river in the sky (seen as the Milky Way) to the Underworld (Fig. II.8). Images of the maize god in his canoe go back to the Olmec, making a timeless tradition in Mesoamerica.[48] This event was followed by the rebirth of the maize god at a place called The Three Stones of Creation. Alnitak, the southernmost star of Orion's belt, is one of these three stones.[49]

Fig. II.8 Maize god (center) descending to the Underworld in canoe. Bone from tomb of Hasaw Ka'an
K'awil, Tikal, Guatemala (redrawn after Miller and Taube 1993: 129).

Orion's belt was represented in Maya art as a turtle (Fig. II.9), and numerous portraits were made of the maize god emerging victorious over death from a split tortoise shell (Fig. II.10). Stuart proposes that this same split, which appears in Maya sky glyphs, is the phonetic *sih* and *sih* means "birth."[50] The maize god was associated with the turtle as early as the Olmec civilization. A jade pectoral depicting the underside of this creature's carapace with the head of the Olmec maize god gives support to the age of this tradition in Mesoamerica.[51] To summarize, Osiris the Egyptian grain god, like the Maya maize god, is murdered by decapitation, travels down a river (possibly the Milky Way of the night sky) to the Underworld in a celestial boat, is associated with the constellation of Orion, and is subsequently reborn.

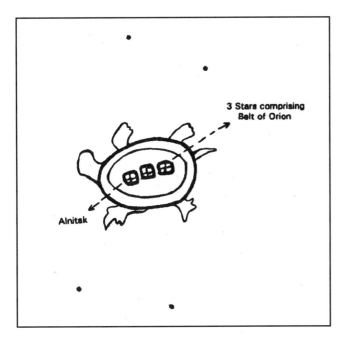

Fig. II.9 Turtle representing constellation of Orion (redrawn after mural, Bonampak, Chiapas, Mexico [overlapping the constellation of Orion, drawn by author]).

Fig. II.10 Hun Hunahpu emerges from a tortoise on a Late-Classic Maya bowl (redrawn after Miller and Taube 1993: 69).

THE REGENERATION OF GRAIN

Both Osiris and Hun Hunahpu were gods of grain, this being their most salient feature. Grain, of course, has a life cycle—it comes to life from a state of dormancy, dies, and is reborn. A Mexican myth relates that plants grew from the buried body of Centeotl, the maize god of Mexican Nahua cultures.[52] In Egypt, grain was considered to be Osiris in the tomb when planted in the ground. When it germinated, Osiris was perceived as coming to life again (Fig. II.11). It was an Egyptian custom to make a figure of Osiris from a linen bag filled with grain.[53] When watered, it sprouted, and Osiris was symbolically reborn. Illustrations show Osiris with a green face and hands—another indication of his vegetative quality. In Mesoamerica the maize god was frequently carved in jade from early Olmec times, the green color of this stone denotes the color of the maize stalk, leaves, and husk.

We find the same concept for the Maya maize god, especially in portraits of his foliated, decapitated head (Fig. II.12).[54] In addition, when the Hero Twins resurrect, this event was symbolized by sprouting corn in their grandmother's house.[55] In essence, the kernels sown were the alter egos of the Hero Twins.[56] The Twins instruct their grandmother that, if the corn planted in her house dies, they die; but if it lives, they remain alive. The maize lived in their grandmother's abode. Germination of seed was considered a sign of rebirth in both Egypt and Mesoamerica. It was a basic tenant in their beliefs that through death comes life. For these ancient cultures death was but a rite of passage to rebirth and continuance in the universe.

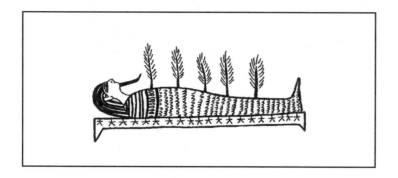

Fig. II.11 Osiris as grain god lying on a sky glyph with stars (redrawn after mural, Valley of the Kings, Egypt).

Fig. II.12 The foliated head of the Maya maize god from a hieroglyph at Yaxchilan, Chiapas, Mexico (redrawn after Freidel, Schele, Parker 1993: Fig. 8:11a).

Rulers Become as Grain Awaiting Rebirth

Among the Maya, Hunahpu, who went through the process of death and rebirth, was the eternal prototype of all kings.[57] To clarify this, it needs to be understood that Maya deceased rulers were equated with Hun Hunahpu the senior maize god, while living rulers were identified with the son(s) of the maize god, Hunahpu in particular.[58] This configuration was identical in Egypt. Osiris appears as a paradigm for Egyptian kings upon their death only, while the living Pharaoh was more closely associated with Horus, the son of Osiris. Even so, the Pharaoh did perform a ritual of renewal during the Sed Festival.[59] This involved a ceremonial walk by the king into a building representing his tomb. He rested, awoke, and when he passed through the doorway of this structure it was as though he was reborn. Thus, although the king was assimilated with Horus during his life, he performed a ritual pertaining to his future integration with Osiris in this ritual of death and rebirth.

The rebirth of Osiris, Hun Hunahpu, the deceased Pharaoh of Egypt and Maya rulers of Mesoamerica, took place at precisely the same time. Both Egypt and Mesoamerica incorporated a 360-day solar calendar that did not quite fill the bill for a complete year. Therefore, they added a five-day "no-name" period to the 360 days. It is during these five epagomenal days that transition took place in both cultures—a period of chaos followed by that of order and rebirth. More important, it was the time when Osiris, Hun Hunahpu, and deceased kings were reborn. In the case of Egyptian tradition, Budge states in his Introduction to the *Egyptian Book of the Dead*: "On the first of these five days Osiris was brought forth; and . . . that the lord of creation was born."[60] These are the five days before the commencement of the New Year. Perhaps significantly the same scenario took place among the Maya. Carmack studied the Quiché Maya culture and the early writings of Ximenez and notices that during this year-end period of five days, the king reenacted a symbolic death and descent to the Underworld where he confronted the Lords of Death as did the Hero Twins. As was the case with the Twins, the king, too, was subsequently reborn.[61] This ritual sounds very much like the Egyptian Sed Festival.

Sacrifice of Substitute King

Another important ceremony held during the Sed Festival may have been the sacrifice of a substitute king on behalf of the living ruler. According to Helck, the victim's death was followed by a symbolic resurrection, which became a realization in the eyes of the Egyptians as the king mounted his throne.[62] It is not known for certain whether a sacrificial victim as a substitute for the king was used in reality or just implied. Even so, as Lurker correctly notes, "New life issued from the murdered god Osiris, the king also, through his death, was to secure the continued stability of his people."[63] Gohary, in her study of Akhenaten's Sed Festival at Karnack, comments that indications were that a mock burial and resurrection using a statue of the king may have been one of the rites of the festival.[64]

Two rituals support this ideology among the Maya. At Piedras Negras, Guatemala, rulers are portrayed climbing a scaffold as they became enthroned (Fig. II.13). The victim rolls to the bottom while the ruler's bloody footprints ascend the ladder to where he sits on his celestial throne surrounded by glyphs pertaining to the sky.[65] The king was thus seen as having died, followed by his resurrection and deification in the heavens.

The Game and Forces of Chaos

The second, another impressive evidence of a substitute sacrifice in Mesoamerica, was the reenactment of a ballgame performed in the *Popol Vuh* played with two teams on a court that represented Xibalba (Fig. II.14). This Underworld locale was understood as a place where the deceased experienced a series of tests in an attempt to defeat the Lords of Death as was accomplished by the Hero Twins. Schele and Freidel show in their study of the Maya ballgame that sacrificial victims were substituted for the king in his role as one of the Hero Twins in the game with the Lords of Death, as described in the *Popol Vuh*.[66] In this game that originally took place in the primordial time of sacred beginnings, both the grain god, Hun Hunahpu, and his son, Hunahpu, lost their heads. It was the son, along with his twin brother, who used magic to deceive the Lords of Death. In the real world where this particular ballgame mimicked the game of creation, the substitute ballplayer lost the game and was sacrificed by decapitation. The king, on the other hand, mounted his throne as though reborn, and figuratively established his victory over death.

Fig. II.13 King sits in his sky throne on Stela 11, Piedras Negras, Guatemala (drawn by Linda Schele, © by David Schele, in Schele and Miller 1986: 112, Fig. II.4).

Fig. II.14 Ballplayer on Panel 2, El Peru, Guatemala (redrawn after Schele and Miller 1986: Fig. VI-12).

In a related vein, we need to mention the Sokar-Osiris-Khentamenthes Festival in which the king performed a dramatic reenactment of the death of Osiris. This reenactment included a battle between the followers of Horus against Seth and his cohorts.[67] This was considered a divine war and a conflict that took place in mythological time. In their attempt for authenticity, the mock battles performed by the Egyptians were so brutal that sometimes death occurred.[68] These battles and the Mesoamerican ballgame ritual had the same agenda—the destruction of the forces of chaos.

FISH AND GRAIN

Returning to the *Popol Vuh*, while the Hero Twins were in the process of tricking the Lords of Death, they allowed themselves to be killed. The Twins jumped into a fire pit after which their bones were ground like maize and thrown into the waters of the Underworld. This part of the legend is significant when we refer to the Ugaritic-Canaanite god, Mot, whose body was not only burned but whose bones were ground before being resurrected. As we will see, this was the same outcome of the Maya Twins.[69]

To continue our story with the Hero Twins, after their ground bones were thrown in a river, they were miraculously turned into fish and reborn a few days later. This portion of the story is beautifully illustrated on a Maya vase (Fig. II.15). Above the figures in the water is a canoe traveling through the Milky Way, which were the waters of the Underworld. Below the canoe is a young man who comes face to face with a fish, both of which appear to emerge from a larger fish/serpent-like creature. Being disgorged from the mouth of fish monsters is a typical theme of rebirth throughout the ancient world.[70] Reents-Budet suggests that one of the *Popol Vuh* Hero Twins has already been reborn, while the other appears as a fish just before his metamorphosis.[71] The Twins were their father's sons and due to their rebirth, their father, the maize god, was also reborn. They all overcame death.

Another place one finds an association of fish with rebirth is at El Tajin, in Veracruz, Mexico (Fig. II.16). A man wearing a fish-mask headdress sits in a sweat bath, which represents a place of purification. In Mesoamerica the waters of the sweat bath were associated with the embryonic fluid of the womb, comparable to the waters of creation.[72] In fact, Eliade writes: "Immersion in the waters signifies, not a definitive extinction, but a temporary reentry into the indistinct, followed by a new creation, a new life."[73] This scene in Mexico is a representation of a fish/man in a transitional condition as he is about to emerge from a state of death into a renewed existence.

Fig. II.15   Hero Twins emerge from a fish monster on lower portion of a Maya vase (drawn after photograph in Reents-Budet 1994: 274).

Fig. II.16   South-central panel of South Ballcourt, El Tajin, Veracruz, Mexico (redrawn after Kampen 1972).

There are interesting aspects to explore in light of Osiris's possible association with fish. According to Zehren, Osiris was visualized as having died in the heavenly river (the Milky Way) by the constellation of Orion.[74] It is plausible that one of the costumes worn by Osiris may be interpreted as containing a fish-scale pattern (Fig. II.17). In Goelet's commentary on the *Egyptian Book of the Dead,* Plate 4 of the Papyrus of Ani, he writes: "Osiris sits on a seat . . . . the two door panels may indicate that Osiris's throne represents the gateway to the Duat [the Underworld]. The pattern on the garment which Osiris wears may represent fish scales, a possible reference to the myth in which Osiris drowns and gets eaten by a fish."[75] On the other hand, the pattern that Goelet suggests are fish scales, may also be construed to be feathers. However, if they are scales, this would be additional support to the concept of Osiris's alliance with the fish, as it was for the *Popol Vuh* Hero Twins when they were turned into fish and subsequently reborn.

Fig. II.17   Osiris in possible fish-scale attire (redrawn after
Papyrus of Ani, Plate 4).

The deceased who became as Osiris in their journey through the Underworld were sometimes manifested in the form of a fish in mummy wrappings. Johnson gives support to this thesis as found in Egypt.[76] A tomb mural in Thebes depicts a huge fish in the process of being embalmed by Anubis (Fig. II.18). Desroches-Noblecourt of the Louvre informed Johnson that in this case the fish represents the deceased who must find his way through the waters of the Underworld. The accompanying murals show the fish going through different stages of its voyage, and we are reminded that the deceased becomes as Osiris.

Fig. II.18   Fish as mummy (redrawn after photograph, Thebes, Deir el-Medinah, Tomb of
Kha'bekhet #2).

The Sun and the Moon

The last point to be considered is the relationship of the heroic Egyptian and Maya sons of the grain gods to the sun and the moon. In the case of Horus, the eyes of his falcon image are significant, the falcon being his prime animal form. One eye of the falcon represents the sun, while the other personifies the moon. We also note that in Egypt the moon may be regarded as the night sun of the Underworld.[77] In one incident, an eye of Horus was plucked out by the Lord of Death yet was magically restored.

Let us compare the eyes of Horus with the *Popol Vuh* Hero Twins. According to Tate the Twins generallly acted in concert.[78] As twins, perhaps they were meant to be considered as two parts of a whole. In an interview conducted by *Parabola*, Dennis Tedlock, as expert on the *Popol Vuh*, explains the role of twins in mythology: "Psychologically, twins are really one—they dramatize a split in a single persona."[79] The Twins ultimately ascend to the sky. One is reborn as the sun (and sometimes as Venus), while the other becomes the night sun, or full moon.[80] As the eyes of Horus represent the sun and the moon, the Hero Twins also, working in unison, represent these two celestial orbs.

Some Mayanists view Hunahpu as the avatar of Venus; yet it is also admitted that some of this deity's iconography was associated with the day sun. D. Tedlock notes that the modern-day Quiché, whose predecessors wrote the *Popol Vuh*, use the same word for Venus in its phase as the morning star, as they do for the day sun.[81] Taube's study of the Mopan Maya version of the *Popol Vuh* confirms that Lord Kin (Sun Lord) in this account, was the principal hero and avatar of the sun.[82] Taube discovers that Lord Kin corresponds to the *Popol Vuh* Hero Twin, Hunahpu. Nevertheless, Hunahpu also appears in the *Popol Vuh* as being reborn as the planet Venus, the morning star. This is extremely interesting when one compares this aspect of Hunahpu to Horus. Anthes shows that Horus is transfigured into the sun according to most texts, but in some Egyptian Pyramid Texts he becomes the morning star, or Venus.[83] It was in later texts that the sun is mentioned as an eye of Horus. Therefore, both Maya and Egyptian accounts describe a son of the grain god reborn sometimes as the sun, and sometimes as Venus.

As to Hunahpu's brother, D. Tedlock reasons that if Xbalanque is a solar deity, more specifically the night sun of the Underworld, then Hunahpu must be the day sun of the upper world.[84] Tedlock then explains that Xbalanque had a definite lunar aspect to his character as the night sun. In Mesoamerica, the moon in its many phases is usually feminine in nature; yet in this case, it is the masculine full moon that represented the night sun. Tedlock also points out that the Quiché Maya metaphorically refer to the full moon as *q'ij*, "sun."[85] Xbalanque is portrayed in art with attributes of a jaguar, such as patches of jaguar skin and/or the ear of a jaguar. It is well known among Mayanists that the jaguar is connected to the night sun.[86] This was also confirmed by Taylor who writes that Xbalanque, the little jaguar sun, became the moon god.[87]

Grain Gods Remain in Underworld

Osiris resurrects and becomes the Lord of the Underworld. Although reborn, he never leaves this place of death and rebirth. In spite of this, one of his titles is ruler of the living.[88] In like manner, Hun Hunahpu is reborn from the ballcourt where he was originally decapitated. To the Maya, the ballcourt represents the Underworld, or Other World, and is related to the place of creation in the night sky of the cosmos.[89] The playing field for the Mesoamerican ballgame consists of a narrow, flat alley between two parallel slope-walled structures. Either end of the ballcourt may be visually compared to the cleft or split in the Mountain of Creation,[90] and it is from this sacred center that Hun Hunahpu is reborn (Fig. II.19 and II.20). This theme is represented in various split objects found in nature, including the tortoise as portrayed in Figure II.10. And so, like Osiris of Egypt, the resurrected Maya grain god remains in the Underworld, even though reborn. The sons of these two gods eventually rise to the sky as celestial lights.

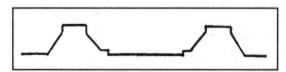

Fig. II.19 Generic Mesoamerican ballcourt
as seen from end.

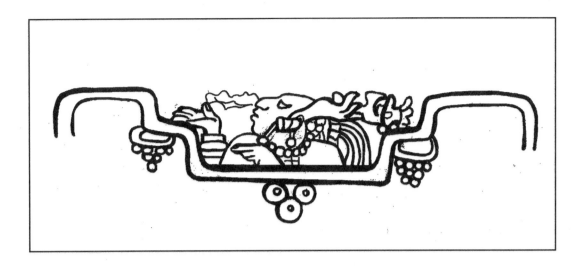

Fig. II.20 Maize god, Hun Nal Ye, reboron from
cleft in Mountain of Creation. Detail
from Stela 1, Bonampak, Chiapas, Mexico
(redrawn after Schele in Gutierrez 1993).

THE DIFFERENCES, AND A TALE OF TWO BROTHERS

There are obvious differences between the elements of these stories from Egypt and Mesoamerica, yet all mythology undergoes some change; old elements are dropped while new aspects are added. The Egyptian "Tale of Two Brothers" is a prime example of this tradition. In fact, not only does this story correspond in many ways to Osiris and Horus, it parallels a familiar theme with the one expressed in the *Popol Vuh* regarding the Hero Twins.

In this Egyptian tale the younger brother Bata equates with Osiris. He too dies and is reborn.[91] The severed phallus of Bata, like Osiris, is thrown into a river and swallowed by a fish. There is also a tree element in the "Tale of Two Brothers." Bata's heart is hung in a pine tree. As we recall, Hun Hunahpu's head is hung in a tree and Osiris's body parts are encased in a tree. Bata then becomes a bull, and when he is sacrificially killed, drops of his blood turn into trees. These trees, containing the essence of the dead Bata, are cut down and some of the splinters fly into the mouth of a noble woman who happens to be Bata's wife. She becomes pregnant. Her son is of royal lineage and eventually becomes king, thus completing the cycle of life, death, and rebirth for Bata. Here again we find a similarity, i.e., conception without a sexual relationship. A woman in the *Popol Vuh* conceives sons from the spittle of the deceased Hun Hunahpu. Isis becomes pregnant from the sperm of the dead Osiris. These stories are of mythological supernaturals who eternally engender themselves, and both Hun Hunahpu and Osiris go through several transformations to reach their objective.

There is also an Egyptian document called the *Westcar Papyrus* that talks about the King's request to cut a man into pieces so the magician can demonstrate his powers of restoration.[92] This is what happens to Bata. His phallus and heart are removed from his body. He is then magically turned into a bull. The bull is then sacrificed and cut up and he magically turns into trees. The trees are cut into pieces, the splinters impregnate a woman, and Bata is magically reborn as the future king.

In the *Popol Vuh* one sees a similar dismemberment scenario. The Twins take turns cutting each other up into pieces, and through their magic restore each other to life. But when the Lords of Death ask that they perform the same magic on them, the Twins do not bring these evil doers to life after killing them. That is how the Hero Twins defeated the Lords of Death in the Underworld.

Another way that Bata's relationship to Osiris is disclosed is in the portion of this legend in which Bata's heart is hung on a tree. According to Tower Hollis, Bata's fate is dependent on the fate of the tree.[93] Osiris also depends on the well-being of the tree in which he was encased. Hollis remarks that it is an old Egyptian belief that whatever happened to the tree, happened to the man. This thinking is in line with the *Popol Vuh* story when the Twins inform their grandmother that if the corn planted in the center of her house lives, they live; if the corn withers and dies, they die. Maize, in Mesoamerica, was considered a kind of tree.

Complexity of Stories

In the late nineteenth century, Boas wisely suggested, "we may safely assume that wherever a story which consists of the same combination of several elements is found in two regions, we must conclude that it's occurrence in both is due to diffusion. The more complex the story is . . . the more this conclusion will be justified."[94] The probability exists that the respective stories of the grain gods in Egypt and Mesoamerica are identical in a sufficient number of ways to show a possible relation and, yet, it is normal and expected that they each take their own departure one from the other.

BRIDGING THE GAP

On the surface, it would appear that the Egyptians and the Maya were not only divided by distance, but by time. However, Stela 25 at Izapa portrays characters from the *Popol Vuh* that may possibly date back as far as 400 B.C. (see Fig. II.5). Several Mesoamericanists, including Stross, believe the decapitated head of the maize god is frequently depicted in Olmec art (Fig. II.21), which, of course, was quite early.[95] If his hypothesis is valid, the sprouting decapitated head of the Maya maize god may rest on an Olmec concept that originated in an era corresponding to Egyptian times when Osiris was worshiped. Another important discovery may also prove to be relevant to the early beginnings of the maize god saga among the Olmec. Recently found were stone sculptures on a pig farm at Rancho El Azuzul near San Lorenzo, Veracruz, Mexico (Fig. II.22). These sculptures portray two nearly identical young men wearing the identifying features of the Olmec maize god. They are one and the same with the *Popol Vuh* Hero Twins.[96] This site takes us back to 900 B.C.[97]

Fig. II.21 Head of decapitated Olmec maize god (redrawn after Stross 1992: 83).

Fig. II.22 Olmec Hero Twins, Rancho El Azuzul, Veracruz, Mexico (drawn after photograph).

There are also many clay figurines from Tlapacoya, Mexico, about 1250–1000 B.C., that depict varying maize symbols on their headdresses. Equally important is the costume of Olmec rulers who dress as ritual ballplayers. The task of these supernatural athletes was to overcome the Lords of Death in the Underworld, thus ensuring the fertility of the cosmos.[98] This being the case, one might find rulers from as early as 1250 B.C. that impersonate or represent Hun Hunahpu, who was First Father (the maize god), and a ballplayer in the creation epic of the *Popol Vuh*. These are all prime examples of the timeless tradition of religious ideology in Mesoamerica.

Traditions evolve and change with time but, in many cases, the basic elements of the myth remain intact. There appears to be good and probable cause to justify a connection between the myths and iconography of these various ancient cultures.

NOTES - Chapter II

1. This chapter is a revised paper by Diane E. Wirth, "Through Death Comes Life: The Dying and Resurrecting Grain Gods of Mesoamerica and Egypt" (paper presented at a conference entitled "The Aesthetics of Enchantment," sponsored by the American Society of Phenomenology, Aesthetics & the Fine Arts, Fourth International Congress, at Harvard Divinity School, Harvard University, Cambridge, Massachusetts, 18-20 April 1998).

2. Personal communication from Allen Christenson to Diane Wirth, October 26, 1998.

3. This time frame takes into account that the Egyptian civilization did not change until it became Romanized and Christianized sometime in the fourth or fifth century A.D. The last dated Egyptian hieroglyphic inscription dates to A.D. 457. Information supplied by John Gee.

4. By 900 A.D. political boundaries of the Maya had greatly disintegrated, and trade routes had changed radically. Their period of fluorescence was over, although a renewal and renovation took place to a certain degree among the Yucatec Maya in the years prior to the Spanish Conquest.

5. Michael D. Coe, *Lords of the Underworld: Masterpieces of Classic Maya Ceramics* (Princeton: The Art Museum, Princeton University, 1978).

6. Carolyn E. Tate, *Yaxchilan: The Design of a Maya Ceremonial City* (Austin: University of Texas Press, 1992), 51.

7. Mary Miller and Karl Taube, *Gods and Symbols of Ancient Mexico and the Maya: An Illustrated Dictionary of Mesoamerican Religion* (New York: Thames & Hudson, 1993), 98.

8. Schele and Freidel, *A Forest of Kings*, 245.

9. Michael Coe, *Breaking the Maya Code*.

10. J. Gwyn Griffiths, *Plutarch's De Iside et Osiride*, (Cardiff, Wales: University of Wales Press, 1970). See also J. Gwyn Griffiths, *The Origins of Osiris and His Cult* (Leiden: E. J. Brill, 1980).

11. Spell 43 in the ancient *Egyptian Book of the Dead* was meant to prevent the deceased from losing his head in the realm of the dead. To quote from Faulkner's translation, "I am a Great One . . . to whom was given his head after it had been cut off. The head of Osiris shall not be taken from him, and my head shall not be taken from me." See, *The Ancient Egyptian Book of the Dead*, Raymond O. Faulkner, trans., Carol Andrews, ed. (1972; rev. ed., New York: Macmillan Publishing Company, 1985), 63.

12. A. J. Spencer, *Death in Ancient Egypt* (1982 Pelican Books; reprint, New York: Penguin Books USA, Inc., 1991), 128.

13. George Hart, *A Dictionary of Egyptian Gods and Goddesses* (London: Routledge & Kegan Paul, 1986), 197.

14. D'Auria, Lacovara, and Roehrig, 34.

15. David P. Silverman, "Divinity and Deities in Ancient Egypt," in *Religion in Ancient Egypt*, Byron E. Shafer, ed. (Ithaca: Cornell University Press, 1991), 29.

16. Brian Stross, "Maize and Blood: Mesoamerican Symbolism on an Olmec Vase and a Maya Plate," *RES* 22 (Santa Monica: Getty Center for the History of Art and the Humanities, 1992), 83.

17. Erik Hornung, *The Valley of the Kings: Horizon of Eternity*, trans. David Warburton (New York: Timken Publishers, Inc., 1990), 116.

18. Dennis Tedlock, *Popol Vuh: The Definitive Edition of the Mayan Book of the Dawn of Life and the Glories of Gods and Kings* (New York: Simon and Schuster, Inc., 1985), 328.

19. Manfred Lurker, *The Gods and Symbols of Ancient Egypt* (New York: Thames and Hudson, 1980), 116. See also Robert Ritner, *The Mechanics of Ancient Egyptian Magical Practices* (Chicago: Oriental Institute, 1993), 76-77.

20. For references to Horus avenging his father's murder, see Miriam Lichtheim, *Ancient Egyptian Literature*, Vol. 2 (Berkeley: University of California Press, 1973-80), 14-23.

21. *Parabola: The Magazine of Myth and Tradition*, an interview with Dennis and Barbara Tedlock, "Where You Want to Be: An Investigation of the *Popol Vuh*," XVIII/3 (New York: Society for the Study of Myth & Tradition, 1993), 51.

22. Erik Hornung, *Conceptions of God in Ancient Egypt: The One and the Many*, trans. John Baines (Ithaca, New York: Cornell University Press, l982), 88-9.

23. Spencer, 146.

24. Erik Hornung, *Idea Into Image*, trans. Elizabeth Bredick (New York: Timken Publishers, Inc., 1992), 178.

25. Schele and Freidel, *A Forest of Kings*, 76, 226.

26. Karl A. Taube, "The Major Gods of Ancient Yucatan," *Studies in Pre-Columbian Art & Archaeology* 32 (Washington, D.C.: Dumbarton Oaks, 1992), 76.

27. For a description of the Underworld, see C. J. Bleeker, "Isis and Hathor," in *The Book of the Goddess Past and Present*, Carl Olson, ed. (New York: Crossroad, 1983), 44; Dennis Tedlock, *Popol Vuh* (1985), 147; E. A. Wallis Budge, *Osiris: The Egyptian Religion of Resurrection*, 2 vols. in one (England: British Museum, 1985; reprint, New Hyde Part, New York: University Books, 1961), I: 107, II: 250; Veronica Ions, *Egyptian Mythology* (Middlesex: Hamlyn Publishing Group, Ltd., 1968), 50; Irene Nicholson, *Firefly in the Night* (London: Faber and Faber, 1959), 35.

28. Dennis Tedlock, *Popol Vuh: The Definitive Edition of the Mayan Book of the Dawn of Life and the Glories of Gods and Kings*, rev. ed. (New York: Simon and Schuster, Inc., 1996), 238-39.

29. Mircea Eliade, *The Sacred and the Profane: The Nature of Religion*, trans. Willard R. Trask (London: Harcourt, Brace, Jovanovich, 1959), 190.

30. E. C. Krupp, *Beyond the Blue Horizon: Myths and Legends of the Sun, Moon, Stars, and Planets* (New York: Harper Collins Publishers, 1991), 236-37.

31. Ibid., 237.

32. Schele and Freidel, *A Forest of Kings*, 255.

33. Personal communication from Dr. Richard Wilkinson to Diane Wirth, October 8, 1999. See also Richard H. Wilkinson, *Reading Egyptian Art: A Hieroglyphic Guide to Ancient Egyptian Painting and Sculpture* (New York: Thames and Hudson, 1992), 75; Alexandre Piankoff, *Le Livre du Jour et le la Nuit* (Cairo: Inst. Fr. d'Arch., 1942), 24, 95.

34. Stephen Quirke, *Ancient Egyptian Religion* (London: British Museum Press, 1992), 36.

35. J. Gwyn Griffiths, *The Conflict of Horus and Seth* (Liverpool: Liverpool University Press, 1960).

36. Michael D. Coe, "The Hero Twins: myth and image," in *The Maya Vase Book*, vol. 1 (New York: Kerr Associates, 1989), 16.

37. Julia Guernsey Kappelman, "Of Macaws and Men: Late Preclassic Cosmology and Political Ideology in Izapan-style Monuments" (Ph.D. diss., University of Texas, Austin, 1997), 9.

38. Evan Hadingham, *Early Man and the Cosmos* (New York: Walker & Co., 1984), 23.

39. E. C. Krupp, *Skywatchers, Shamans and Kings* (New York: John Wiley & Sons, Inc., 1997), 288.

40. For a complete translated of this text, see J. de Horrack, "Louvre Papyrus No. 3248," *Bibliotheque Egyptologique*, XVII (1878), 110-37.

41. Hadingham, 23.

42. Krupp, *Beyond the Blue Horizon*, 32.

43. Ibid., 219.

44. Wilkinson, *Reading Egyptian Art*, 155.

45. Virginia Lee Davis, "Identifying Ancient Egyptian Constellations," *Archaeoastronomy* 9 (1985), 102-4. For an example of an opposing view, see Rolf Krauss, "Astronomische Konzepte und Jenseitsvorstellungen in den pyramidentexten," *Aegyptologische Abhandlungen* 59 (Wiesbaden: Harrassowitz, 1997).

46. See also Jane B. Sellers, *The Death of Gods in Ancient Egypt* (New York: Penguin, 1992), 97, 165.

47. *Egyptian Book of the Dead: The Book of Going Forth by Day*, trans. Raymond Faulkner and Ogden Goelet, Jr., ed. Eva Von Dassow (San Francisco: Chronicle Books, 1994), plate 16, chapter 58.

48. Karl A. Taube, "The Olmec Maize God," *RES* 29/30 (Cambridge, Massachusetts: Peabody Museum of Archaeology and Ethnology, Harvard University, 1996), 62.

49. Richard A. Wertime and Angela M. H. Schuster, "Written in the Stars: Celestial Origin of Maya Creation," *Archaeology* 46/4 (1993), 26-27.

50. Referenced in Linda Schele and Nikolai Grube, "Some Revisions to Tikal's Dynasty of Kings," *Texas Notes on Precolumbian Art, Writing, and Culture* 67 (Austin: Center of the History and Art of Ancient American Culture of the Art Department, University of Texas, 1994), 7.

51. Taube, "The Olmec Maize God," 69, Fig. 22.c.

52. Thelma D. Sullivan, "The Mask of Itztlacolichqui," *Actas del XLI Congreso Internacional de Americanistas, Mexico, 1974*, 2 (Mexico, 1976), 259.

53. R. T. Rundle Clark, *Myth and Symbol in Ancient Egypt* (New York: Thames and Hudson, 1959), 118.

54. David A. Freidel, "Children of the First Father's Skull: Terminal Classic Warfare in the Northern Maya Lowlands and the Transformation of Kingship and Elite Hierarchies," in *Mesoamerican Elites*, Diane Z. Chase and Arlen F. Chase, eds. (Norman: University of Oklahoma Press, 1992), 107.

55. Tedlock, *Popol Vuh* (1985), 42, 349.

56. Rafael Girard, *Esotericism of the Popol Vuh*, trans. Blair A. Moffett (Pasadena: Theosophical University Press, 1979), 173.

57. Michael D. Coe, "The Hero Twins," 169.

58. Michael D. Coe, "Death and the Ancient Maya," in *Death and the Afterlife in Pre-Columbian America*, E. P. Benson, ed. (Washington, D.C.: Dumbarton Oaks, 1975), 91.

59. Greg Reeder, "Running the Heb Sed," *KMT* 4/4 (1993), 65.

60. E. A. Wallis Budge, *The Book of the Dead: The Papyrus of Ani* (New York: Dover Publications, 1967), xlix.

61. Robert M. Carmack, *The Quiche Mayas of Utatlan* (Norman: University of Oklahoma Press, 1981), 149.

62. H. W. Helck, "Rp't auf dem Thron des Geb," *Orientalia* 19, cited in Hugh Nibley, *Abraham in Egypt* (Salt Lake City: Deseret Book Company, 1981), 46.

63. Lurker, 12.

64. Jocelyn Gohary, *Akhenaten's Sed-festival at Karnak* (New York: Kegan Paul International, 1992), 1.

65. Linda Schele and Mary Ellen Miller, *The Blood of Kings: Dynasty and Ritual in Maya Art* (New York: George Braziller, Inc., in association with the Kimbell Art Museum, Fort Worth, TX, 1986), 111.

66. Linda Schele and David Freidel, "The Courts of Creation: Ballcourts, Ballgames, and Portals to the Maya Otherworld," in *The Mesoamerican Ballgame*, Vernon L. Scarborough and David R. Wilcox, eds. (Tucson: University of Arizona Press, 1991), 291.

67. See for example Rudolf Anthes, "Mythology in Ancient Egypt," in *Mythologies of the Ancient World*, Samuel Noah Kramer, ed. (Garden City, New York: Doubleday, 1961), 73.

68. Personal communication from Geoffrey Graham to Diane Wirth, October 5, 1997.

69. Cyrus H. Gordon, *Before Columbus: Links Between the Old World and Ancient America* (New York: Crown Publishers, 1971), 154-58.

70. Peter T. Furst, "House of Darkness and House of Light: Sacred Functions of West Mexican Funerary Art," in *Death and the Afterlife in Pre-Columbian America*, Elizabeth P. Benson, ed. (Washington, D.C.: Dumbarton Oaks Research Library, 1975), 34; Mircea Eliade, *Rites and Symbols of Initiation: The Mysteries of Birth and Rebirth* (London: Harvill Press, 1958), 63.

71. Dorie Reents-Budet, *Painting the Maya Universe: Royal Ceramics of the Classic Period* (Durham: Duke University Press, 1994), 274.

72. Rex Ashley Koontz, "The Iconography of El Tajin, Veracruz, Mexico" (Ph.D. diss., University of Texas, Austin, 1994), 77, 79, 82.

73. Mircea Eliade, *Images and Symbols*, 152.

74. Erich Zehren, *The Crescent and the Bull: a Survey of Archaeology in the Near East*, tran. James Cleugh (New York: Hawthorn Books, Inc., 1962), 265, 267.

75. *Egyptian Book of the Dead*, 156.

76. Buffie Johnson, *Lady of the Beasts* (New York: Harper Collins Publishers, 1990), 252-53.

77. E. A. Wallis Budge, *From Fetish to God in Ancient Egypt* (London: Oxford University Press, 1934; reprint, New York: Dover Publications, 1988), 182.

78. Carolyn E, Tate, *Yaxchilan*, 51.

79. *Parabola*, 48.

80. Dennis Tedlock, *Popol Vuh* (1985), 342; Miller and Taube, 136.

81. Dennis Tedlock, "Myth, Math, and the Problem of Correlation in Mayan Books," in *The Sky in Mayan Literature*, Anthony F. Aveni, ed. (New York: Oxford University Press, 1992), 35.

82. Taube, "The Major Gods of Ancient Yucatan," 63.

83. Anthes, 89-90.

84. Dennis Tedlock, "Myth, Math, and the Problem of Correlation in Mayan Books," 264.

85. Ibid., 265.

86. Floyd G. Lounsbury, "The Identities of the Mythological Figures in the Cross Group Inscriptions of Palenque," in *Fourth Palenque Round Table, 1980,* gen. ed. Merle Greene-Robertson; vol. ed. Elizabeth P. Benson, VI (San Francisco: Pre-Columbian Art Research Institute, 1985), 54; Schele and Freidel, *A Forest of Kings*, 414.

87. Dicey Taylor, "Painted Ladies: Costumes for Women on Tepeu Ceramics," in *The Maya Vase Book*, 3 (New York: Kerr Associates, 1992), 521.

88. George Hart, *Egyptian Myths* (Austin: University of Texas, 1990), 33.

89. Mary Ellen Gutierrez, "Ballcourts: The Chasms of Creation," *Texas Notes on Precolumbian Art, Writing and Culture* 53 (Austin, The Center for the History and Art of Ancient American Culture, Art Department, University of Texas, 1993).

90. Ibid., 2; Schele and Freidel, *A Forest of Kings*, 418.

91. Susan Tower Hollis, *The Ancient Egyptian "Tale of Two Brothers": The Oldest Fairytale in the World* (Norman: University of Oklahoma, 1990).

92. Ibid., 87.

93. Ibid., 124.

94. Franz Boas, "Dissemination of Tales Among the Natives of North America," *Journal of American Fold Lore* 6 (1891).

95. Stross, "Maize and Blood."

96. *Olmec Art, Arquelogia Mexicana* (Mexico, 1997), 37.

97. Richard A. Diehl and Michael Coe, "Olmec Archaeology," in *The Olmec World in Ritual and Rulership* (Princeton: The Art Museum, Princeton University, in association with Harry N. Abrams, Inc., 1997), 15.

98. Douglas E. Bradley and Peter David Joralemon, *The Lords of Life: The Iconography of Power and Fertility in Preclassic Mesoamerica* (Indiana: The Snite Museum of Art, University of Notre Dame, 1992), 18, 31.

CHAPTER III

CREATION AND RECREATION

Creation myths were reenacted yearly, or periodically, by ancient cultures of the Near East and Mesoamerica. Traditions involved in these cyclical performances vary, yet were oftentimes similar to an amazing degree. In fact, these similarities are so numerous and detailed that they may only be explained as a result of culture borrowing. This raises questions concerning the theory of total isolationism as opposed to a consideration of early voyages to the Americas. Parallel ceremonies associated with the creation will be reviewed in this chapter.

REENACTMENT OF CREATION

Ancient kings renewed their earthly kingdoms and their right to the throne by performing a ritual reenactment of the creation and bringing all things to life as the gods did at that pristine moment in time. Eliade, an exacting student of comparative religion, informs us that this means: "What he [the king] does has been done before. . . . The gesture acquires meaning and reality solely to the extent to which it repeats a primordial act."[1] The primordial act is, of course, the creation of the world—the moment in time considered among the most sacred in history. By re-creating this hallowed act with great pomp and circumstance at a temple site, continuity in the kingdom was established. In other words, the whole of the community (its rulers, and the religious center) became sanctified and revitalized through renewal rituals. In essence, this is what Eliade means by the myth of the eternal return; the return to the beginning of sacred time for its duplication and perfection of the future. As a result of these ceremonies, the community experienced sacred time and sacred time was one and the same with the First Time—the day of creation. Man became contemporary with creation and the past and present became one.

Building Dedications and Other Ceremonies

Apparently this tradition existed in ancient Mesopotamia (now eastern Syria and Iraq), Egypt, Israel, India, and Greece.[2] This concept was also prevalent in Mesoamerica. Creation-oriented rituals were often performed at the dedication of a new territory or building; at the onset of a new war; or at the coronation ceremony of a new king.[3] The key word here is new, as in the newly created earth, which was sacred and pure at the moment of its conception. All this took place at the temple site, which was considered the sacred center, the axis of the earth and heaven where creation took place—the portal where men communicated with the gods.

ORDER VERSUS CHAOS

Hero gods had to overcome evil supernaturals in order for creation and life to come to fruition. This scenario was a metaphor for controlling the forces of nature and bringing chaotic physical matter into an organized state. Creation and order were inseparably connected in sacred rites of the First Time.

Slaying the Monster

Children's stories of heroes slaying dragons and saving the kingdom are but tales evolved from very old and less fanciful traditions. For example, Babylonian myths tell of the god, Marduk, who split the body of Tiamat, a great sea monster who represented chaos (Fig. III.1). With the pieces of Tiamat's body, Marduk created the heavens and the earth, setting all things in their proper order.[4]

We find the same monster of chaos in Mesoamerica among central Mexican cultures. Using the *Histoyre du Mechique* as her source, Heyden describes a similar Mesoamerican concept of the creation. A great monster is torn, limb from limb, with parts of its body becoming the mountains, valleys, and vegetation.[5] Whether a monster is defeated and cut into pieces to create the world, or a hero figure conquers the forces of evil associated with death, the end result was the same. Chaos and death are overcome. Life and order triumph.

Fig. III.1 Tiamat (monster of chaos) defeated by Marduk on Babylonian cylinder seal (drawn after photograph in Ward 1910).

THE COUNCIL OF GODS

Before all was set in its proper place, early accounts tell of a council of gods whose prime directive was to organize the world for the habitation of man. Often overlooked is Genesis 1:26 that reads, "and God [Elohim] said, Let us make man in our image." The Hebrew word, Elohim, is plural, yet translated as God in the New Testament, rather than Gods. This passage should be translated: "and the Gods said, Let us make man in our image." *Us* and *our* are plural pronouns, which certainly refers to at least two and probably more than two Gods. On the subject of one Supreme God over the Gods, Dahood, a highly respected biblical scholar, remarks: "The picture of God in the midst of the assembly of Gods recurs again and again in the Psalter [Psalms]."[6] This Father God is the one worshiped in the scriptures, with no other in authority over Him.

Fig. III.2 Maya Vase of the Seven Gods (courtesy of Michael Coe).

Among the Maya, the creation involves a council of supernatural beings who discuss and plan the act of creation together.[7] The council of Maya gods are depicted on the Vase of the Seven Gods (Fig. III.2). In the Genesis-like story related in the Quiché Maya's *Popol Vuh*, the creation is accomplished by more than one god, and follows a somewhat similar pattern to that described in the Old Testament.

Then came the word. Tepeu and Gucumatz came together in the darkness, in the night, and Tepeu and Gucumatz talked together. They talked then, discussing and deliberating; they agreed, they united their words and their thoughts.

Then while they meditated, it became clear to them that when dawn would break, man must appear. Then they planned the creation, and the growth of the trees and the thickets and the birth of life and the creation of man.[8]

The Word

Comparable to the Hebrew account in Genesis and Egyptian sources that state the creation took place through God's word,[9] the same was true in Mesoamerica where it was held that the creation started with the utterance of a word, and that which was uttered appeared.[10] To finish the act of creation, a hieroglyph at Palenque, Chiapas, Mexico, reads "It is done."[11]

NEW YEAR CEREMONY

In that the creation was the supreme act of all time, it was considered the most sacred event to have ever taken place. In order for the good fortune of renewal to occur in a polity, this moment from the ancient past needed to be incorporated into the present cycle of time. For this reason, New Year ceremonies were inaugurated. Each New Year was as though the creation took place all over again.[12] As Hornung remarks about this time of year in Egypt: "The beginning of the New Year revises the world and repeats creation. The Egyptians called the year 'that which rejuvenates itself' (renpet). New Year's Day . . . signals the return of creation."[13] In addition, the Hebrew word for year, *shannah,* derives from the verb to repeat.[14]

New Year festivities were held at different times depending on the culture. For some it was during the harvest when crops bore fruit and then died, for others the winter solstice when the sun returned to its course from its progress south, or the spring when vegetation is reborn. Whatever the time of year, the symbolism was the same. Order and rebirth were again established through sacred ritual as it was at the beginning of time.

Western cultures visualize the current year-end as an old man ready to enter the grave; whereas the New Year is represented as a young child with bright eyes and an eager smile as he ushers in a period of new beginnings. In addition to this symbolism, people congregate, eat, dance, sing, and make a joyous noise when the hour of the New Year strikes at midnight. It is also a time of order, renewal, resolutions, and goals. Like many traditions performed in our day, New Year celebrations take place without regard to their origins. Among ancient cultures, however, such rites were well understood and considered sacred.

A Time of Renewal

By reenacting the creation scenario during New Year festivals, Mesoamerican and ancient Middle Eastern kings were the prime source of revitalization for the community. Prior to a king's accession to the throne or renewing his right to rule, the polity was likened to a time of chaos and confusion, which was the state of the cosmos before the creation. Like the hero god/creator whom the king impersonated, he went through a ritual combat with evil and chaotic forces and was figuratively killed and resurrected. Along with his personal success and enthronement, or renewed rulership, the king was thought to bring life and vitality to his people. Crops were assured, battles would be won, and everyone would prosper as a result of the king's re-creating the events of the First Time.

These ceremonial acts were prevalent in most Near Eastern, New Year festivals and lasted for literally thousands of years.[15] For example, although the Persian Empire reached its height hundreds of years after the earlier Babylonian empire, which included some of the same lands now comprised of Iran and Iraq, it carried over many traditions linked to kingship and ritual with very little deviation from its predecessors'. Comparable to their kings of old, the Persian king became his god's adopted son and the representative of his people on earth. Order in the cosmos was reestablished by him at the time of the New Year festival, called Nauruz, when the king took the role of his god and reenacted the First Time. In an inscription at Susa, King Darius (521–486 B.C.) proclaims that he performed the work of his god, for he, like his god, made the world excellent.[16] This roleplaying may have included the primeval battle necessary to overcome chaos, which took the form of a monster. There are a number of reliefs depicting the king fighting a monster and a victory over this enemy, assuring creative order for the coming year. Sacred processions also took place during the Persian Nauruz Festival, which no doubt were derived from earlier customs of the land. This continuity of traditions over time, from the Babylonian through the Persian Empires, is a prime example of how Old World practices were slow to change compared to our fast-paced world of modern technology.

Stretching the Cord

These yearly or periodic performances of creation entailed a wide range of activities for ancient cultures. One of the oldest traditions pertaining to these rituals provided a way to establish sacred boundaries. In the Near East, cosmological alignments and measurements were believed taken at the time of the creation.[17] On a Neo-Sumerian stela, a god presents the ruler with implements for laying out the temple ground plan. These items are a rod and measuring cord (Fig. III.3).[18] Rituals involving the measuring of sacred space were reminiscent of the Creator's measuring the universe. Performing this ceremony in the Near East was oftentimes called Stretching the Cord. Four corners were established and, more importantly, this rite brought together the realms of heaven and earth.[19] Since rulers impersonated the role of their high god, it was most appropriate for the Egyptian Pharaoh to Stretch the Cord (Fig. III.4).[20] In ancient Israel one finds a similar tradition.[21] Several verses in Job come to mind with regard to stretching the cord for measuring boundaries at the time of creation. God asks Job the following questions:

Fig. III.3 Detail from the Neo-Sumerian Urnammu Stela (redrawn after Lundquist 1994: 106).

> Where wast thou when I laid the foundations of the earth? declare, if thou hast understanding. Who hath laid the measures thereof, if thou knowest? or who hath stretched the line upon it? Whereupon are the foundations thereof fastened? or who laid the corner stone thereof; When the morning stars sang together, and all the sons of God shouted for joy?[22]

Examining some of the particulars of New Year ceremonies in the Near East, we find unusual corresponding ideas in Mesoamerica. It was essential that sacred space be created for the site where these rites were to be performed. Measuring space with a cord was as important to the Maya,[23] as it was to Old World cultures. These sacred centers became associated with the First Time of creation when space was partitioned by the gods with measuring ropes. Girard studied rituals of the Chortis Maya in Honduras and their ceremonies dealing with the beginning of new cycles of time. The action of measuring space and separating the sky from the earth started the new calendar year. This Maya act of measuring rejuvenated the existing world.[24] The *Popol Vuh* makes reference to measuring the sky and

Fig. III.4 Stretching of the Cord ceremony, Temple of Amun and Re-Horakhty Amada, Nubia (redrawn after Wilkinson 1994: Fig. 135).

earth at the time of creation;[25] and from the *Chilam Balam of Tizimin* we read: "Now it should be said of the four gods that they stretched out the earth. And when they had finished stretching out the earth, they planted the red Imix tree."[26]

The Lacandon Maya of Chiapas, Mexico, also believed that the cords of the creator gods stretched to mark the four cardinal points;[27] and among other Maya groups, god impersonators stretched ropes around the area to be sanctified. As Kubler and C. Gibson note, the Aztec month, Tititl as shown in the Tovar Calendar commentary, translates as stretching, and a drawing in this account depicts "a man as one who stretches something with a cord, in order to indicate that the gods thus stretch and sustain the machine of the world."[28]

Ritual Procession

Another way of designating the parameters of sacred space was through a ritual procession or dance that circumambulated the area. In the Middle East men and women participated in dances to accomplish certain objectives of the Egyptian Sed Festival, which was their festival of renewal. Although not held annually, it was a reinstatement of the Pharaoh. Some dances by the men appear to represent ritual combat,[29] which may have had to do with overcoming chaos at the time of creation. However, it is the processional dance that is of significance here. The Pharaoh made a circuit of a designated area as part of the Sed Festival. This circuit was called "Dedication of the Field" or "Circuit of the Wall" (Fig. III.5).[30] When the king circled a designated area of his kingdom, he was symbolically traversing the heavens as the gods were known to do.[31] This custom was also popular among the ancient Hebrews of the Near East. As Patai notes, the king made such a procession once a year, namely on New Year's Day. His route was from the gates of the city to the temple and back.[32]

Fig. III.5   Egyptian king performing ritual at his Sed Festival (redrawn after Brandon 1975: Fig. 402).

Rulers of Egypt also followed a processional path through the temple, and the temple structure replicated the entire cosmos.[33] Like the Egyptian Pharaoh whose circuitous dance represented the movement of the sun,[34] Maya rulers took a ceremonial stride through the temple to the interior and back with the idea that their journey into the temple represented the sun's path through the heavens.[35]

In ancient times, to encircle a sacred center transformed physical space into the more spiritual cosmological geography of the heavens—the two becoming as one. Wosien comments: "In dance ritual . . . [the king] . . . undertook to represent his god, celebrating and commemorating his god's measured movements in creation. . . . By dancing out again and again the original Mystery of Creation, the dancer . . . is put in touch with the primal event."[36] The measuring of space, organizing matter, and setting order in the universe, were viewed as accomplished by the dance of a god around his sacred realm. Thus, it was important for mortal men to reenact the creation dance of the gods.

In Mesoamerica, one finds a great deal of information on circumambulation. Hieroglyphic texts on stelae and stone lintels tell of ritual dance. For example, processions were performed by the Quiché and Tz'utujil Maya during New Year ceremonies, and these processional lines often wound their way to four nearby mountains.[37] If mountains were not in the vicinity, Bassie-Sweet regards the heaps of stone placed on four sides of a town, as noted by Tozzer, as representing mountains at the cardinal points.[38] These symbolic mountains stood for ritual entrances that were markers for New Year ceremonial processions. Similar to cultures of the Near East, these parade-like circuits surrounding sacred areas replicated the structure of the cosmos and charged the earthly space with power from above.

Apparently this phenomenon was Pan-Mesoamerican as it was also dramatized by the Aztec. We know, for example, that just before the advent of New Year ceremonies, promenades involving both rulers and commoners took place around Tenochtitlan, the site upon which today's Mexico city is built. This was done with purifying the nation as the prime, symbolic objective, reaffirming the interrelationship of the social and the cosmic orders (Fig. III.6).[39] As MacLeod finds regarding other Mesoamerican traditions: "A count of footsteps is far more than mechanical formula, for it gives birth to the world."[40]

Fig. III.6   Aztec ritual dance of circumambulation (redrawn after
Durán 1963: Trat. 2, Lm. 11).

All in all, there were various kinds of dances and processions performed by these ancient cultures and, in many cases, they were merely variations of a theme: the creation and its related aspects of rejuvenation, life, order, and cohesion. These dances/processions were very similar to those performed in our time in Mexico and Central America,[41] and are rich in music, color, and costume.

Sacred Space and Purification

Sacred space, whether in the Old or New World, became the axis of the world and could be re-created at different locations. When sacred space was established, it needed to be purified, as all needed to be made ready for the area designated to represent the place of creation. Evil and all uncleanliness were removed from sacred areas and the surrounding community in different ways. Common to Babylonian, Israelite, and Mesoamerican peoples was a symbolic loading of sin/evil onto an object, which was then ceremonially removed from the sacred center.[42]

In the Near East, evil was sometimes removed by lighting bonfires, especially at the turn of the New Year.[43] In Mesoamerica the essence of evil was often transferred by a priest to a pile of burning copal (incense made from tree sap) in a bucket and then removed from the area.[44] Incense was also used among the Hebrews as a means of purification;[45] e.g., in ancient Israel on the day the New Year commenced special emphasis was made of ridding one's self of all evil.[46]

As early as the Babylonian empire, cleansing and/or renovation of the temple was part of the New Year ceremony.[47] The same was performed in Israel during Yom Kippur when not only the sanctuary but all the vessels and people were cleansed.[48] In fact, it was absolutely imperative that priests in Egypt, Israel, and Mesoamerica go through purification ceremonies before entering their respective temples. As Krupp noted, purification of people and sacred sites in preparation for New Year festivals was not a simple matter of washing and cleaning—it represented the fresh, purified state that renewal brings.[49]

Rebuilding Edifices

Rebuilding temples in Mesoamerica was common (Fig. III.7), and ceremonies of purification and renewal were performed on such occasions. By superimposing layers of renovated surfaces, the original sacred space continued on through the generations. The power of the past remained in the present through rituals of renewal.[50] Whether or not temple rededication rites were performed during New Year festivities is not known. However, Tozzer suggests that the large number of replastered walls of some ruins indicate yearly renewal rites.[51] Both the dedication and rededication of a temple in various cultures of the Near East were quite common during New Year festivities. For example, the original dedication of the Temple of Solomon in ancient Israel took place at the New Year in the seventh month at the Feast of Tabernacles, which, in a sense, represents the creation of the world.[52] Rededication rites ensured not only the temple's purified and sacred state, but the cosmic renewal of the community in which the temple stood.[53]

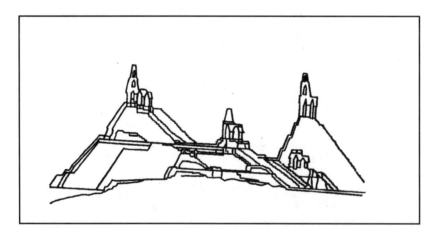

Fig. III.7   Temples renewed by building a new structure over the old.
Tikal, Guatemala (redrawn and adapted after W. Coe 1968).

Measuring sacred space, circumambulating the area, and purification rites, applied to temples in both the Near East and Mesoamerica. Building a temple was comparable to the original act of creation.[54] In line with this perception, the cornerstone of a building was, and still is, a very important part of any building—especially temples. According to Eliade: "To build a temple or a city is equivalent to reiterating the 'contstruction' of the Universe. . . . The cornerstone is located at the 'Center of the World'."[55] In the Near East it was a common custom to deposit sacred objects under the cornerstone. It is therefore no surprise that a sacred cache was traditionally placed under cornerstones in Mesoamerica.[56]

New Fire

Kindling a new fire was also essential to New Year activities. These fires had special significance in the Old and New Worlds, and were connected to the sun's birth. Kings played an important role in these rites as they, too, represented the sun. At Copan, Honduras, several stelae portray the deceased king dressed as the jaguar night sun facing west in the direction of the setting/deceased sun. The other side of these stelae face east, the direction of the new sun, and depict the new king who represents the living and burning sun.[57]

New fires built at the time of a king's renewal or accession to the throne, especially during a New Year festival, were of great significance in the Near East.[58] Lurker, for example, notes that fires were extinguished at the death of a king in Kordofan in the Sudan, and lit when a new king ascended the throne.[59]

This practice also took place among the Aztec. Motecuhzoma commenced his reign in 1507 A.D., which happened to fall at the end of an important cycle. This august occasion was commemorated with a New Fire Ceremony so, in the case of Motecuhzoma, the festival satisfied a ritual for both the birth of his rule and the rebirth of a new cycle of time.[60] And among the Maya, Sedat writes that fire-related rituals appear to refer to inaugural ceremonies.[61]

In Mesoamerica there are two major calendars: the 365-day solar calendar and the 260-day sacred calendar. The first day of each of these two calendars, occur simultaneously—only once every fifty-two years. The important New Fire Ceremony was performed at this synchronized moment in time. Edmonson is of the opinion that New Fire Ceremonies appeared in Mexico among the Olmec, dating back before the seventh century B.C. and may even date to 200–300 years earlier.[62] Today the Maya still make great bonfires on New Year's Day.[63]

As mentioned, Egyptian kings had a strong affiliation with the sun. Lurker informs us that it was the Pharaoh himself who kindled a new fire at the beginning of the Sed Festival to ensure light and life, and the king's reinvestiture and enthronement.[64] To reiterate, these new fires symbolized the original fires of creation and the greatest fire of all, the living sun. According to Sellers, the ceremony that kicked off the Egyptian Sed Festival was called 'Lighting of the Flame,' and involved a procession of torches.[65] One finds the same in ancient Israel. Sukkot, or the Feast of Tabernacles, was the primary festival held anciently in Israel and celebrated the beginning of their year. Prior to the Hebrews, a similar ceremony was commemorated by the Canaanites. Besides singing and praising their god, they, like other ancient cultures, made grand processional dances, including a spectacular torch dance at night.[66]

Among the Mexica of Mexico, a New Fire Ceremony was held every fifty-two years, which was the end of the major cycle of time, as already mentioned. Fifty-two sticks were bundled together and used to create the new fire. This new fire was frequently started on the chest of a sacrificial victim (Fig. III.8) with the belief that the blood debt would provide the sun with energy.[67] This rite guaranteed the sun's continuance for another fifty-two years. All in all, it ensured the rebirth of time. In the *Borgia Codex* (pp. 33, 46), a new fire is drilled atop a mirror on a sacrificial victim. The region where this was performed is called *tlalxicco*, which, as Taube notes, means earth navel. In addition to sacrifices, many people performed auto sacrifice, a self-inflicted, blood-letting sacrificial penance.[68] One of the occasions upon which this was dramatized was at the lighting of a new fire.[69] This was perhaps a way for the protagonist to proclaim his part in giving blood to the sun as a personal offering and having a role in the rebirth of the new cycle.

Fig. III.8 New Fire created on the chest of a sacrificial victim (redrawn after *Florentine Codex*).

After a sacred fire was lit, relay runners went from place to place to rekindle all fires that were extinguished to mark the death of the old cycle.[70] This, too, like the aforementioned ceremonies, is another reenactment of creation. The end of the year was comparable to a flame that died—it was the end of a cycle. The new cycle burst upon the scene with a fresh new glow, symbolized by the new fire.[71] For the Mexica of Mexico, the new fire was believed to come through a cosmic fire drill.[72] When a fire was kindled for a New Year ceremony, the person accomplishing the task was likened to the god who brought forth fire at the moment of creation. New fires were also lit at the dedication of buildings, especially temples.[73] This, too, is connected to the fires of creation as the new temple is the prime symbol of the creation and cosmos.

The Five "Empty" Days

Some of the rites mentioned to this point were conducted just before the onset of the New Year. The Mesoamerican solar calendar of 365 days was actually 360 days with an additional five "empty" or "nameless," unlucky days placed at the end to complete the year. The Egyptians had a similar system, adding five epagomenal days to their 360-day solar year.[74] These days were more or less empty days as well since they belonged to neither the previous nor oncoming year.[75]

In Mesoamerica among the Aztec, these days were known as *nemontemi,* "the days unfit for work."[76] Although all work ceased at this time, the air bustled with activity as rites were performed to combat the chaos that these five days represented.

The Maya of San Juan Chamula, for example, still conduct a festival of games that are performed with the intent of destroying the old world and creating a new one.[77] Stanton describes his visit to San Juan Chamula in Chiapas, Mexico, at a time when preparations were being made for the mid-winter festival of renewal called *Ch'ay K'in.*[78] This particular renewal literally means "lost days,"[79] and *ch'ay* alone carries the connotation of "death."[80] These five days are spent in utter confusion, representing an upside-down world, a time of chaos similar to the period before the primordial creation. There is cross-dressing, mock battles, and men costumed as howler monkeys, performing mischievous antics that, again, represent chaos. All this mayhem is finally dealt with as *pasiones* represent the sun. The *pasiones* are religious men who fast, abstain from sex, and take the fire walk representing the path of the sun. Once accomplished, this ritual ensures the restoration and rebirth of the universe. As Taube observes: "The new year festival is a period ending rite that symbolically constitutes the destruction and creation of the world."[81] This tradtion goes back hundreds of years among the Maya.

The Creation Play

All these events lead us to the theatrical portion of renewal rites. Ancient texts found in the Near East indicate that creation scenarios were read and/or acted out during special times of the year, especially during New Year festivities. Among the Babylonians and Assyrians this activity was the primary cultic event of the religious calendar.[82] In Mesopotamia, priestly manuals were produced as a guide for performing rituals in the temple for their New Year Akitu Festival. This creation account, the *Enuma Elish,* was written around 1700 B.C., although the basis for its traditions come from much earlier. *Enuma Elish* means, "as it once happened above."[83] The objective of this performance was, of course, to reestablish order in the cosmos and the kingdom, and to reaffirm the gods and the king, their earthly representative.[84]

Ritual Combat

A crucial part of this recitation was the story of Marduk's triumph over Tiamat, i.e., the victory of their creator gods over the forces of chaos. Oesterley compares the combat between Marduk and Tiamat to a fight described in later interpretations of the Bible, referring to a conflict and victory over Tehom. He concludes: "A ritual combat—was at one time represented in the Israelite New Year festival."[85] Gray supports this premise when he wrote that the theme included the victorious conflicts of God with the powers of chaos.[86] Oesterley notes that creative acts were recited from Psalms as well.[87] In their book, *Hebrew Myths: The Book of Genesis,* Graves and Patai demonstrate that the creation account in the first chapter of Genesis presented an underlying theme similar to the myth of Marduk and Tiamat.[88] And today the creation account in the Bible is read on the final day of Sukkos, the Feast of Tabernacles, the festival originally celebrated as the Hebrew New Year.

The Shabako Stone is one of the oldest Egyptian creation texts and was dramatized by actors while the account was recited by a priest, whom Sethe appropriately calls the "theaterdirektor."[89] Bell describes a reenactment scene portrayed on an Egyptian pectoral. The king is shown defeating his enemies. According to Bell, this particular act constituted reiterating and redoing creation by reenacting what the creator gods did.[90]

Other Egyptian texts are full of creation accounts that were recited. The king took part in many of these rites and his roleplaying was that of the creator gods in primeval times. In fact, everything the Pharaoh did was considered an act of creation. For example, both Sesostris I and Thutmosis I repeated the acts of creation, doing what their Father, Re, did before them.[91] And it is said that Ramesses II grounded the world anew, as in creation.[92]

Once again, we note the same concept appearing in Mesoamerica where the king played the role of deity. Houston informs us that most pre-Columbian texts were meant to be performed, and a great many of these texts were linked to stories told in the *Popol Vuh*—the myths of creation.[93] In the Near East this performance was conducted at the temple, and the New Year ritual in Mesoamerica also appears to have taken place at the temple.

Raising the World Tree

One of the major acts of the creation reenactment (the action that set all things in place) was raising the World Tree. In Egypt the king officiated at the ceremony by raising a pole called the Djed-pillar (see Fig. VI.14). This event was held at daybreak during the Sed Festival of renewal.[94] Baring and Cashford explain the significance of raising a pillar at this momentous point in time. "The raising of the pillar meant that the spirit of the corn had not been killed in the cutting down of the corn. . . . Sometimes the pillar is drawn as a tree with lopped off branches . . . signifying the Tree of Life as the Axis of the World."[95] A bare tree trunk was also used in the New Year Festival in Assyria.[96]

In Mesoamerica the tradition of raising the World Tree, in the form of a pole, took place during the New Year ceremony.[97] This was symbolic of the event when First Father separated the sky from the earth at the moment of creation. At the end of a Maya solar year, which was called a *Tun*, a stela was erected. The setting up of a vertical stela at the end of a year also symbolized the raising of the World Tree as part of the creation scenario. Chapter VI contains a complete discussion of the raising of this sacred pole/tree.

Rebirth and Renewal of King

Another ritual concerning renewal in which the king was involved should be added to this list of similarities. Every New Year in Mesopotamia the king performed a rite in which he disappeared into an underground vault, away from the seeing eyes of the public. The sole purpose of this act was to show that he could overcome death. The king's royal clothes were removed and, at the end of three days, he emerged triumphant as though reborn, demonstrating that he overcame death and was authorized to rule another year.[98]

Townsend discusses a ritual sequence performed by Aztec rulers that involved a separation from the public, not unlike that which was performed by the Babylonians. Using as his source the works of Mendieta and Sahagún, Townsend explains that the ruler changed his royal clothes to dress in a simple loincloth, which "may be seen as a sign of returning to a state of simplicity, to a symbolic time of origin, to the beginning of things."[99] The ruler was then dressed with emblems of death, including a veiled face. He proceeded to a building, separated from the temple, where he hid for four days. On the day of emergence the ruler was purified through a ritual bathing as though born anew.

At Palenque the great ruler, Pakal, is portrayed on the Oval Palace Tablet (Fig. III.9) wearing a simple loincloth while being presented his royal crown. Like a newborn child, Pakal's lack of clothing at his accession to the throne rested on the significance of a rebirth, the same as in the Middle East. Also relevant are scenes of the Maya maize god on polychrome vessels where he is given clothing after his rebirth.[100] New clothing was associated with the rebirth of the New Year among the Maya when images of the gods were redressed during the festivities.[101] Offerings

Fig. III.9   Pakal in simple attire receives his crown. Oval Palace Tablet, Palenque,
Chiapas, Mexico (redrawn after Schele and Freidel 1990: Fig. 6.7).

of clothing were also made to gods at this time of the year in Egypt.[102]

One of the themes running through these theatrical productions, in which the king plays a major role, was victory over death. In both Egypt and Mesoaptamia the king represented the dying and resurrecting god in the annual festival. In addition to the rite of seclusion mentioned above, this could be accomplished by roleplaying in which the king vanquished his enemies or demons represented by men in monster masks. In the case of Mesoamericans, a ballgame was played after which the losers lost their lives.

Sacrifice and Renewal

The act that makes this scenario work is sacrifice. According to Eliade, the purpose of ancient sacrifice was "to restore the primordial unity, that which existed before the creation."[103] Sacrifice played a major role in most Near-Eastern rites. During New Year festivals, a choice victim was sacrificed with the idea that the living king, for whom the sacrifice was a surrogate, appeared to resurrect. This concept was essential to the renewal of all things in a new age. Rosenberg corroborates this when he writes, "[in] the ancient Canaanite cult of Jerusalem . . . periodically the King, or a substitute for the King, had to be offered for sacrifice."[104]

This, of course, was notably true of the Aztecs. In Egypt, blood from the victims ran down channels in the altar into alabaster bowls.[105] In Mesoamerica, blood offerings were also poured into bowls. In both places, the victims were usually prisoners of war. Derchain finds that the main objective of the Egyptian New Year rite was to preserve the universe, which was in constant danger of collapse. The only way to renew the cosmos, including the earth, was through ritual sacrifice.[106] This tradition sounds a familiar ring to students of the religious philosophy of Mesoamerican culture. The Egyptians and other people of the Near East, however, did not perform human sacrifice to the extent that some Mesoamerican cultures achieved.

In Chapter II, it was shown that rulers in Egypt and in Mesoamerica had an affinity for grain. It is important to note that when the grain was cut, the king symbolically died. When the seed of the corn burst back to life, the king was reborn. "Through death comes life," was a concept essential to understanding sacrifice and the reason these ancient cultures found this bloody ritual necessary for the well-being and rebirth of the cosmos. Kings were not killed, but substitutes, who took their place, were sacrificed. On this theme in the Old World, *Man, Myth and Magic* reports: "The king who is killed, the god who dies, is the grain of wheat that falls to the ground. The new king, the risen god, is the reborn crop of the next season."[107] In some cultures, plants or animals were offered as a substitute for the life of the giver. However, in Mesoamerica, human sacrifice, whether that of a victim or through auto-sacrifice, was the rule rather than the exception.

SUMMARY

Similar to Mesoamerican cultures, the Egyptians perceived the creation not as a onetime occurrence but as something that could be repeated, becoming as new and perfect as at the time of its origin.[108] Chaos existed prior to creation and if rituals of the cosmic drama were not performed, it was believed everything would collapse and return to its original, formidable state. The beginning of the Egyptian New Year, along with all faithfully performed rituals symbolic of the First Time, assured the world of its continuance. As Freidel, Schele, and Parker remark: "Creation and recreation were and are at the heart of being Maya."[109] So, in essence, each year the world was symbolically recreated. Once again, we are looking at a surprisingly significant number of similarities that occurred oceans apart.

Until the mid-1970s the Mixe of Oaxaca, Mexico, still bathed in streams to cleanse themselves of evil on New Year's Day and, as their people did for hundreds of years, they put on new clothes, starting the year afresh. Fires were lit; prayers were said; sacrifices were made (usually of fowl); a feast was prepared; new municipal authorities were installed in local governments; ancestors were petitioned to aid the new authorities for the coming year; and processions took place accompanied by music. Much of this is still performed today, yet as modernization and influence of the Catholic and other Christian churches increase, old traditions gradually change to accommodate demand.[110]

New Year festivals in the ancient Middle East contained the following elements: the creation of sacred space, the purification of that space, the lighting of new fires, a visual representation of the dying and resurrecting god, a recitation of the creation myth, a triumphant god/king whose battle is a ritual combat, a sacred marriage, and a grand procession often led by a king/god. With the exception of a sacred marriage rite, all these elements are found in Mesoamerican rites of renewal. This does not mean that sacred marriages did not take place in the New World, but that they are an element of the scenario not yet determined.

The performances discussed in this chapter symbolize the greatest cosmic drama of all time—the creation. As heir to the procreator/god, the king was responsible for the continuation of life and all that belonged to his kingdom. Although this mighty burden rested on his shoulders, his people were allowed to participate in this accomplishment when they performed in song, dance, procession, purification, fasting, and feasting. When the community joined in roleplay along with the king, it was as though each individual was able to contribute to the rebirth of time and space. In a way, these New Year celebrations commemorated the birthday of the world, both past and present, and they will undoubtedly do so for many years to come.

NOTES - Chapter III

1. Mircea Eliade, *The Myth of the Eternal Return: Or, Cosmos and History*, trans. Willard R. Trask (Princeton: Princeton University Press, 1954), 5.

2. Ibid., 121.

3. Eliade, *The Sacred and the Profane*, 81-82.

4. Nahum M. Sarna, *Understanding Genesis* (New York: McGraw Hill, 1966), 4; Donimique Collon, *First Impressions: Cylinder Seals in the Ancient Near East* (Chicago: University of Chicago Press, 1987), 178; *Enuma Elish: The Seven Tablets of Creation*, trans. and ed. L. W. King, vol. I (London: Luzoc and Co., 1902; reprint, Escondido, California: The Book Tree, 1999), LXXXII.

5. *Histoyre du Mechique* (1965), 108, cited in Doris Heyden "Caves, Gods, and Myths: World-View and Planning in Teotihuacan," in *Mesoamerican Sites and World-Views*, Conference at Dumbarton Oaks, October 16-17, 1976, ed Elizabeth P. Benson (Washington, D.C.: Dumbarton Oaks, 1981), 6. The *Histoyre du Mechique* is known through a sixteenth-century French translation of a lost Spanish original.

6. Mitchell Dahood, *Psalms II: 51-100* (New York: The Anchor Bible, Doubleday, 1968), 269. In addition, John Tvedtnes has noted that the concept of "planning sessions" at the time of creation is suggested in several Jewish texts, namely Tosefta to TB Nedarim 39b, and TB PesaHim 54a. Personal communication from John Tvedtnes to Diane Wirth, March 24, 1999.

7. David Freidel, Linda Schele, and Joy Parker, *Maya Cosmos: Three Thousand Years on the Shaman's Path* (New York: William Morrow & Company, Inc., 1993), 69.

8. Adrián Recinos, Delia Goetz, and Sylvanus G. Morley, *Popol Vuh: The Sacred Book of the Ancient Quiché Maya* (Norman: University of Oklahoma Press, 1950), 82.

9. Budge, *From Fetish to God in Ancient Egypt*, 117, 381; Hornung, *Idea Into Image*, 43-44.

10. Freidel, Schele, and Parker, *Maya Cosmos*, 65.

11. Linda Schele, *Workbook for the XVIth Maya Hieroglyphic Workshop at Texas* (Austin: Department of Art and Art History and the Institute of Latin American Studies, University of Texas, 1992), 152.

12. Mircea Eliade, *Myth and Reality*, trans. Willard R. Trask (New York: Harper & Row, 1963), 40.

13. Hornung, *Idea Into Image*, 52.

14. Personal communication from John Tvedtnes to Diane Wirth, March 24, 1999.

15. John Weir Perry, *Lord of the Four Quarters: The Mythology of Kingship* (New York: Paulist Press, 1991), 20-22.

16. John R. Hinnells, *Persian Mythology* (New York: Peter Bedrick Books, 1985), 103.

17. Giorgio de Santillana and Hertha von Dechend, *Hamlet's Mill* (Boston: David R. Godine, 1977), 3.

18. John M. Lundquist, "What is a Temple? A Preliminary Typology," in *Temples of the Ancient World: Ritual and Symbolism*, Donald W. Perry, ed. (Salt Lake City: Deseret Book Co., and Provo, Utah: FARMS, 1994), 106.

19. John M. Lundquist, *The Temple: Meeting Place of Heaven and Earth* (New York: Thames and Hudson, 1993), 13.

20. Santillana and von Dechend, 56; Hornung, *Idea Into Image*, 118.

21. See also Rev. 11:1-2, where an angel from heaven showed a future temple to John and gave him a rod to measure various parts of the temple.

22. Job 38:4-7.

23. Schele, *Workbook for the XVIth Maya Hieroglyphic Workshop*, 148, 246; Freidel, Schele, and Parker, 115, 126, 163.

24. Rafael Girard, *Los Mayas: Su civilizacion, su historia, sus vinculaciones continentales* (Mexico: Libro Mex. Editores, 1966), 33.

25. Dennis Tedlock, *Popol Vuh* (1996), 63-64, 220.

26. Maude W. Makemson, *The Book of the Jaguar Priest: A Translation of the Book of Chilam Balam of Tizimin, with Commentary* (New York: Henry Schuman, 1951), 41.

27. Robert D. Bruce, *Lacandon Dream Symbolism* (Mexico, D.F.: Ediciones Euroamericanas Klaus Thiele, 1975), 31.

28. George Kubler and Charles Gibson, *Skywatchers, Shamans and Kings* (New York: John Wiley & Sons, Inc., 1951), 34.

29. S. G. F. Brandon, *Man and God in Art and Ritual* (New York: Charles Scribner's Sons, 1975), 329.

30. Sellers, 104, 200.

31. Reeder, 68.

32. Patai, *On Jewish Folklore*, 140.

33. Hornung, *Idea Into Image*, 116.

34. Lundquist, *The Temple*, 14; Reeder, 68.

35. Schele and Freidel, *A Forest of Kings*, 435.

36. Marie Gabriele Wosien, *Sacred Dance: Encounter with the Gods* (New York: Thames and Hudson, 1974), 13.

37. Barbara Tedlock, *Time and the Highland Maya*, rev. ed. (Albuquerque: University of New Mexico Press, 1982), 99.

38. Diego de Landa, "Landa's Relación de las Cosas de Yucatán" in *Papers of the Peabody Museum of American Archaeology and Ethnology* 18, Alfred M. Tozzer, ed. (Cambridge, Massachusetts: Harvard University, 1941), 139, cited in Karen Bassie-Sweet, *From the Mouth of the Dark Cave* (Norman: University of Oklahoma Press, 1991), 180.

39. Richard Frazer Townsend, *State and Cosmos in the Art of Tenochtitlan* (Washington D.C., Dumbarton Oaks, 1979), 47.

40. Barbara MacLeod, "The 819-Day-Count: A Soulful Mechanism," in *Word and Image in Maya Culture*, William F. Hanks and Don S. Rice, eds. (Salt Lake City: University of Utah Press, 1989), 124.

41. Evon Z. Vogt, *Zinacantan: A Maya Community in the Highlands of Chiapas* (Cambridge, Massachusetts: The Belknap Press of Harvard University Press, 1969).

42. Theodor H. Gaster, "Seasonal Ceremonies," in *The Encyclopedia of Religion*, Mircea Eliade, ed., vol. 13 (New York: Macmillan Publishing Company, 1987), 148.

43. Ibid., 149.

44. Verbal communication from Linda Schele to Diane Wirth, December, 1992.

45. Brandon, 334.

46. Hayyim Schauss, *The Jewish Festivals*, trans. Samuel Jaffe (New York: Schocken Books, 1938), 121.

47. Gaster, 149.

48. Ibid., 148.

49. E. C. Krupp, *Echoes of the Ancient Skies: The Astronomy of Lost Civilizations* (New York: Harper & Row, 1983), 199.

50. Richard Fraser Townsend, "Coronation at Tenochtitlan," in *The Aztec Templo Mayor*, Elizabeth Hill Boone, ed. (Washington, D.C.: Dumbarton Oaks, 1987), 377-78.

51. de Landa, 151.

52. Personal communication from John Tvedtnes to Diane Wirth, March 24, 1999. See also Schauss, 173; 1 Kings 8:1-3; 2 Chron. 5:2-4.

53. Lundquist, *The Temple*, 8.

54. Ibid., 22; Brandon, 82; Evan Hadingham, *Early Man and the Cosmos* (New York: Walker & Co., 1984), 168-69; Linda Schele, "House Names and Dedication Rituals at Palenque," in *Vision & Revision in Maya Studies*, Flora S. Clancy and Peter D. Harrison, eds. (Albuquerque: University of New Mexico Press, 1990), 156.

55. Mircea Eliade, *Symbolism, The Sacred, and the Arts*, Diane Apostolos-Cappadona, ed. (New York: Crossroad, 1988), 113.

56. Tate, *Yaxchilan*, 33.

57. Claude-François Baudez, *Maya Sculpture of Copán: The Iconography* (Norman: University of Oklahoma, 1994), 131.

58. Patai, *On Jewish Folklore*, 149.

59. Lurker, 12.

60. Cecelia F. Klein, "The Ideology of Autosacrifice at the Templo Mayor, in *The Aztec Templo Mayor*, Elizabeth Hill Boone, ed. (Washington, D.C.: Dumbarton Oaks, 1987), 349.

61. David W. Sedat, "Preclassic Notation and the Development of Maya Writing, in *New Theories on the Ancient Maya*, Elin C. Danien and Robert J. Sharer, eds. (Philadelphia: University Museum, University of Pennsylvania, 1992), 86.

62. Munro S. Edmonson, *The Book of the Year: Middle American Calendrical Systems* (Salt Lake City: University of Utah Press, 1988), 20-22, 27, 100, 146.

63. Barbara Tedlock, 35.

64. Lurker, 12.

65. Sellers, 220.

66. Schauss, 121, 170-73, 183.

67. Jane Stevenson Day, *Aztec: The World of Moctezuma* (Niwot, Colorado: Denver Museum of Natural History and Roberts Rinehart Publishers, 1992), 44.

68. Karl A. Taube, "The Temple of Quetzalcoatl," *RES* 21 (Santa Monica: Getty Center for the History of Art and the Humanities, 1992), 79-80.

69. Klein, "The Ideology of Autosacrifice," 339.

70. Townsend, *State and Cosmos*, 62.

71. Emily Umberger, "Events Commemorated by Date Plaques at the Templo Mayor: Further Thoughts on the Solar Metaphor," in *The Aztec Templo Mayor*, Elizabeth Hill Boone, ed. (Washington, D.C.: Dumbarton Oaks, 1987), 441.

72. Alfredo López Austin, "The Masked God of Fire," in *The Aztec Templo Mayor*, Elizabeth Hill Boone, ed. (Washington, D.C.: Dumbarton Oaks, 1987), 275.

73. Sahagún, *Florentine Codex*, Bk. 5: 194.

74. Sellers, 39.

75. Lewis Spence, *Ancient Egyptian Myth and Legends* (New York: Dover Publications, Inc., 1990), 65.

76. Gaster, 148.

77. Freidel, Schele, and Parker, 116.

78. Doug Stanton, "South of the Border, Upside-Down Mexico Way," *Outside Magazine* (February 1997).

79. Personal communication from Dr. Brian Stross to Diane Wirth, January 18, 1998.

80. Personal Communication from Allen Christenson to Diane Wirth, October 26, 1998.

81. Karl A. Taube, "The Ancient Yucatec New Year Festival: The Liminal Period in Maya Ritual and Cosmology," Vol. 1 (Ph.D. diss., New Haven: Yale University, 1988), 2.

82. Henri Frankfort, *Kingship and the Gods* (1948; Chicago: University of Chicago Press, 1978), 319.

83. *Enuma Elish*, 1.

84. W. G. Lambert, "Myth and Ritual as Conceived by the Babylonians," *Journal of Semitic Studies* 13 (1968), 106.

85. W. O. E. Oesterley, "Early Hebrew Festival Rituals," in *Myth and Ritual*, S. H. Hooke, ed. (London: Oxford University Press, 1933), 129.

86. John Gray, *Near Eastern Mythology* (New York: Hamlyn Publishing Co., 1969), 108.

87. Oesterley, 129.

88. Robert Graves and Raphael Patai, *Hebrew Myths: The Book of Genesis* (New York: McGraw Hill, 1966), 31; see also Sarna, 22; Theodore H. Robinson, "Hebrew Myths," in *Myth and Ritual*, S. H. Hooke, ed. (London: Oxford University Press, 1933), 176.

89. K. Sethe, *Das 'Denkmal memphitischer Theologie', der Schabakostein des British Museum*, Pt. 1 of *Dramatische Texte zur altäag Mysterienspielen* (Leipzig: J. C. Hinrichs, 1928), 17.

90. David Moyer, "Temples, Tombs and the Egyptian Universe: an ARCE Brooklyn Museum Symposium Report," *KMT* 5/2 (1994), 64.

91. Erik Hornung, "Politische Planung u. Realität im Alten Aegypten," *Saeculum* 22 (1971), 50-52.

92. Hornung, *Idea Into Image*, 53.

93. Stephen D. Houston, *Hieroglyhs and History at Dos Pilas* (Austin: University of Texas Press, 1993), 97.

94. Gohary, 16.

95. Anne Baring and Jules Cashford, *The Myth of the Goddess: Evolution of an Image* (New York: Viking Arkana through Penguin Books, 1991), 242.

96. Henri Frankfort, *The Art and Architecture of the Ancient Orient* (Baltimore: Penguin Books, 1970), 137.

97. Freidel, Schele, and Parker, 414.

98. François Thureau-Dangin, *Rituals Accadiens* (Paris: Leroux, 1921); Frankfort, *Kingship and the Gods*, 320.

99. Townsend, "Coronation at Tenochtitlan," 391-93.

100. Michel Quenon and Genevieve le Fort, "Rebirth and Resurrection in Maize God Iconography," in *The Maya Vase Book*, vol. 5, Barbara Kerr and Justin Kerr, eds. (New York: Kerr Associates, 1997).

101. Yuri Knorozov, *Maya Hieroglyphic Codices*, trans. Sophie D. Coe (Albany: Albany Institute for Mesoamerican Studies, State University of New York, 1982), 26.

102. Anthony Spalinger, "Some Remarks on the Epigomenal Days in Egypt," *Journal of Near Eastern Studies* 54/1 (1995), 40, 42.

103. Eliade, *The Myth of the Eternal Return*, xiv.

104. R. A. Rosenberg, "Jesus, Isaac, and the 'Suffering Servant,'" *Journal of Biblical Literature* 84 (1965), 388.

105. E. A. Wallis Budge, *Tutankhamen: Amenism, Atenism and Egyptian Monotheism* (London: Martin Hopkinson and Company, 1923; reprint, Mineola, New York: Dover Publications, Inc., 1991), 62.

106. P. Derchain, "Le Papyrus Salt 925," *Memories of the Academie Royale de Belgique* 58 (Belgium: Palais des Academies, 1965), I: 11.

107. *Man, Myth and Magic*, vol. 2, Richard Cavendish, ed. (Long Island, New York: Marshall Cavendisk Corp., 1970), 271.

108. Hornung, *Idea Into Image*, 39.

109. Freidel, Schele, and Parker, 107.

110. Frank J. Lipp, *The Mixe of Oacaca* (Austin: University of Texas Press, 1991), 140-46.

CHAPTER IV

FISH TRADITIONS

The iconography of the fish and its relation to the human embryo and birth process in Mesoamerican and Middle Eastern thought will be the focus of this chapter. This aquatic creature is one of the oldest images of regenerated life, according to Baring and Cashford.[1] In fact, the fish was the central image of fertility and rebirth in Chaldean myths regarding Oannes, the fish god.[2] Moreover, in the Old World the fish was often an emblem of the mother goddess, sometimes representing her womb and, indirectly, fertility.[3] Apparently, in primitive mythologies the goddess of rebirth was associated with the symbol of the fish more frequently than were male deities.[4] A fine example of this is at Malta, a site known for its mother goddess iconography. An ivory fish containing a spiral design was found buried with a child resting in a fetal position. Besides the fish and labyrinth imagery, other objects of the grave were artistic renderings of bird and serpent designs, emblems representing rebirth associated with the mother goddess.[5]

FISH, SHELL, AND THE WOMB

Fig. IV.1   Boetian vase, 700 B.C. found near Thebes (redrawn after Gimbutas 1989: 259).

An example found in Greece depicts a fish in proximity to the womb of the woman (Fig. IV.1). Gimbutas suggests that the Greek word *delphis*, meaning "dolphin," and *delphys*, the word for "womb," may support the probable relationship between the womb and the fish.[6]

In Maya art, the flattened head of a fish (Fig. IV.2a & b) was worn on the attire of women and in some instances on men.[7] Their net-beaded skirts indicate these individuals were associated with the earth and fertility.[8] Regardless of the person's gender, the fish head was worn at the apron position directly over the area of the womb. This grapheme, sometimes read as *xok*, "shark," can also mean "waist" or "hips" in Yucatek,[9] and in several Maya dialects present a close relation to the word for "woman."[10]

a.

b.

Fig. IV.2   Front and side view of *Xoc* fish head and shell from mid-section of figure:
a. Naranjo Stela, Guatemala. b. Stela 1, Caracol, Belize.

In this particular design, the mouth of the fish rests on a spondylus shell grapheme. In Mesoamerican tradition, Taylor proposes that inasmuch as the spondylus shell is often scraped to bring out its interior reddish color, it may be connected to the womb.[11] Eric Thompson identifies glyph T606 as a shell (Fig. IV.3)[12] and, as to its meaning, Dütting interprets this glyph as "life,"[13] and Schele as "the child of."[14] The shell (the cowrie shell in particular) was held as a symbol of fertility throughout Egyptian history and oftentimes represent female parts.[15]

In light of the placement of the fish on figures associated with fertility, the fish may be symbolic of the womb, where life develops and is ultimately born. P. Furst explains that persons swallowed by fish-type monsters represent "death-and-rebirth beliefs and rituals in both the Old and New World" (Fig. IV.4).[16] We are reminded of the story of Jonah, who was swallowed by a fish for three days before he was spewed out;[17] Matthew likens Jonah's experience inside the fish to the death and resurrection of Christ.[18] The fish in these cases are, therefore, associated with the womb.

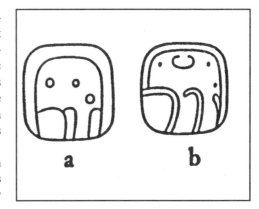

Fig. IV.3 T606 Shell graphemes (redrawn after J. E. S. Thompson 1962).

Fig. IV.4 Fish swallowing man, Colima, Mexico (drawn after photograph in P. T. Furst 1975: 34).

Fig. IV.5 Shell motif on fish on Maya bowl, Tikal Museum, Guatemala.

Another example of this symbolism can be seen on a Maya vase depicting the rebirth of the maize god.[19] In this scene the young moon goddess, who may be equated with Blood Woman of the *Popol Vuh*, presents a shell and *xok* fish head to her husband, the maize god,[20] thus corroborating the association of fish and shell with rebirth. At the Tikal Museum in Guatemala there is a Maya bowl with a shell motif inside the body of a fish (Fig. IV.5), again showing a relation between the shell and fish. To further substantiate this theme, the lid on a Maya terracotta bowl depicts the sun god with a four-petaled, flower-sun glyph on his cap, paddling his way through the waters of the Underworld. On his back is a fish with a shell motif (Fig. IV.6). The sun god's objective and destination through the dark Underworld is rebirth in the east. In discussing the womb-like quality of the shell, Eric Thompson quotes the interpreter of the *Vatican A Codex* stating: "Just as the fish issues from the shell, so emerges man from the womb of his mother."[21] This theme is visually portrayed in the *Dresden Codex* (Fig. IV.7). The tomb in many ancient cultures of the world represents the womb of the earth,[22] a concept that was certainly true in Mesoamerica. Of all the tombs discovered to date on the western hemisphere, one of the more spectacular is that of the tomb of Pakal in Palenque (see Fig. VI.26). The design on the sarcophagus lid in this tomb is a dramatic piece of cosmological art embodying many elements of life, death, and rebirth.[23] Under the rectangular lid is a most unusual sarcophagus carved in a uterine shape.[24] It is also plausible that this chamber represented the outline of a fish (Fig. IV.8) as well as a womb. The

Fig IV.6   Lid of a covered Maya bowl with sun god and fish. Housed at Dallas Museum of Art (redrawn after Hellmuth 1987: 109).

Fig. IV.7 A deity emerges from shell as a newborn child (redrawn after *Dresden Codex*).

Fig. IV.8   Carved uterus-shaped insert in sarcophagus of Pakal, Palenque, Chiapas, Mexico.

final resting place of Lord Pakal was designed as a place of emergence—a place of rebirth from the womb of the earth.

FISH AWAIT BIRTH OR REBIRTH

Although the fish in Mesoamerica is associated with the shell and womb, it is also viewed as a human embryo. The wet, slippery body of the fish, its shape, and the fact that it lives in water may be the rationale behind the iconography of this creature. Taube notes the appearance of a human fetus in its early stages and remarks: "It looks like a fish."[25] Therefore, in Mesoamerican symbolism, fish apparently could represent the womb yet, as will be demonstrated, it was more closely allied with the contents within the womb—the embryo in transition.

In ancient Egypt, fish are part of funerary symbolism as its presence was believed to guarantee new life.[26] In addition, the common *bulti* fish in Egypt is a round in shape, is often of a bright reddish color, and has a long dorsal fin. Due to its red color this fish is associated with the sun, which is reborn each day. Fish are carved on Egyptian scarabs, symbols of the sun, indicating a quality of regeneration and resurrection.[27] Wilkinson explains the symbolism of the *bulti* fish: "The spirit of the deceased was believed to rise from the waters of the afterlife as the sun had risen from the primeval lake."[28] The *bulti* is often drawn with vertical lines on its body, which is the hieroglyph for water. According to Wilkinson, since these lines are positioned vertically as opposed to the more common horizontal position for a water hieroglyph, the *bulti* may have been portrayed as swimming up toward the surface of the symbolic rebirth.[29]

Johnson may have evidence to support this thesis as found in Egypt. The tomb mural mentioned earlier at Deir el Medinah, Thebes, displays a huge *bulti* fish in the process of being embalmed by Anubis (see Fig. II.18). The deceased is here visualized as a fish, winding its way through the embryonic waters of the Underworld before its rebirth at dawn.[30]

Von Sadovszky demonstrates how fish symbolism from Vettersfelde, Ireland, can also be found 1,200 years earlier at the Temple of Byblos in the Middle East. He states that the Irish word *bradán* means "large fish," but can also be interpreted as "life" and "soul."[31] These meanings go back to ancient times and may indicate a common origin.

The foregoing sets the stage for the "fish" equals "human embryo" iconography. Freidel, Schele, and Parker write that the souls of infants came through the *Ol* portal (the opening to and from the supernatural Otherworld) to find bodies growing for them in the wombs of Maya women.[32] Many fish motifs in Mesoamerican art appear to symbolized the human fetus awaiting birth either into this world from the thirteenth heaven where souls enjoy a premortal state,[33] or the next stage of rebirth (resurrection) after passing through this mortal existence.

First Stage—Birth into the World

Analyzing birth into mortality in Mesoamerica, which will be referred to as the first stage, we need to look to an earlier, premortal existence when the creator/couple begat offspring.[34] This came to pass in a garden of delights, often referred to as Tamoanchan, a place containing waters and mist. Taube writes that the fish painted in the Teotihuacan Mythological Animals Mural in the valley of Mexico, may "represent . . . fish before they became humans. In other words, they may represent the ancestors in their journey to the present human world."[35] Taube also states that there was a widespread association of fish with the origin of mankind.

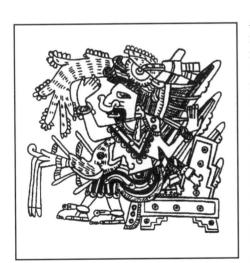

Fig. IV.9   Mexican goddess, Mayauel, nurses a fish (redrawn after *Borgia Codex* 16).

Another example in the *Borgia Codex* portrays Mayauel in her role as an earth goddess nursing a fish (Fig. IV.9). The fish was an obvious alternate manifestation for a human infant. There is also a scene on Altar O at Copan that is interesting (Fig. IV.10). A fish is exhibited directly over a child standing next to his father. The fish may represent the child's soul or co-essence, due to the fact that its association with birth and lineage is apparent. There is a ruling fish family at Copan.[36] The father figure rests his hand on his thigh, which is a recognized symbol of fertility in Mesoamerica.[37] In Egypt, the thigh is also equated with the concept of fertility.[38]

Fig. IV.10 Altar O, Copan, Honduras (redrawn after Maudslay 1889-1902, Vol. I: Pl. 85).

Fig. IV.11 Child descends from realm above
for birth, *Borbonicus Codex*
(Seler 1902-1903: 24).

Fig. IV.12 Child descends for birth, Stela 10,
Izapa, Chiapas, Mexico (redrawn
after Norman 1976: 109).

In the *Borbonicus Codex* a child descends from its heavenly home to a
mother figure as she gives birth (Fig. IV.11).[39] The earliest illustration of this
particular theme, according to Norman, may be depicted on Stela 10 at Izapa,
Chiapas, Mexico (Fig. IV.12).[40] Floating above a reclining figure with a
swollen abdomen is a child who may be coming from the heavens to enter its
earthly mother's womb. Dütting reads the combination of glyphs T187 and
T758:110 as referring to the heavenly shelter from where the children or suck-
ling ones descend.[41] Among the Chol Maya, "to touch the earth" and "to see
or experience the earth/world," are metaphors for birth.[42] Bowen and
Anderson find a similar birth expression at Palenque. It reads, "he came to the
world," or as these epigraphers explain, ". . . its metaphorical equivalent 'he
touched the earth'."[43]

The idea of a soul descending from the heavens at birth was not exclusive
to the Maya for we also find it in Oaxaca, Mexico. A carved stela from a tomb
in Suchilquitongo is a fine example in pictographic form of the birth metaphor
(Fig. IV.13). Starting at the top, the jaguar head represents the family lineage
of the individual being born. At the center is a glyph for the sky, and the feet
below indicates that this person emerged from the sky as an infant. A. Miller
translates the column containing this birth statement as, "In the Year N
(sixteenth year in the cycle), descended from the sky (was born) of the 'Jaguar-
Tied Bundle' lineage family (family name) Lord 12 O (calendar name), 4th
born of Lord 13 O (birth-order name)."[44]

Sahagún records an Aztec song that celebrated the premortal birth of
Cinteotl, the corn god: "Cinteotl is born in the place of rain and mist, where
the children of men are made, where the jeweled fish are sought."[45] The
jeweled fish are symbolic of the precious human souls sent to mortal parents
to be raised on earth. Seler notes that Michoacan, which he equates with the

Fig. IV.13 Suchilquitongo, Oaxaca,
Mexico (redrawn after
A. Miller 1991: Fig. 4).

Maya Tamoanchan, means "the Place of the Fisher," and holds that this locale may be identified in scenes where gods were portrayed catching fish with a hand net as is the case in the *Borgia Codex* (Fig. IV.14).[46] Dütting is in accord with Seler when he states there is a definite correlation between "the making of children with the capture of fishes," which he views as "human embryos." The occasion of these fish being caught in the heavenly ocean was the ritual that took place just prior to the physical birthing process on earth. As we will see, the catching of fish was also important to the second stage, where a rebirth took place after death.

Fig. IV.14   A god snares fish in the waters of the upper world (redrawn after *Borgia Codex* 13).

Second Stage—Rebirth

If the first stage of the life cycle is viewed as an embryo awaiting birth into this finite world, the second stage would be the deceased's transition from mortality to a resurrected condition, which constitutes rebirth. Greene-Robertson notes that the roof and roofcomb of the Temple of the Cross at Palenque are covered with fish.[48] This particular roof represents the waters of the Underworld and may therefore be considered a place where the ancestors await their rebirth or the second stage of their journey.

Of all the stelae at Izapa, none is more complex nor more enigmatic than Stela 5 (Fig. IV.15). Containing symbolism of cosmic proportions, this stela includes the following elements: celestial panel, fruit-laden World Tree, ancestral beings, supernatural deities, water, serpents, birds, and fish. It is the latter, the fish, which are of interest to this chapter. On Stela 5, two fish rise in smoke columns above an incense burner and two fish hang from the celestial panel high above an elderly couple seated below at the far left. The fish may represent the old man and woman who some scholars suggest to be First Father and First Mother, in their transition from life to immortality. On the other hand, as proposed by McDonald, the two fish may represent the Hero Twins of the *Popol Vuh* when they turned into fish and were subsequently reborn.[49]

It is well established that illustrations and myths of the sacred World Tree were widespread throughout Mesoamerica. To the Maya, for example, it is comparable to a ladder connecting this world to the next. It was set up at the time of creation at the center of the earth and is the means for men to ascend through the many-layered heavens to the topmost heaven where the gods live.[50] On Stela 5, the fruit of this Tree makes this journey possible. The heavens, the Tree, the fruit, the fish, and the ancestral couple, led to a complete life cycle—the constant and integral nature of timeless lineage. Stela 5 at Izapa may be one of the more significant carvings in all of Mesoamerica. The Tree of Life theme was of equal importance in the ancient Near East, having similar iconographic elements.[51] This theme is more thoroughly addressed in Chapter VI.

Fig. IV.15   Fish on Stela 5 (at top left and middle, left of tree), Izapa, Chiapas, Mexico
(from Norman 1976: Part 2, 165).

Fig. IV.16   Gods catch fish, Tikal Bone (redrawn after Norman 1976: 89).

CAPTURING FISH

Dütting brings to our attention an illustration portraying symbolism of the second stage or rebirth. This is a unique fishing scene carved on a bone from Tikal, Guatemala (Fig. IV.16).[52] The supernaturals catching fish on this bone are described as varioius deities—sometimes Chak,[53] or as GI of the Palenque Triad.[54] Chak is the rain god supreme among the Maya. Schele and Freidel identify god GI as Hunahpu of the *Popol Vuh*, the Hero Twin named after his father Hun Hunahpu, or First Father.[55] However, Schele reminds us that the relationship between Chak and First Father is yet unresolved; that both First Father in his guise as GI, and Chak in his human form, wear shell earflares and a fish barbel.[56] Perhaps Chak (GI of the Palenque Triad) and Hun Hunahpu (or his namesake Hunahpu), are all aspects of what was originally a male god who, in the process of time, was manifested as a variety of deities, each containing some of his multifarious attributes.

According to Looper, when Chak is fishing he is in the act of removing fish from below the surface waters of the Underworld and bringing them up to the earthly realm. Chak could do this because he was able to open the portal between the supernatural and the real worlds.[57] In that the Tikal Bone (see Fig. IV.16) showing a god fishing was buried in the tomb of a Tikal lord, it would appear in this case that the rebirth would apply to the deceased ruler.

Symbolism behind the capturing of fish was important in Mesoamerica. There are some cases where Dütting associates the Maya glyph *chukah*, "capture," which Proskouriakoff calls the "prisoner glyph," with "capture for birth." Dütting held that this refers to the "capturing of fishes/human embryos from the mythological lake." The act of catching fish for their birth, either into this world or their rebirth into the next world, is of significance. On the Creation Stone from Palenque, Chak is designated in the hieroglyphic text as "the daytime fisherman, the nighttime fisherman."[58] One of the two glyphs comprising the name of Chak is a head topped by a heron with a fish in its mouth (Fig. IV.17). Perhaps as a daytime fisherman, Chak catches fish for this world, as the Mexican version in Figure IV.14 expresses. As a nighttime fisherman, the fish are caught for rebirth in their second stage of transition after death. Dütting also notes there may be an association of this capturing rite with a tradition held by the Aztec. They viewed a woman to be taking a captive when she delivered a newborn child.[59] In his *Historia,* Sahagún writes:

Fig. IV.17 Creation Stone, Palenque, Chiapas, Mexico, (redrawn after Greene-Robertson 1991: 273).

> And when the baby had arrived on earth, then the midwife shouted; she gave war cries, which meant that the little woman had fought a good battle, had become a brave warrior, had taken a captive, had captured a baby.[60]

Fig. IV.18 God catches fish, Stela 1, Izapa, Chiapas, Mexico (redrawn after Norman 1976: 86).

Whether in stage one or stage two, fish were symbolically perceived to be captured for birth. This scenario can also be seen at Izapa on Stela 1 (Fig. IV.18). Norman identifies the fishing god on this stela as Chak and found the upper portion of this stela to represent a celestial scene. The figure with umbilical cord may be interpreted as "the passage of man into postmortal life."[61] This ties in well with the theme of fish being caught as they anticipate the process of rebirth. Similar to the Tikal Bone, Stelae 22 and 67 at Izapa, depict deities in boats floating on water containing fish, although these deities are not in the process of catching fish. Even so, these scenes may portray Tamoanchan, where fish await their birth on earth presided over by fishing gods who are responsible for their capture.

In Egypt, a somewhat minor tradition may be similar to catching fish in Mesoamerica; in this case, the deceased await rebirth and are prohibited. An account of this practice is in Spell 153 of *The Book of the Dead,* which says that the fishing gods specifically caught the inert ones who were wanderers after death.[62] Spell 153 gives instructions to the deceased for escaping from the net. The vignettes to this spell are illustrations of clap traps for birds and a fishing net for fish (Fig. IV 19). Parkinson of the British Museum views the imagery of the fish as follows: "The inert ones are the unresurrected dead who are like fish, in that they lie in the waters of chaos; in the spell the deceased states that he will not be caught in the traps used to trap them."[63]

Fish-in-hand Glyph

This discussion leads to Dütting's theory that the fish-in-hand glyph, T714 (Fig. IV.20a), may be linked to the concept of grasping of fishes/embryos for birth.[64] Grube finds a Maya phonetic spelling for the fish-in-hand glyph, *tzak,* meaning "to take hold of."[65] He notes that the fish-in-hand sign is sometimes found with the T670 form (Fig. IV.20b), which also contains a hand and is sometimes used in the "child of mother" glyph, or with a *ya* prefix, meaning "son of mother." In cases where the *ya* prefix is not attached to this sign, it reads "to grab" or "to take." As Grube remarks: "Thus, both the 'fish-in-

Fig. IV.19 Vignette to *The Book of the Dead,* Spell 153 (redrawn after Naville 1886: plate CLXXVIII).

hand' form [T714] and the T670 form of G1 [of the Supplementary Series] have the same basic meaning." In addition, Figure IV.20c is composed of a hand holding the *k'u* sign, which means "divine." Grube proposes that this reading "refers directly to the image of a fish grabbed by a hand."[66]

Winters suggests that it is now an "accepted view that the fish-in-hand glyph is also connected with lineage and ancestry," and that "bloodletting and blood of ancestry are concepts inextricably intertwined."[67] In this group of related glyphs we may see a possible connection of fish, child, divine or precious, and the act of capturing (grasping, taking, or conjuring a supernatural being).

Fig. IV.20 Maya hand glyphs: a. T714 Fish-in-Hand glyph, middle wall of Casa Colorada, Chichen Itza, Yucatan, Mexico; b. a form of T670, hand holding a *K'u* head; c. *K'u* infixed into hand instead of a fish, Stela 21, Yaxchilan, Chiapas, Mexico.

Proskouriakoff was the first to propose that the fish-in-hand rite portrayed in Maya art was used to express the belief in the ability to conjure up a deceased ancestor;[68] however, there is apparently another interpretation depending on the circumstances. Dütting argues that on occasion this ritual was, "rather a quest for noble offspring, a ceremony performed to evoke the birth of a child of noble lineage."[69] This would again relate to the first stage of birth. Then Dütting goes on to support the second rebirth when he notes that this rite was also performed after the death of rulers, "perhaps to evoke their rebirth or resurrection."[70] To date, studies show that the first known fish-in-hand glyphs were incorporated during the Early-Classic Period. Some of the sites where this glyph is exhibited are Copan, Palenque, Chichen Itza, and Yaxchilan.[71]

God K is identified as a god of descent, a god of lineage and fertility.[72] Kelley determines that the presence of God K in certain texts probably connects the birth of important persons in Maya royalty;[73] and Winters finds God K's glyphic head follows the fish-in-hand glyph in at least thirteen texts, denoting an association with procreation and lineage.[74]

Fig. IV.21 First Father on upper portion of Stela 2, Seibal, Guatemala (drawn after photograph).

Birds Capturing Fish

The sides of the sarcophagus lid in Pakal's tomb at Palenque records the name of one of his female ancestors, Na-Sak-K'uk,' which translates as "Lady White Bird." Regarding the interpretation of this female ruler's name, Schele notes that her name recalls that of the ancestral goddess, First Mother, referred to in mythological texts at Palenque. The main sign of her name was a bird head, which may be that of a heron. Schele reports that D. Tedlock interprets the name of First Mother as Na-Sak-Bak-Ha', which, in short, means "Lady Egret" or "Heron," and went a step farther and found her asso-ciated with Xbaquiyalo, the first wife of Hun Hunahpu in the *Popol Vuh*.[75] In light of this, the egret (heron) with fish in its mouth on the headdress of First Father on Stela 2 at Seibal, Guatemala (Fig. IV.21), may be a zoomorphic variant of First Mother. Stuart notes that a water bird with fish in its mouth worn in the headdress of a ruler at Palenque, may be a public display for that ruler's association with GI, or First Father (the maize god),[76] a general concept also suggested by Peterson.[77]

As noted, in Maya art the egret/heron often holds a fish while perching on the headdress of a ruler or deity. According to Stuart, a heron with fish in its mouth can mean "captive," and both the word for "heron" and "captive" may be translated in Mayan as *bak*.[78] Other translations of *bak* are "child" and "bone."[79] Recalling the Aztec belief that deliverance of a child at birth was comparable to the process of capturing, it is understandable why the Maya chose *bak* to mean "captive" or "child," in addition to "heron" and "bone." Perhaps there is an association here with the meaning of the heron's role of capturing fish, especially in light of the role of the mother goddess as a guardian of the birth process, which act is comparable to capturing a soul.

In the Old World, certain predatory birds are associated with the mother goddess. In Egypt, it is most certainly the vulture,[80] and bird-headed goddesses are prevalent in early Mesopotamia.[81] The owl, of which the Mesoamerican moan bird is a type, is associated with both death and rebirth from prehistoric times.[82]

ORIGIN OF GRAIN/MAIZE

Recalling the story of two fish from the *Popol Vuh*, the denizens of Xibalba believed they tricked the great ballplayers, Hunahpu and Xbalanque, into jumping to their death leaping into an oven in the Underworld. Their bones were ground like corn and scattered in a river, yet on the fifth day the Twins turned into fish and appeared again in human form.[83] This scenario is discussed in Chapter II with special focus on the Maya vase illustrated in Figure II.15. The hidden meaning of this story is the relation of man to corn. It is essential to understand that in Mesoamerica man was believed to be made of maize. This part of the *Popol Vuh* story refers not only to the birth of maize, but to the birth of man. As was demonstrated, this happened at the moment the earth-turtle's shell was cracked to allow for the emergence of both maize and man.[84]

In Sumerian mythology the earth was split open and the flesh of mankind sprouted at the mythological site of the Mountain of the Gods. The cracking open of the earth's primordial crust was accomplished with an ax used by Enlil, the storm god.[85] The myth is the same in Mesoamerica. Monument 23 at Quirigua, Guatemala, depicts Chak, the storm god, using his lightning ax to open the earth for both the emergence of maize and mankind.

MAIZE, FISH, AND MEN

In that fish were associated with grain, and grain had a bearing on the makeup of man, an analysis of these traditions need qualifying in both Mesoamerica and the Near East.

Fish and Maize in Mesoamerica

A myth known as the *Story of Hómshik* told by the native speakers of the Sierra Popoluca language of Veracruz, Mexico, contains another version of the origin of maize. Here also the hero, Hómshik, is killed. His bones are ground like maize and then thrown in the water.[86] Due to the fact that the maize god's remains were immersed in water, his rebirth was assured.[87] Water is the element that activates the soil—the means whereby birth is allowed to take place.[88]

The myth not only shows Hómshik dying as the maize god but, as a result of his conquest over death, he is reborn as the flesh of mankind.[89] The Huichol of Mexico also viewed a newborn as sacred maize, yet for the duration of the first five days of the child's life it was thought to be comparable to a fish before it truly became human.[90] This, too, shows a clear connection between human, maize, and fish in Mesoamerica.

Although not previously suggested by Mayanists, it is proposed here that the Initial Series Introductory Glyph on Stela D at Copan presents more than appears on the surface (Fig. IV.22). The Maya were fond of multilayered meanings in their visual arts, and another interpretation may be linked to this Introductory Glyph, especially in light of its whole-body representation as opposed to the more conventional use of phonetic sounds read from glyphs. Harris suggests that the central figure is the maize god; and this may be the case.[91] On the other hand, there is an

Fig. IV.22 Introductory glyph from Stela D,
Copan, Honduras (d rawn after
photograph).

example in Maya art of a conflation of the Maya maize god and the moon goddess,[92] and the Copan example may be a similar juxtaposition. The maize god was not normally associated with the moon, the curved object behind the figure. In light of the motifs of corn and fish that flank the individual, this may be enough to identify this supernatural person as Xquic (or Xkik'), "Blood Woman," who was associated with the young moon goddess, the mother of Hunahpu and Xbalanque;[93] or she may be Xmucane, the grandmother of the Hero Twins whom M. Coe equates with Ix Chel, the old moon goddess and ancestress.[94]

In the *Popol Vuh*, Blood Woman needs to prove to her mother-in-law, Xmucane, that she was impregnated by the deceased Hun Hunahpu. She was given a test to prove her identity and is sent to the fields to obtain corn. Although there is only a single clump of corn in the garden, Blood Woman produces a net full of maize ears, thus establishing beyond doubt that she is who she claims to be.[95]

The *Popol Vuh* tells another story related to corn that may have a bearing on the Introductory Glyph on Stela D at Copan. We already learned of this tale in a previous chapter, but to reiterate, the Hero Twins plant corn in their grandmother's house and explain to her that if the corn dies, they would die. On the other hand, if the corn grows, this would be a sign of their rebirth.[96] Hunahpu and Xbalanque trick the lords of the Underworld by planning their own death. After their ashes are cast into the river, they turn into fish. The corn flourishes in their grandmother's house—the prophetic sign that they succeeded in Xibalba and live again. This is interesting because according to Girard, some Maya groups see a relationship between fish and corn. For example, the fish was believed to be the soul/co-essence of maize.[97]

Aside from the fact that man was considered to be molded from ground maize, a visual connection may have been made with fish scales and kernels of corn.[98] The fish on Stela D at Copan are positioned in a vertical stance, not how fish are ordinarily viewed as they swim (see Fig. IV.22). Furthermore, it is not difficult to equate fish scales with grains of corn. An example of fish with a pronounced appearance of kernels or scales comes from Chichen Itza, Yucatan (Fig. IV.23). And at Palenque there is a maize motif with leaves facing down instead of upward, with a split tail and fish-like fins (Fig. IV.24). Moreover, a figure in Maya art known

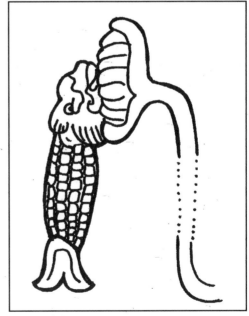

Fig. IV.23 Fish with kernels/scales, Chichen
Itza (redrawn after Maudslay
1889-1902, Vol. IV:Pl. 83).

as the Jester God presents a three-part element identified by Fields as a maize sign.[99] Several of these Jester Gods are combined with a ring-tailed fish (Fig. IV.25), giving further support to the association of fish and maize.

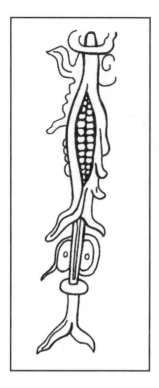

Fig. IV.24 Maize with fish tail and fins, Temple of the Sun, Palenque, Chiapas, Mexico (drawn after photograph).

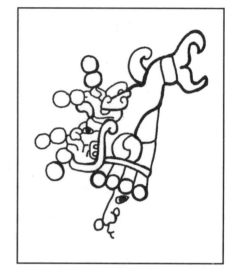

Fig. IV.25 Maya Jester God with a ring-tailed fish, Loltun Cave, Yucatan (redrawn after Miller and Taube 1993: 105).

Fig. IV.26 Pictograph of fish/maize by Tomatlan River, Jalisco, Mexico (redrawn after Mountjoy 1982: 119).

Fig. IV.27 *Nal* "maize" glyph (redrawn after *Dresden Codex*).

Among the Huichol of Nayarit, Mexico, *mu'ri iku'ri,* "fish," is identified phonetically with *iku'ri,* "corn."[100] Perhaps the relationship between fish and corn is the reasoning behind two seers summoned by Hunahpu and Xbalanque, named Xulu and Pacam, persuading the Xibalbans to specifically grind the bones of the Hero Twins on a stone,[101] just as maize is refined into corn meal. The powder from their bones turned into fish when nurtured by water.

A pictograph in Jalisco near the area of the Huichol Indians presents another persuasive piece of evidence to sustain a connection between maize and fish (Fig. IV.26). Not only is a fish depicted, but the body appears to be divided into kernels of corn. Lumholtz explains: "Green corn is called 'black fish' and ears of corn are depicted . . . by the painting of a fish, which is called by the Mexicans '*bagre*'."[102]

To further support an affiliation of fish with corn, Girard refers to a Chorti ritual to ensure the growth of maize. He explains that fish were brought from the temple fountain, no doubt in similitude of the Hero Twins' episode in the *Popol Vuh*. Girard concludes that removing the fish from the water was comparable to bringing maize up from the Underworld waters.[103] And although Maya words for fish and maize are not homophonous, examples of the *nal* "maize" glyph in the *Dresden Codex* look remarkably like fish heads, yet this glyph is clearly translated as "maize" (Fig. IV.27).

Another convincing discussion on the relationship of fish and maize appears in an article by Stross where he shows a clear symbolic equivalence between fish and maize as early as the second century A.D. on La Mojarra Stela 1, which was discovered in Veracruz, Mexico. The headdress of the protagonist is topped by a fish (actually a shark) whose body is composed of maize motifs, umbilical cord/rope, blood, and four small fish that are attached to the back of the mother fish. Together these symbolic elements compose the body of a stylized fish (Fig. IV.28).[104]

Fish and Grain in the Middle East

Returning to Egypt, we are reminded of the myth of the grain god, Osiris, and his association with the fish as discussed in Chapter II. Osiris occasionally wears a costume that may contain a fish pattern, and the deceased, who emulate Osiris in death, are sometimes portrayed wrapped in mummy form as fish (see Figs. II.17 and 18.) It may be significant that the Egyptian hieroglyph for a man's body or corpse contains a fish sign (Fig. IV.29). In Egyptian, fish is read *XA* and the word for corpse is *XAy.t*.[105] It is Hornung's opinion that this is due to the fact that deceased corpses were thought to exist in the watery abyss as fish before their resurrection.[106]

Fig. IV.28 A portion of the headdress worn by a ruler on La Mojarra Stela 1, Veracruz, Mexico (redrawn after George Stuart in Winfield Capitaine 1988: 8, Fig. 8).

Fig. IV.29 Egyptian hieroglyph for "body" or "corpse" (redrawn after Budge 1967: 247

There is another clue from Egypt indicating that fish and grain were symbolically linked. A late Egyptian practice held during the Harvest Festival involved the trampling of fish underfoot (albeit the fish represented the Pharaoh's enemies) and, according to Egyptologist Watterson, may equate with the trampling of grain.[107]

Various myths refer to the creation of man, yet Egyptologists mention little regarding the substance of which men were made among these people. The god, Khnum, fashioned the bodies of men on a potter's wheel.[108] Therefore, it is assumed that in Egyptian thought, humans were believed to be made of clay. However, there is a text inscribed on the sarcophagus of Ankhnesneferibra that speaks of grain, which was used to create mankind.[109]

Patai also demonstrates that there is a similarity between the newborn human child and grain in the ancient Near East. He explains that the Jews of Kurdistan consider infants similar to grain and are often placed in a sieve, a winnow, or other agricultural implement such as a kneading trough.[110] Therefore, even though men were considered to be made of clay or the dust of the earth, they were still closely associated with grain in that they were considered the fruit of the womb of the earth.

FISH SYMBOLIC OF TRANSITION

As noted previously, examining fish and their possible relationship to the death and rebirth aspect of Stela 5 at Izapa (see Fig. IV.15), we find a pair of fish at the tip of ascending smoke eating the fruit of the Tree. It may be assumed that corresponding fish hanging from the celestial panel are there as a result of not only death but rebirth, after having eaten of the life-giving properties of the fruit of the World Tree. As noted before, these two fish may symbolically represent the old couple below, in a state of transition before rebirth. This being the case, it is probable that the elderly couple on Stela 5 at Izapa represents the ancestral pair of several Mesoamerican cultures, e.g., Cipactonal and his consort Oxomoco among the Nahua,[111] and Xpiyacoc and Xmucane as referenced in the *Popol Vuh*. Both these sets of ancestors are synonymous with First Father and First Mother.[112] The aged couple were obviously at a transitional point in life when they would soon pass from mortality to immortality. The fish logically represent their souls after death, wherein they ate of the fruit of the Tree in order to be reborn, and ascend to the highest heaven via the smoke vehicle of incense. The *Egyptian Pyramid Text of Pepi II,* describes how the deceased's soul ascends into heaven by means of incense, which is burnt on his behalf.[113]

In Old World mythology two fish represent the sign of Pisces. Nothing indicates that this is the case in Mesoamerica. Nevertheless, Scott's findings are of interest here. Referring to the sign of the two fish in the zodiac, he discovered an old interpretation of the symbolism of the two fish. According to ancient lore they represent the heavenly marriage of true mates. Having learned the value of the fruit of the Tree of Life they partook of the fruit. No longer separated, they are joined by divine law in the heavens.[114] Whether this realistically ties in with the fish and World Tree on Stela 5, the tradition is worthy of mention.

The Ballgame and the Hero Twins

When a Maya ruler played ball he reenacted what the Hero Twins accomplished before the dawn of creation as is expressed in the *Popol Vuh*. In at least two cases rulers are shown wearing a fish as part of their respective costumes. On Panel 7 at Yaxchilan, Chiapas, Mexico, a ruler by the name of Bird-Jaguar wears the accouterments of a ballplayer with the net skirt of the maize god and a fish on his back (Fig. IV.30). Another ruler on Stela 1 from La Amelia, Guatemala, dances over his captive, symbolized as a jaguar, after defeating him in a ballgame.[115] This victor also carries a fish on his back with only the tail being exposed. The fish attached to these costumes may exemplify the concept of a transition that took place after the Hero Twins won their ballgame over the Lords of Death in Xibalba, killed themselves, turned into fish, and were afterwards reborn.

Fish, Serpent, and Rebirth

Dütting suggests that the fish-in-hand grapheme, T714 (see Fig. IV.20a), may be read as "come to life" or "be born," and that the fish held in a hand signified a human embryo.[116] Most fish-in-hand glyphs are shown in scenes where

Fig. IV.30   Bird Jaguar, Panel 7, Yaxchilan, Chiapas, Mexico
(redrawn after Freidel, Schele, and Parker 1997:
Fig. 8: 16b).

bloodletting paraphernalia are exhibited. Bloodletting rituals were used among the Maya for various and sundry reasons as a means to an end. One explanation is that it was to give birth to the gods.[117] As Grube maintains, the fish-in-hand verb "refers to something that happened as a result of bloodletting rather than to the sacrifice itself."[118]

In Winters' study of the fish-in-hand glyph, she finds it frequently allied with a serpent or serpents.[119] One type is a double-headed serpent with figures coming out of its mouths, sometimes in the form of a ceremonial bar carried in the arms of royalty (Fig. IV.31). Dütting holds the opinion that some ceremonial serpent bars are associated with rebirth, renewal of life, and/or procreation.[120] Therefore, the double-headed serpent, whether in its U shape, or represented as a ceremonial bar, had among other things, an element of sacredness, of royal lineage, and of life.

The other occasion where the fish-in-hand glyph was prominent was when a human figure emerged from the mouth of a snake—the so-called Vision Serpent (Fig. IV.32). This rising serpent in cases where a head of an ancestor materializes was of great significance, especially when the fish-in-hand glyph was also present. Many Mayanists suggest that this scene represents the conjuring up of an ancestor by the individual performing bloodletting as a personal sacrifice.[121]

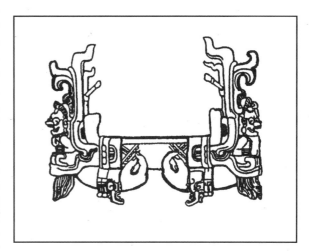

Fig. IV.31   Ceremonial serpent bar, Copan, Honduras (redrawn after Spinden 1975: 50).

Fig. IV.32   Rising "Vision Serpent" from
Structure 21, Lintel 15, Yaxchilan,
Chiapas, Mexico (drawn after
photograph).

Fig. IV.33   Birth of Bird Jaguar from
mouth of serpent, Structure 20
Lintel 13, Yaxchilan, Chiapas,
Mexico (redrawn after Tate
1992: 195).

Perhaps, however, this is not always the case. Dütting writes that in "the 'fish-in-hand rite,' a deceased ancestral lord . . . was invoked for his rebirth or resurrection."[122] Using Stela 25 in Dos Pilas, Guatemala, as a test, Stuart demonstrates that "the Maya believed they materialized gods through their bloodletting rites and that they conceived of this action as a kind of birth."[123]

Concerning Lintel 13 on Structure 20 at Yaxchilan (Fig. IV.33), Stuart suggests that the human figure emerging from the Vision Serpent is none other than the heir to the throne. The unborn individual is brought up by the serpent to qualify his pre-mortal, supernatural state before birth. This is the hoped for, deified child of royal lineage.[124] Regarding this particular lintel, which we view in our illustration in part, Brisko observes that the serpent is shedding its skin. This process in itself is a worldwide symbol of rebirth. In addition, Brisko states that the "serpent passes through the uterine area of the woman," who holds the snake, which further verifies that the heir to the throne was visualized in a magnificent scene of symbolic birth.[125] The bloodletting rituals, often exhibited together with Vision Serpents, were no doubt associated with the act of giving birth in that blood issues from the womb at this momentous occasion. Houston and Stuart suggest that emergence from the mouth of a serpent may be a metaphor for birth,[126] and Ciaramella provides numerous examples to illustrate that a coiled snake symbolizes birth.[127]

Altar O at Copan (see Fig. IV.10) mentioned previously, is also significant here. Carved on the edges of this altar are several sky serpents that display *ahau* (T535) glyphs attached to their tails, which may be read "son of father."[128] Baudez suggests that the royal male figures on Altar O may be viewed as emerging from the jaws of one of these serpents.[129] This, too, supports the birth/emergence theme from the mouths of serpents. So, whether the fish-in-hand ritual implies a materialization of an ancestor through obtaining a vision, the resurrection of a deceased person, or the hoped for birth of a future heir to the throne, a type of birth or rebirth is inferred in all instances.

We might add that Bassie-Sweet views the serpent as the sky serpent of the cave—the Underworld, from which deities emerged as they are being born.[130] It is also significant that M. Pohl notes a Chorti belief that the fish is the offspring of the serpent.[131] Cohodas, too, finds the serpent to be a symbol of birth with the mouth of the serpent representing the point of emergence from the womb. "By depicting himself with the serpent, the ruler demonstrates that like the sun he has been transformed in the Underworld and now emerges reborn as the child of the earth goddess, and fit to rule as a divine king."[132] It is no surprise that the supernatural Hero Twins in the *Popol Vuh* emerge from the mouth of a serpent/fish monster as portrayed on the Maya vase shown in Figure II.15, which was previously discussed.

The Egyptian *Book of Gates* tells a remarkable story of rebirth that may be equated to scenes of rebirth from the mouth of Mesoamerican serpents. Hornung states that during the final hour of the deceased in the Underworld, the most pictorial descriptions of their rebirth appear when the sun god, together with the deceased, is "pulled backward through the body of an enormous serpent. . . . They enter the serpent's tail as venerable, gray- haired, infirm individuals whose lives are essentially over, and then they emerge from the serpent's mouth as children."[133]

SUMMARY

The Mesoamerican fish appears to be a valid grapheme to denote the pre- or postmortal soul waiting to be caught in the net of a fishing god for its transition into the next stage of its evolution. The concept of capturing fish for birth or rebirth is related to the process of parturition, in that delivering a child is metaphorically compared to the capturing of a soul. Symbolically this is accomplished by a fisher, whether Chak or a fishing bird such as the heron. As to the latter, Cohodas views fishing birds as a symbol for the rebirth of maize, and a generic rebus for rebirth.[134] This concept ties significantly to the metaphor that the human embryo equals fish, which equals corn, which equals man.

A fish was used to represent a human embryo due to the natural habitat of a fetus in a watery embryonic fluid before birth. In the mind of the Mesoamerican, it was necessary to catch the fish from supernatural waters where they lived with the gods. Water, in turn, is the catalyst for fertility and serves to bring about rebirth in the life cycle of maize, which is also symbolized by the fish. Man not only needed maize for sustenance to perpetuate his race but, according to Mesoamerican tradition, he was created from maize.

The process of birth was also associated with blood since the newborn, accompanied by blood, issues forth at the time of birth from the womb. The living supplied their sacrificial blood as a sign and token to ensure the birth of an heir to the throne, or the rebirth and ultimate deification of an ancestor, as the case may be. Thus, one sees an eternal round of life—death and rebirth—incorporated within the symbolism of fish in the art of Mesoamerica.

Less detailed information is known regarding fish symbolism in the Middle East. However, parallels do exist between the significance of fish iconography from that part of the world and the same in Mesoamerica. In addition to Egypt's association of fish to rebirth and fertility, it is noteworthy that in Jewish thinking the concept of having progeny was comparable "to be like fishes, to multiply like fish."[135] Barren, Moroccan, Jewish women were even known to swallow fish that contained a fish within its mouth. As Patai comments on this custom: "The symbolism of the fish within another fish, indicating the desired position of the child in the womb of the mother, is obvious enough."[136]

Common features of this tradition from both locales include: (1) the fish is an image of fertility and rebirth, (2) the fish often represents the womb of a woman, (3) the grain gods of Egypt and Mesoamerica are both associated with fish, (4) the fish is symbolic of transition before rebirth, (5) shells and fish are associated with rebirth, (6) fishing gods catch fish (souls), (7) fish are portrayed in conjunction with burial settings, and (8) rebirth may also take place from the mouths of fish or serpents.

NOTES - Chapter IV

1.   Baring and Cashford, 414.

2.   Ibid., 63.

3.   Elizabeth E. Goldsmith, *Life Symbols* (New York: G. P. Putnam's Sons, 1928), 206; Marija Gimbutas, *The Language of the Goddess* (San Francisco: Harper & Row, 1989), 258-59.

4.   Joseph Campbell, *The Masks of God: Primitive Mythology* (New York: Penguin Books, 1987), 388.

5.   Ibid.

6.   Gimbutas, *The Language of the Goddess*, 263.

7.   Tom Jones, "Jaws II: Return of the Xoc," in *Sixth Palenque Round Table, 1986*, vol. 8, Merle Greene-Robertson and Virginia M. Fields, eds. (Norman: University of Oklahoma Press, 1991), 252.

8.   Information display, Stelae 1 and 2, El Peru, Guatemala, Peabody Museum, Harvard University, 1995.

9.   Ralph L. Roys, "Personal Names of the Maya of Yucatan," in *Carnegie Institution of Washington* Pub. 523, Contrib. 31 (Washington, D.C.: Carnegie Institution of Washington, 1940): 35, 44.

10. Jeffrey J. Miller, "Notes on a Stelae Pair Probably from Calakmul, Campeche, Mexico," in *Primera Mesa Redonda de Palenque, Part I*, Merle Greene-Robertson, ed. (Pebble Beach, California: Pre-Columbian Art Research, 1974), 154.

11. Taylor, 522.

12. J. Eric S. Thompson, *A Catalog of Maya Hieroglyphs* (Norman: University of Oklahoma Press, 1962), 229.

13. Dieter Dütting, "The Great Goddess in Classic Maya Religious Belief," *Zeitschrift Fur Ethnologie* V/III (1976): 141.

14. Linda Schele, *Workbook for the XVth Maya Hieroglyphic Workshop of Texas* (Austin: Department of Art and Art History and the Institute of Latin American Studies, University of Texas, 1991), 70.

15. Richard H. Wilkinson, *Symbol & Magic in Egyptian Art* (New York: Thames and Hudson, 1994), 16.

16. Peter Furst, "House of Darkness and House of Light," 34.

17. Jonah 1:17.

18. Matthew 12:40.

19. Justin Kerr, *The Maya Vase Book* vol. 1 (New York: Kerr Associates), Fig. 7, Kerr File No. 1004.

20. Taylor, 523.

21. J. Eric S. Thompson, *Maya Hieroglyphic Writing*, Pub. 589 (Washington, D.C.: Carnegie Institution of Washington, 1950), 133.

22. For example, in Egypt the sarcophagus was called *mwt*, which also means "mother." In other Semitic languages, the root *mwt* means "to die." John Tvedtnes notes that "the grave was seen as a return to the womb in preparation for rebirth," in ancient Near Easter belief. See John A. Tvedtnes, "Burial as a Return to the Womb in Ancient Near Eastern Belief," *Newsletter and Proceedings of the Society for Early Historic Archaeology* 152 (Provo, Utah: SEHA, 1983); Old Testament verses that equate "grave" with womb: Proverbs 30:16; Job 10:19.

23. Schele and Miller, 268-69, 285.

24. Mary Ellen Miller, *The Art of Mesoamerica from Olmec to Aztec* (New York: Thames and Hudson, 1986), 128.

25. Karl A. Taube, "The Teotihuacan Cave of Origin: The iconography and architecture of emergence mythology in Mesoamerica and the American Southwest," *RES* 12 (Cambridge, Massachusetts: Peabody Museum of Archaeology and Ethnology, Harvard University, 1986): 77.

26. Carol Andrews, *Amulets of Ancient Egypt* (Great Britain: British Museum Press, and Austin: University of Texas Press, 1994), 93.

27. Ibid., 11, 67.

28. Wilkinson, *Reading Egyptian Art*, 111.

29. Ibid.

30. Johnson, 252-53.

31. Otto J. von Sadovsky, *Fish Symbol and Myth* (Budapest: Akadémia Kiadó, 1995), 29-32.

32. Freidel, Schele, and Parker, 218.

33. Bernardino de Sahagún, *Historia General de las Cosas de Nueva Espana* vol. 1 (Mexico City, Mexico: Editorial Nueva Espana, 1946), 608.

34. Ibid.; Henry B. Nicholson, "Religion in Prehispanic Central Mexico," in *Handbook of Middle American*

Indians, vol. 10/1, Robert Wauchope, ed. (Austin: University of Texas Press, 1971), 411; J. Eric S. Thompson, *Maya Hieroglyphic Writing*, 115.

35.   Taube, "The Teotihuacan Cave of Origin," 53, 76.

36.   Barbara Tedlock, 140.

37.   Mary Ellen Miller, *Maya Art and Architecture* (London: Thames & Hudson, Ltd., 1999), 53.

38.   Clark, 160.

39.   Eduard Seler, *Codex Vaticanus B*, trans. A. H. Keane (Berlin and London, 1902), 23, 25.

40.   V. Garth Norman, *Izapa Sculpture* 30/2 (Provo, Utah: New World Archaeological Foundation, Brigham Young University, 1976), 110, 264.

41.   Dieter Dütting, "Aspects of Polyvalency in Maya Writing: Affixes T12, T229, and T110," in *Sixth Palenque Round Table, 1986*, gen. ed. Merle Greene-Robertson, vol. ed. Virginia M. Fields, vol. 8 (Norman: University of Oklahoma Press, 1991), 281.

42.   Kathryn J. Josserand, "The Narrative Structure of Hieroglyphic Texts at Palenque," in *Sixth Palenque Round Table, 1986,* gen. ed. Merle Greene-Robertson, vol. ed. Virginia M. Fields, vol. 8 (Norman: University of Oklahoma Press, 1991), 19.

43.   Sharon Bowen and Lloyd Anderson, "The Palenque Emblem Bird *mat* and *Matawil*," in *U Mut Maya*, eds. Carolyn and Tom Jones, 8 (Arcata, California: U Mut Maya, 1994), 49-50.

44.   Arthur G. Miller, "The Carved Stela in Tomb 5, Suchilquitongo, Oaxaca, Mexico," *Ancient Mesoamerica* 2/2 (1991): 222.

45.   Sahagún, *Florentinne Codex*, Bk. 2: 212.

46.   Seler, *Codex Vaticanus B*, 154.

47.   Dütting, "The Great Goddess," 44-45.

48.   Personal communication from Merle Greene-Robertson to Diane Wirth, October 17, 1991.

49.   Andrew J. McDonald, "Izapa's Stela 5 in a Mesoamerica Setting" (1999).

50.   J. Eric S. Thompson, *Maya Hieroglyphic Writing*, 72.

51.   E. A. S. Butterworth, *The Tree at the Navel of the Earth* (Berlin: Walter de Gruter & Co., 1970); Roger Cook, *The Tree of Life* (New York: Avon Books, a division of The Hearst Corporation, 1974).

52.   Dütting, "The Great Goddess," 42-43.

53.   Norman, 89; Karl A. Taube, "The Iconography of Rain and Lightning in Ancient Maya Myth and Ritual,"(paper presented at a symposium, *Origins: Creation and Continuity: Mythology and History in Mesoamerica*, VIIIth Texas Symposium, University of Texas, Austin, 1992).

54.   Dieter Dütting, "On the Astronomical Background of Mayan Historical Events," in *Fifth Palenque Round Table, 1983,* gen. ed. Merle Greene-Robertson, vol. ed. Virginia M. Fields, vol. VII (San Francisco: Pre-Columbian Art Research Institute, 1985), 271; Diane Winters, "A Study of the Fish-in-Hand Glyph, T714: Part I," in *Sixth Palenque Round Table,1986*, gen. ed. Merle Greene-Robertson, vol. ed. Virginia M. Fields, vol. 8 (Norman: University of Oklahoma Press, 1991), 243.

55.   Schele and Freidel, *A Forest of Kings*, 245-51.

56.   Linda Schele, *Workbook for the XVIth Maya Hieroglyphic Workshop at Texas* (Austin: Department of Art and Art History and the Institute of Latin American Studies, University of Texas, 1992), 152.

57.   Matthew G. Looper, "The Dances of the Classic Maya Deities *Chak* and *Hun Nal Ye*," (master's thesis, Austin: University of Texas, 1991), 71.

58.   Verbal communication from David Stuart, Harvard University, to Diane Wirth, Spring 1995.

59.   Dütting, "The Great Goddess," 101.

60.   Sahagún, *Florentine Codex*, Bk. 6: 167.

61.   Norman, 87, 91.

62.   *Egyptian Book of the Dead*, 123.

63.   Personal communication from Dr. Parkinson, Dept. of Egyptian Antiquities, British Museum, to Diane Wirth, June 9, 2000.

64.   Dütting, "The Great Goddess," 113.

65.   Noted in Schele, *Workbook for the XVth Maya Hieroglyphic Workshop*, 43, 79, 80b.

66.   Ibid., 87-88.

67.   Winters, 234-36.

68.   Tatiana Proskouriakoff, "Historical Date in the Inscriptions of Yaxchilan, Part I," *Estudios de Cultura Maya* 3 (1963): 156.

69. Dütting, "On the Astronomical Background," 270.
70. Ibid.
71. Ibid., 233.
72. Bassie-Sweet, 29.
73. David H. Kelley, *Deciphering the Maya Script* (Austin: University of Texas Press, 1976).
74. Winters, 239.
75. Schele, *Workbook for the XVIth Maya Hieroglyphic Workshop*, 113, 120. See also Dennis Tedlock, *Popol Vuh* (1985), 369; Dennis Tedlock, *Popol Vuh* (1996), 351.
76. Merle Greene-Robertson, Alfonso Morales, and David Stuart, "Cross Group Project Discovers Tomb, Throne and Limestone Panel in Palenque," *Pre-Columbian Art Research Institute* 28 (June 1, 1999).
77. Jeanette Favrot Peterson, *Precolumbian Flora and Fauna: Continuity of Plant and Animal Themes in Mesoamerican Art* (La Jolla, California: Mingei International, 1990), 76. The heron was also associated with Osiris, and is often depicted sitting on his sacred willow tree. See Wilkinson, *Reading Egyptian Art*, 91.
78. Verbal communication from David Stuart, Harvard University, to Diane Wirth, Spring 1995.
79. Brian Stross, "Glyphs on Classic Maya Vessels: The Introductory Formula of the Primary Standard Sequence," in *Seventh Palenque Round Table*, gen. Ed. Merle Greene-Robertson, vol. ed. Virginia M. Fields, vol. IX (San Francisco: The Pre-Columbian Art Research Institute, 1989), 193.
80. In Egypt the vulture was a symbol of the Goddess Mut. Her name not only means "mother," but aldo "death." Predatory birds such as the vulture were often equated with death. See Wilkinson, *Reading Egyptian Art*, 85; Tvedtnes.
81. Erich Neumann, *The Great Mother*, trans. Ralph Manheim (Princeton: Princeton University Press, 1974), 164, 272.
82. Gimbutas, *The Language of the Goddess*, 190-91.
83. Dennis Tedlock, *Popol Vuh* (1985), 45.
84. Freidel, Schele, and Parker, 93.
85. Perry, 62.
86. Kay Sammons, "Rhetorical Functions of Parallelism in Sierra Populuca" (Ph.D. Diss., University of Texas, Austin, 1995), 51.
87. Ibid., 88.
88. In Egypt during the 18th Dynasty, some Egyptian tombs had water-pools were thought to immerse mummies for the purpose of purification and rebirth. These waters represented the Primordial Waters of the earth. See Tvedtnes.
89. Sammons, 55.
90. Robert M. Zingg, *Los Huicholes: Una Tribu de Artistas*, 2 vols., trans. C. Paschero (Mexico: INI, 1982), I: 394, 410.
91. John Harris, "Mayan Hieroglyphs Represented by Whole Human Bodies" *The Codex* 6/1 (Philadelphia: University of Pennsylvania Museum of Archaeology and Anthropology, October 1997): 24.
92. Taube, "The Olmec Maize God," Fig. 12c, 55.
93. Dennis Tedlock, *Popol Vuh* (1985), 328. Xquic was the second wife of Hun Hunahpu.
94. Michael D. Coe, *The Maya*, 5th ed. (New York: Thames & Hudson, 1993), 178.
95. Dennis Tedlock, *Popol Vuh* (1985), 40.
96. Ibid., 42, 349.
97. Rafael Girard, *Esotericism of the Popol Vuh*, 260.
98. Rafael Girard, *Le Popol Vuh* (Paris: Payot, 1972), 208.
99. Virginia Fields, "The Iconographic Heritage of the Maya Jester God.," in *Sixth Palenque Round Table, 1986*, gen. ed. Merle Greene-Robertson; vol. ed. Virginia M. Fields, vol. 8 (Norman: University of Oklahoma Press, 1991).
100. Carl Lumholtz, "Symbolism of the Huichol Indians," in *Memoirs of the American Museum of Natural History*, vol. 1 (New York: American Museum of Natural History, New York, 1900), 55.
101. Dennis Tedlock, *Popol Vuh* (1985), 148.
102. Lumholtz, 214.
103. Rafael Girard, *Los Mayas Eternos* (Mexico City: Antigúa Libereria Robredo, (1962), 77-117.
104. Brian Stross, "Maize and Fish," *RES* 25 (Santa Monica: Getty Center for the History of Art and the Humanities, 1994).

105. Personal communication from John Gee to Diane Wirth, December 15, 1999.

106. Hornung, *Valley of the Kings*, 90.

107. Barbara Watterson, *The House of Horus at Edfu: Ritual in an Ancient Egyptian Temple* (Stroud, Glousester-shire: Tempus Publishing Ltd., 1998), 110.

108. Hart, *A Dictionary of Egyptian Gods*, 110.

109. Quirke, 58.

110. Patai, *On Jewish Folklore*, 386-88.

111. M. Wells Jakeman, "Stela 5, Izapa, Chiapas, Mexico, a Major Archaeological Discovery of the New World," *Special Publication* 2 (Provo, Utah: The University Archaeolgical Society, 1958), 13-19.

112. Dennis Tedlock, *Popol Vuh* (1985), 369.

113. Budge, *Osiris*, II: 255.

114. Oral E. Scott, *The Stars in Myth and Fact* (Caldwell, Idaho: Caxton Printers, Ltd., 1942), 136-37.

115. Freidel, Schele, and Parker, 360-61.

116. Dieter Dütting, "Lunar Periods and the Quest for Rebirth in the Mayan Hieroglyphic Inscriptions," *Estudios de Cultura Maya* XVI (1985), 135-36.

117. Schele, *Workbook for the XVth Maya Hieroglyphic Workshop*, 43.

118. Note in Ibid., 86.

119. Winters, 235-36.

120. Dütting, "The Great Goddess," 73, 132.

121. George Kubler, *The Art and Architecture of Ancient America: The Mexican, Maya and Andean Peoples* (Baltimore: Pelican Press, 1962); Peter T. Furst, "Fertility, Vision Quest and Auto-sacrifice: Some Thoughts on Ritual Bloodletting among the Maya," in *The Art, Iconography, and Dynastic History of Palenque, Part III*, Merle Greene- Robertson, ed. (Pebble Beach, California: Pre-Columbian Art Research Institute, 1976); Schele and Freidel, *A Forest of Kings*.

122. Dütting, "Lunar Periods and the Quest for Rebirth," 131-32; "The Great Goddess," 132.

123. Noted in Freidel, Schele, and Parker, 445.

124. David Stuart, "Blood Symbolism in Maya Iconography," *RES* 7/8 (New York: Cambridge University Press, 1984): 19.

125. Jo Ann Brisko, "Aztec Goddesses: A Historical Perspective" (master's thesis, San Jose State University, 1993), 133.

126. Stephen Houston and David Stuart, "The *Way* Glyph: Evidence for 'Co-essences' among the Classic Maya," *Research Reports on Ancient Maya Writing* 30 (Washington, D.C.: Center for Maya Research, 1989), 7.

127. Mary A. Ciaramella, "The Lady with the Snake Headdress," in *Seventh Palenque Round Table 1989*, gen. ed. Merle Greene-Robertson, vol. ed. Virginia M. Fields, vol. IX (San Francisco: Pre-Columbian Art Research Institute, 1989), 208.

128. Kornelia Kurbjuhn, "Busts in Flowers: a Singular Theme in Jaina Figurines," in *Fourth Palenque Round Table 1980*, gen. ed. Merle Greene-Robertson; vol. ed. Elizabeth P. Benson, vol. VI (San Francisco: Pre- Columbian Art Research Institute, 1985), 163.

129. Baudez, 92.

130. Bassie-Sweet.

131. Mary Pohl, "Ritual Continuity and Change in Mesoamerica: Reconstruction the Ancient Maya Cuch Ritual," *American Antiquity* 46 (1981): 525.

132. Marvin Cohodas, "Some Unusual Aspects of Cross Group Symbolism," in *Tercera Mesa Redonda de Palenque*, eds. Merle Greene-Robertson and Donnan Call Jeffers, vol. IV (Palenque, Chiapas, Mexico: Pre-Columbian Art Research, 1978), 222.

133. Hornung, *Idea Into Image*, 105-06.

134. Marvin Cohodas, "The Iconography of the Panel of the Sun, Cross, and Folidated Cross at Palenque: Part III," in *The Art, Iconography and Dynastic History of Palenque*, Merle Greene-Robertson, ed. (Pebble Beach, California: Pre-Columbian Art Research, Robert Louis Stevenson School, 1976), 164.

135. Patai, *On Jewish Folklore*, 348.1

136. Ibid., 349.

CHAPTER V

SYMBOLISM IN GENEALOGY

Old Testament writings prove the Hebrews were dedicated to genealogical record keeping. They were, in fact, renowned for it. Ancestral lists of kings from Mesopotamia and the well-preserved records of the Egyptians also testify to the importance of genealogy in the ancient Middle East. In addition, portraits of the deceased, especially those made by the Egyptians, are significant. Perhaps this tradition was comparable to the modern practice of keeping photographs of deceased relatives.

Mesoamerican cultures also considered lineage important and often reflected on their ancestors, especially on The Day of the Dead.[1] In the area of the Isthmus of Tehuantepec, Mexico, the people still refer to their revered ancestors as "old people of the clouds."[2] In Maya art, this is exactly where the ancestors were sometimes portrayed (Fig. V.1). The dots around the S-curved cloud in which the ancestor floats, may represent water droplets or perhaps lineage blood according to Stuart.[3] Similar dotted chains associated with hieroglyphs are translated to read, "of noble blood" or "descendant."[4] Marcus notes that the Maya word for "great-grandmother," *c'aa'na'*, has a close similarity to the word for "sky dweller," *c'aanal*.[5] Floating ancestral figures were depicted in art since the late Olmec period around 500 B.C. (Fig. V.2).

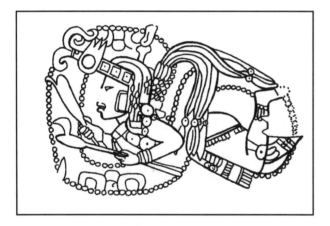

Fig. V.1 Maya ancestral figure at top of Stela 4, Ucanal, Guatemala (redrawn after Marcus 1992b: 297, Fig. 9.25a).

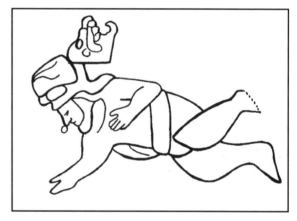

Fig. V.2 Detail of deceased, floating Olmec ancestor on Stela 3, La Venta, Tabasco, Mexico (redrawn after Drucker et al. 1959: Fig. 67).

GENEALOGICAL RECORDS

Although genealogies were given orally and passed from one generation to the next among various cultures throughout the Americas, it is in Mesoamerica that we find over a dozen writing systems, many of which contain genealogical records. These records are written in stone as well as in the accordion-like picture books called codices. As will be demonstrated, the similarity between the symbolism associated with genealogical record keeping in the Old World and among Mesoamerican peoples runs much deeper than one would expect.

Except for the day glyphs, it has only been in the last few decades that researchers are now able to read most Maya hieroglyphic texts, a process that requires an understanding of both Maya logograms and phonetic glyphs.[6] Dates of birth, rulership, conquests, marriages, and deaths, can now be interpreted concerning the lives of many rulers. Histories recorded for the most part on stone stelae include additional useful information such as the names of parents and grandparents, often going back to distant ancestors.[7] In some cases the lineage head took on the name of the lineage's founding father.[8]

Proper names were the key to classical decipherments in the Near East, which is true of the phonetic decipherment of Maya glyphs as well.[9] Hopkins discusses the research of several scholars who investigated certain Maya hieroglyphs referred to as relationship glyphs. They often occur in parentage statements.[10] These texts contain the genealogy of named rulers, as well as glyph compounds reading "child of mother," "child of father," etc. (Fig. V.3).

The Dumbarton Oaks Tablet, purportedly originating near the great Maya city of Palenque, illustrates the importance of family lineage by using ancestral portraits (Fig. V.4). The central figure, K'an-Hok'-Chitam II (a.k.a. Kan-Xul in earlier studies), was named after an ancestor. To his right is his mother, Lady Tz'ak-Ahaw (a.k.a. Lady Ahpo-Hel in earlier studies), and to his left is his father, the great king Pakal.[11] The mother holds a figure of what Mayanists refer to as God K, identified by a serpent leg and smoking celt on the forehead. This deity was associated with lineage and was the "guardian of human descendants."[12] The father figure, Pakal, holds what is regarded as a personified tree, a prominent emblem associated wth ancestry.[13]

Fig. V.3 K'uk'-Balam's genealogical statement at Palenque, Chiapas, Mexico. Detail from Tablet of the 96 Glyphs (redrawn after Linda Schele in Hopkins 1991: Fig. 3).

Fig. V.4 Dumbarton Oaks Tablet, K'an-Hok'-Chitam II and his parents, Palenque, Chiapas, Mexico, (drawn by Linda Schele, © by David Schele, in Schele and Miller 1986: 275, Fig. VII.3).

Back to their God(s)

The firstborn son of Pakal, Kan B'alam, contributed greatly to the splendor of Palenque, listing his ancestry back to the first founder of the dynasty. Then it goes back to an even more remote time to the ancestral gods from whom his royal line is believed to descend.[14] It is general knowledge that Egyptian rulers claimed their lineage from the gods, and a similar type of accounting may have been used by Luke when he wrote the genealogy of Christ (Luke 3:23–38). The King James Version states that Cainan ". . . was the son of Enos, which was the son of Seth, which was the son of Adam, which was the son of God" (Luke 3:37, 38).

Ancestor Veneration and Validation

Significant to both Mesoamerica and Egypt was a veneration of ancestors and the ideology that accompanied this belief. This tradition had its roots in the desire for lineage validation. There are many similarities to other cultures, but we are going to focus on the institution of divine kingship in which ancestor homage was a basic tenet of these two cultures.[15]

In Maya art, ancestral beings often look down on their progeny or stand close by, which signified the protagonist's royal lineage. For example, on Stela 29 at Tikal, a king holding emblems of his rank and power is accompanied by a floating apparition of his "dynastic ancestor from whom he received the right to rule."[16] In Egypt one find's the same thing. Fairman clearly explains this practice and veneration of ancestors and kingship when he states: "The rites of the coronation not only made him [the heir] the divine king, the presence of the royal ancestors showed that he was accepted by them, he was of their essence, he was filled with the spirit of the ancestors, and in that spirit he ruled unchallenged."[17]

Family Tree

A. Miller's research shows that genealogy was an important preoccupation of the Mesoamerican community.[18] In illustrations of the family tree, a twisted umbilical cord was an essential symbol of artistic expression associated with family lineage. This motif appears in an interesting post-Conquest sixteenth-century genealogical tree of the Maya Tutul Xiu family (Fig. V.5). A bearded figure, who is the founder of his lineage, has a twisted umbilical cord extending from his neck to his waist. Out of this historic person's loins a tree emerges similar to European representations of genealogical trees. The fruits of the tree are his descendants. There is a Spanish influence in this illustration, yet many other elements (the tree, the fruit, the cord), are in keeping with Mesoamerican tradition.

Humans and Trees

Eric Thompson states that the Maya spoke of related people being on the same stem of a fruit tree.[19] In fact, in Mesoamerica the human body was viewed as having the attributes of a tree; the

Fig. V.5 Genealogical Tree of the Xiu Family of Mani in Yucatan (courtesy of Peabody Museum of Archeaology and Ethnology, Harvard University).

children produced by humans were considered as flowers, fruit, or branches.[20] Thompson also observes glyphs on the thigh of the founder of the Tutul Xiu dynasty. These glyphs depict flowers, and the mother figure behind the Tutul Xiu patriarch has a rather similar design on her garment.[21] The flower motif represents the souls of progeny, and the thigh was a symbol of fertility among both the Egyptians and the Maya.[22] In Oaxaca, hundreds of miles west of where the Maya live, a male femur from the thigh of an ancestor was kept by Zapotec rulers and gave the heir his hereditary right to rule (see Fig. I.15a).[23]

According to Widengren, the Sumerians of Mesopotamia hailed newly enthroned kings as "the shoot," which were regarded as a branch of the Tree of Life.[24] The Hebrew religion presents a striking similarity. The Old Testament scriptures are full of references to descendants as shoot, stem, and branch.[25] Tvedtnes notes that the term *zerac* can refer to either a "plant" or "human posterity." Similarly, the Aramaic *bar*, "son," is identical to the Semitic words meaning "grain" or "seed."[26]

The metaphor for the human body as a tree was of great significance to Mesoamerican cultures. In Maya inscriptions, for example, the founder of a lineage was called "sprout-tree-house-root."[27] Even today Maya grandparents call their grandchildren sprouts. The Tzutujil Maya speak of a sprouting plant as *xlexa,* which translates as "his face came out." Similarly, when children are born it is said they sprout; and Carlsen and Prechtel note that grandparents are often addressed as "Big Tree" or "Big Vine," a title of great respect.[28] Also important are other terms relating to human body parts and trees. Among the Tzutujil [Maya], the space beneath a person is *r'xie*, "at a person's root." The space in front of a person is *chuech,* "at its fruit." Behind a person is *tz'nj,* "at its bark." A person's feet are called *r'kan*, "trunk." The Tzutujil word for hand is *r-k'a'* and may be interpreted as "branch."[29] Our last example, also from Carlsen and Prechtel, is the word for "face" and for "fruit," which is *uech,* also meaning "children."[30]

From stems, branches, or shoots of trees, grow fruits or blossoms. This is especially significant among the Maya. Unlike fish, which represented a soul in transition before birth or rebirth, living souls may be represented as flowers. They were often portrayed as flowers in reference to genealogical lineage. Mathews suggests from his reading of glyphs at Copan that the portrayal of a flower hanging from an umbilical rope attached to the heavens represents the "flower soul" of a person (Fig. V.6).[31] The fact is, when a person died it was sometimes written that "the flower soul died." Stuart finds a death statement and translates *ch'ay sak-nik-nal* as "expired, the white-flower thing."[32] This tradition's true counterpart may be found in the ancient Near East where a drooping lotus held in the hand of the deceased king indicates his death.[33]

Many depictions of the World Tree in Mesoamerica contain bell-shaped objects on the ends of branches (Fig. V.7). These are representations of white flowers and imply human souls that were created by First Father. As Freidel, Schele, and Parker explain, "We are the blossoms of that tree."[34] Today the Maya still use this symbolism, only in a highly stylized form. Almost unrecognizable, the flowers at the ends of the modern tree/cross now appear as mere circles (Fig. V.8).

Goodenough, in his voluminous work on Jewish symbols, describes the murals in the Dura Europos Synagogue, which were discovered in 1932. One of them above the Torah shrine contains a representation of a tree with the twelve sons of Jacob (Israel) portrayed beneath its spreading branches (Fig. V.9). Goodenough claims the tree was linked to life in two ways: (1) the Tree of Life and salvation, which led to the supernal throne; and (2) in this case, it is a tree associated with the life and lineage of the family of Israel.[35] This symbolism is also familiar with other Old World cultures where genealogy charts are visualized as a tree. For this

Fig. V.6 A god holding a flower soul, Copan, Honduras (redrawn after Schele *Proceedings* 1992: 226)

reason, the association of the tree and its branches or roots representing human lineage is of even more significance when found in Mesoamerica.

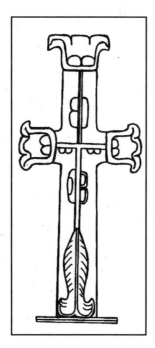

Fig. V.7 Tree cross with bell-shaped
flowers. Detail from Temple
of the Cross, Palenque,
Chiapas, Mexico.

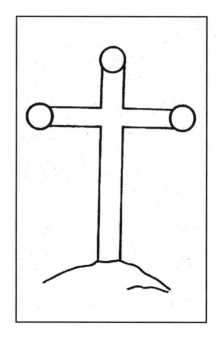

Fig. V.8 Modern Maya Tree-cross
(circles represent flowers).

Fig. V.9 Mural above Torah Shrine at the Dura Europos Synagogue, near today's eastern frontier of
northern Syria (redrawn after photograph, Goodenough 1964: Plate 30).

According to Aztec legend, the split tree represents the garden in Tamoanchan, a mythological location comparable to what the western world refers to as Paradise. It is the "house of descent," "the place of birth," and "the place where gods and men originated."[36] This may be the motive that Mesoamericans, like many other cultures, expressed their genealogical roots as coming from a tree in which the descendants are sometimes referred to as branches, shoots, or flowers of the original World Tree.

Scholars have determined that some Mesoamerican trees and plants often stand for genealogy and bloodlines.[37] For example, the Aztec visualized the fetus as a shoot from the maguey cactus.[38] The Mixtec culture (which was an earlier group that settled around 1000 A.D. in the valley of Oaxaca, Mexico) compared trees to ancestors who watched over their descendants as the full grown plant or tree protects the bud.[39] The Mixtec were often depicted as born from trees. In the *Selden Codex* a man emerges from a cleft in a tree with his umbilical cord still attached (Fig. V.10). The left serpent wrapped around the tree represents clouds, denoted by its scroll motif. The other serpent is bordered by star eyes, making it the night sky.[40] A single eye is placed at the tree's center. These emblems not only connote cosmic forces but also the living aspect of the genealogical tree. Referring back to Figure II.13 of Stela 11 at Piedras Negras, the wooden scaffold with a ladder may be connected to the lineage tree from which the acceding lord was reborn.[41] In addition, the ruler on this stela wears a frog headdress, which signifies birth.[42]

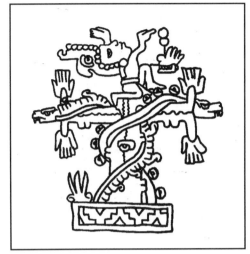

Fig. V.10 Man born from split trunk of a tree (drawn after *Selden Codex*).

Fig. V.11 Fragment of a Zapotec genealogical slab dating to A.D. 600-900. Matatlan, Oaxaca (redrawn after M. Orsen in Marcus 1992a: 233, Fig. 14.3).

It is not surprising that the Mixtec associated descent from trees because the Zapotec (an even earlier culture from the Valley of Oaxaca in Mexico) also depicted genealogical scenes of great significance. In a study by Marcus, royal Zapotec genealogical portraits and texts are explained. Figure V.11 is a Zapotec marriage scene from Matatlan, Oaxaca. A bearded man and his spouse sit below an open mouth representing the jaws of heaven from which descends a plant/tree with leaves. This is an image of divine blessing for the lineage of this couple. The female figure holds a staff/tree with leaves, topped by a bird's head. In addition, the slab gives the names of the seated couple as well as their relatives whose heads are represented beneath them at the corners.[43]

Among the Maya we can look to Palenque for the same tradition. Pakal had one of the more magnificent burials in all of Mesoamerica. In a stone inside his tomb the names and death dates of his ancestors are recorded. Their portraits are arranged around his sarcophagus where they are depicted emerging from trees that grow from cracks in the earth (Fig. V.12. Metaphorically, these cracks represent the point of emergence from the womb of the earth. This symbolism conveys rebirth for this ruler's ancestors. A long text gives the names of thirteen ancestors or relatives and, possibly, the names of two children of the marriage couple.

Fig. V.12   Ancestors of Pakal emerge with tree symbolism from cracks in the earth. Side of sarcophagus, Temple of Inscriptions, Palenque, Chiapas, Mexico (drawn by Linda Schele, © by David Schele, in Schele and Miller 1996: 284).

Seven Tribes

In *The Annals of the Cakchiquel Maya*, reference is often made to four tribes whose branches were separated from an original grouping of seven lineages. "Thus, then, we were four families who arrived at Tulán, we the Cakchiquel people, oh, our sons! so they told us. . . . And these four branches which began were the tribes. . . . From the west we came to Tulán, from across the sea."[44]

Durán (a Dominican friar who lived thirty-two years among the natives of Mexico in the sixteenth century) writes of the seven tribes. According to native legends, these seven lineages believed their god promised them this land, and they were a people he held dear to his heart.[45] In fact, Sahagún equates cave symbolism of the seven tribes with boats. He suggests these tribes crossed the waters in search of the terrestrial paradise.

> Concerning the origin of these peoples, the report that old men give is that they came by sea from the north, and true it is that they came in some wooden boats but it is not known how they were hewn, but it is conjectured by a report found among all these natives that they came from seven caves, and that these seven caves are the seven ships or galleys in which the first settlers of this land came, as gathered from likely conjectures.[46]

The caves from which the seven lineages or branches emerge is of great significance in Mesoamerican symbolism. It is closely associated with birth and creation. Mesoamericans regarded the damp interior of a cave as comparable to a womb. There are several representations of the seven genealogical tribes in Mesoamerica, some emerging from caves. A prime example is an illustration of Chicomoztoc (seven caves), showing the origin of the Tolteca-Chichimeca in Mexico (see Fig. VIII.23). Each petal of the flower-shaped design represented a cave (womb) or tribe from which ancestors emerged. This subject is discussed in more detail in Chapter VIII.

SUMMARY

Similarities between Old World and Mesoamerican traditions regarding genealogical record keeping, symbolism of the tree and tree/plant parts with ancestral lines, and iconographic art forms symbolic of a place of emergence and birth, give additional support to pre-Columbian voyages to the New World.

NOTES - CHAPTER V

1. Carmichael, Elizabeth and Chloë Sayer, *The Skeleton at the Feast: The Day of the Dead in Mexico* (Austin: University of Texas Press, 1991).

2. Marcus, Joyce, "Royal Families, Royal Texts: Examples from the Zapotec and Maya," in *Mesoamerican Elites,* Diane Z. Chase and Arlen F. Chase, eds. (Norman: University of Oklahoma Press, 1992), 286.

3. Taube, Karl A., "A Study of Classic Maya Scaffold Sacrifice," in *Maya Iconography,* Elizabeth P. Benson and Gillett G. Griffin, eds. (Princeton: Princeton University Press, 1988), 184, 221.

4. Dütting, "On the Astronomical Background of Mayan Historical Events."

5. Marcus, "Royal Familes, Royal Texts," 298.

6. Coe, Michael D., *Breaking the Maya Code.*

7. Coe, Michael D., *The Maya,* 4th ed. (New York: Thames & Hudson, 1987), 187; Schele and Miller, 14.

8. Carmack, 63.

9. Justeson, John S., "The Representational Conventions of Mayan Hieroglyphic Writing," in *Word and Image in Maya Culture,* William F. Hanks and Don S. Rice, eds. (Salt Lake City: University of Utah Press, 1989), 25.

10. Hopkins, Nicholas A., "Classic and Modern Relationship Terms and the 'Child of Mother' Glyph (TI:606.23)," in *Sixth Palenque Round Table,* 1986, vol. 8, Merle Greene-Robertson, gen. ed., Virginia M. Fields, vol. ed. (Norman: University of Oklahoma Press, 1991), 255-65.

11. Schele, Linda, "The Xibalba Shuffle: A Dance After Death," in *Maya Iconography,* Elizabeth P. Benson and Gillett G. Griffin, eds. (Princeton: Princeton University Press, 1988), 308.

12. Dieter Dütting, "Birth, Inauguration and Death in the Inscriptions of Palenque, Chiapas, Mexico," in Tercera Mesa Redonda de Palenque, eds. Merle Greene-Robertson & Donnan Call Jeffers, vol. IV (Palenque, Chiapas, Mexico: Pre-Columbian Art Research, 1978), 197.

13. Schele, "The Xibalba Shuffle," 308.

14. Schele and Freidel, "The Courts of Creation," 217, 218.

15. Watterson, 123; Schele and Miller, 14.

16. Schele and Freidel, *A Forest of Kings,* 141.

17. Fairman, H. W., "The Kingship Rituals of Egypt," in *Myth, Ritual, and Kingship,* S. H. Hooke, ed. (Oxford: Claredon Press, 1958), 104.

18. Miller, Arthur G., "The Iconography of the Painting in the Temple of the Diving God, Tulum, Quintana Roo, Mexico: The Twisted Cords," in *Mesoamerican Archaeology: New Approaches,* Norman Hammon, ed. (London: Duckworth, 1974), 175-77.

19. Thompson, J. Eric S. *A Commentary on the Dresden Codex, Memoirs of the American Philosophic Society,* 93 (Philadelphia: American Philosophical Society, 1972), 8.

20. Furst, Jill Leslie McKeever, *The Natural History of the Soul in Ancient Mexico* (New Haven: Yale University Press, 1995), 86.

21. J. Eric S. Thompson, *A Commentary on the Dresden Codex,* 8.

22. Clark 1959, 160; Diane Wirth and Brian Stross, "The 'le' Motif: Symbol of Lineage and Fertility Among the Olmec and Maya," in *U Mut Maya VI,* Carolyn and Tom Jones, eds. (Bayside, California: U Mut Maya, 1997), 81-90.

23. Lind, Michael and Javier Urcid, "The Lords of Lambityeco and Their Nearest Neighbors," *Notas Americas* 9 (1983), 80.

24. Widengren, Geo, *The King and the Tree of Life in Ancient Near Eastern Religion,* vol. 4 (Wiesbaden, Germany: Uppsala Universitets Ärsskrift, 1951), 20-22.

25. See, for example, Ps. 1:3-5; 52:8; 128:3; Jer. 11:19; 17:6, 8; Isa. 11; 24:13; Ezek. 31; Zech. 4.

26. Personal communication from John Tvedtnes to Diane Wirth, April 1, 1999.

27. Freidel, Schele, and Parker, 447.

28. Carlson, Robert S. and Martin Prechtel, "The Flowering of the Dead: An Interpretation of Highland Maya Culture," *MAN* 26 (1991), 28.

29. Personal communication from Brian Stross to Diane Wirth, April 1998.

30. Carlson and Prechtel, 29.

31. Schele, Linda, *The Proceedings of the Maya Hieroglyphic Workshop,* March 14, 15, 1992, Phil Wanyerka, ed. and transcriber (Austin: University of Texas, 1992), 226.

32. Noted in Freidel, Schele, and Parker, 183.

33. Gray, 101.

34. Freidel, Schele, and Parker, 183.

35. Goodenough, E. R., *Jewish Symbols in the Greco-Roman Period* (New York: Pantheon, 1964), 10: 2:200.

36. Laurette Séjourné, *Burning Water* (New York: Vanguard Press, 1956), 118.

37. Millon, Clara, et. al., *Feathered Serpents and Flowering Trees,* Kathleen Berrin, ed. (San Francisco: The Fine Arts Museums of San Francisco, 1988), 161.

38. Sahagún, *Florentine Codex,* Pt. 6: 142.

39. Heyden, Doris, "Metaphors, Nahualtocaitl, and Other 'Disguised' Terms Among the Aztecs," in *Symbol and Meaning Beyond the Closed Community: Essays in Mesoamerican Ideas,* Gary H. Gossen, ed. *Studies on Culture and Society,* vol. 1 (Albany: Institute for Mesoamerican Studies, University of Albany, 1986), 40.

40. Furst, Jill Leslie, "The Tree Birth Tradition in the Mixteca, Mexico," *Journal of Latin American Lore* 312 (Los Angeles: UCLA Latin American Center, 1977), 190.

41. Taube, "A Study of Classic Maya Scaffold Sacrifice," 341.

42. Ibid., 343.

43. Marcus, "Royal Families, Royal Texts," 223-59.

44. Recinos, Adrián and Delia Goetz, *The Annals of the Cakchiquels* (Norman: University of Oklahoma, 1974), 44-45.

45. Durán, Fray Diego, *The Aztecs: The History of the Indians of New Spain,* Doris Heyden and Fernando Horcasites, translators. (New York: Orion Press, 1964), 9.

46. Sahagún, *Historia General de las Cosas de Nueva Espana,* Introduction.

CHAPTER VI

THE KING AND THE WORLD TREE

The objective of this comparative study in this chapter is to show a similar relationship between the role of kings and the World Tree in Middle Eastern cultures, and a parallel belief system held by Mesoamerican peoples, more particularly the Maya and their predecessors the Olmec. Religious concepts endured among the ancient cultures of Mesoamerica for lengthy periods of time. For example, pyramids perceived as sacred manmade mountains were constructed for over a thousand years. The Aztecs, Toltecs, Mixtecs, Zapotecs, and Maya were profoundly influenced by the Olmec (the earliest civilization in Mexico) thriving from approximately 1500-400 B.C. After the demise of their far-reaching culture, many Olmec sacred traditions managed to pass from one generation to the next throughout Mesoamerica. We shall see that the Olmec ideology revolving around the king and his relation to the World Tree made a substantial impression on Mesoamerican peoples for years to come. This may be likened to the magnificent Greek civilization that left an enormous imprint on the western world.

THE KING AS SERVANT AND/OR DIVINE

The ruler was of prime importance to his people, whether in Mesoamerica or anywhere else in the ancient world when there existed kings. Something unique about Mesoamerican kings as well as their counterparts in the Middle East, is that many were considered divine and/or a conduit for revelation from their god(s). In Israel the case was slightly different. The king was considered more than a mere man. He was regarded as a special servant of the divine king, the king of kings, who is God. The ruler of an earthly kingdom, when and if he was a righteous man, became the agent and spokesman for God. In other words, the king's right to rule his domain was likened to a shadow of God's rule on earth. The king, in and of himself, was nothing without the power and authority of his priesthood, which was given to him by God.[1] This type of tradition was popular in Mesopotamia, Syria, and Palestine.[2]

Kings in both Mesoamerica and the Middle East often wore the costume of their deity and/or the emblems of their priesthood. By doing so, they became sacred, or at least as was the case in Israel, were recognized as God's representative on earth. Furthermore, although the king in Israel was not considered divine, God did say of King David's heir, "I will be his father, and he shall be my son."[3] There is obviously a parental connection between Israel's God and his people, and especially to chosen heirs to the throne. In fact, Patai points out that according to later Jewish tradition, the new king symbolically became as a one-year-old child, who, when anointed, became the son of God.[4]

Gray notes that in Israel, King David was put in charge as the executive of the divine power over the forces of chaos in history.[5] This is significant in that this facet of kingship was of equal importance to Mesoamerican kings. First, let us consider the concept of order as opposed to chaos. The Old Testament speaks of God as the king who triumphs over chaos (Psalm 89). This has reference to the beginning of time, the day of creation when all was set in order. The king held the same role. He was the one expected to keep balance and order in the earthly kingdom, and was supposed to ensure that it would run as smoothly as the day the world was created. The king should be able to do this as he was the spokesman for God. He was the one who knew the heart of God. The king in Israel was "the Lord's anointed."[6] There is no doubt that ideally there was to be a personal relationship between the king and his God at all times.

The New Year festival in particular (a religious highlight of the year in ancient Israel) was a time when the kingship of God and his appointed king on the earth were sustained in light of their ability to conquer the forces of chaos and maintain a continual state of order. As discussed in Chapter III, this was accomplished through ritual that involved a reenactment of the creation symbolizing a renewal and harmony of all things. Thus, the king in Israel, although he himself was not divine, held a sacred role—a sacred calling as the anointed of the highest Divine King of heaven. To show a connection between kings of the Old and the New World, we also need to review the Sumerian, and then the Egyptian symbolism behind the enthroned king.

Among the Sumerians of Mesopotamia we find a close parallel to the Hebrew culture, which was a later development. More often than not the Sumerian king was also considered the servant his god, and only in a few cases was the king believed to be deified.[7] In both Mesopotamia and Israel a New Year festival reenacted the moment of creation. The prime objective of this roleplaying was to establish the king as the one to conquer chaos and through these rituals he was able to revitalize his kingdom.

Unlike Israel and Mesopotamia, where the king was considered a chosen vessel who spoke for the Divine King, the king of Egypt, Pharaoh, not only uttered words for the highest god but was thought to be his literal son—becoming fully deified after his death and resurrection. Although considered sacred, the Pharaoh was a servant of Ra, required to carry out the commands of his divine father, and to perform rituals that reenacted the creation of the world. The Egyptian ruler was expected to conquer death and play out the entire cosmic drama to set all things in order again for his earthly reign, which was a metaphor for a new creation.[8]

In Mesoamerica we note a slightly different pattern, which is somewhat like that of Israel and Mesopotamia, yet much closer to Egyptian tradition. In recent years Mesoamerican scholars deciphered hieroglyphic texts describing royal genealogies. These texts, along with scenes portrayed on stelae, tell us much about Maya royalty. For example, according to Marcus:

> By maintaining the belief that as a group they had enjoyed a separate, divine descent, Maya royalty remained the only individuals who could serve as mediators between the secular commoners, on the one hand, and the divine supernatural beings . . . on the other. . . . Reciting myth and participating in special rites served to establish and reenact the sacred links between the rulers and the divine.[9]

The Maya went to great lengths to establish this divine ancestral connection. Kan-B'alam, the son of the great King Pakal of Palenque, falsified his genealogy. According to Schele and Freidel, this was done to reflect his ancestral ties with the founder of the dynasty, and even beyond to divine, supernatural beings who were the first to establish order.[10] Moreover, the birth date of both his father, Pakal, and that of his grandmother fell on the same day as that of the Creatrix. As Schele and Mathews explain: "By creating affinities between himself [Pakal] and a supernatural being from the remote past, he declared himself to be made of the same stuff as the gods."[11] M. Coe also makes a comment on this subject that is noteworthy: "The rulers were descended from the gods, and a king probably became identified with his lineage god after death."[12] Consequently, both Pakal and Kan-B'alam became the offspring of divinity—their eventual place among their supernatural ancestors being established without question in the historical records of Palenque. Yet we must note that Mesoamerican ancestral gods were not worshiped in the same manner, nor were they thought of in the same way as the western world perceives the concept of gods. These ancestors were honored, respected, and petitioned, but they fall more in the category of sacred entities or supernaturals beings than they do as gods.[13]

Since the Maya king was thought to descend from divine royalty, he became the conduit for his gods' messages to the people. This is identical to the function of kings in the ancient Middle East. Referring to the role of king in Canaan, Gray notes that kings performed sacrifices on behalf of the community and were the channel for divine blessings and revelation, which would be passed on to the people.[14] This concept was just as much at home in the Near East as it was in Mesoamerica.

VICARIOUS SACRIFICE

The king's association with sacrifice is parallel in the Old World and Mesoamerica. In the Middle East the cosmos and men were thought to be periodically regenerated as a result of sacrifice. This could be accomplished through vicarious sacrifice where an unblemished victim or burnt offerings were used as a substitute for the king. As previously noted in Chapter II, the substitute king is of extraordinary interest, for it was thought that a captive died vicariously for the king in order that the people might live.[15] In the Egyptian rite called the Sed Festival, a substitute king was often sacrificed followed by a symbolic resurrection of the king. This rebirth became a realization in the eyes of the Egyptian populace when the king mounted his throne as the ruler for a new period of years.[16] According to Eliade, the purpose of sacrificial rites in the Old World was to restore the primordial unity—that which existed before the creation. This was certainly true of Mesoamerican cultures.[17]

Sacrifice among the Maya could be in the form of burnt offerings, bloodletting by kings (a form of self-sacrifice), or the sacrifice of human victims—the more royal the better. Sometimes a Maya king performed rituals in the temple to symbolize his descent into the Underworld where he would overcome the Lords of Death through sacrifice. By doing so, he reenacted mythological events recorded in the *Popol Vuh*. Schele and Freidel observe that the king's objective was to bring back life and prosperity for his people.[18] Just as the Hero Twins of the *Popol Vuh* conquer death and become resurrected as the sun and the moon, so, too, it was thought that the king and his people would be reborn in a like manner. In fact, Kan-B'alam of Palenque declared himself a living incarnation of the sun.[19] This was also true of Osiris in Egypt who, like the sun, symbolically died and was reborn each day.

In their study of the Maya ballgame, Schele and Freidel show that sacrificial victims were substituted for the king in his role as one of the *Popol Vuh* Hero Twins, playing the game in Xibalba with the Lords of Death. The ballcourt itself was considered the realm of the Underworld.[20] The theme of substitute sacrifice is also seen on stelae at Piedras Negras, Guatemala. On Stela 11 in particular, Schele and M. Miller explain that the king already climbed to his celestial throne (see Fig. II.13). The upper niche where the king sits is identified with the cosmic realm. It was there that the victim sat just before his death, after which he was thrown to the bottom of the ladder.[21] The victims on Piedras Negras stelae were sacrificed vicariously for the king. We know from hieroglyphic texts of accession scenes that the sacrificed lord was considered the *k'ex,* or "substitution" for the new king.[22]

Substitute sacrifice had similar implications among the Aztec. A handsome youth in perfect health and without blemish was lavished upon for a year, given privileges of royalty, education, entertainment, and was even considered a god. This ritual veneration was followed by the young man's death.[23] He was clearly a substitute for the royal sacrifice. When the king came out of his temple it appeared as though he died and was reborn. Among the Israelites, animals selected for sacrifice were without blemish the same as the Aztec's chosen youth. Patai's study of African rituals led him to conclude that their rites originated in the ancient Near East. In fact, very much like the Aztec youth who was wined and dined before his demise, an African victim, "after having been fed, clothed, and treated in all aspects as a king for the duration of a month, was presented to the king and then killed—again in order to prolong the life of the king."[24]

KING AS GUARDIAN/GARDENER

In his capacity as ruler, and as one who keeps his kingdom in order as the gods do in the universe, the king is also regarded as the guardian of nature. In other words, if the king ensures rain, the crops survive as well as the people. If he protects his realm from enemies, his kingdom remains intact. If the king is chosen as a spokesman for the gods, his people benefit from their wisdom coming from the king's sacred word. The king is the supreme guardian, much as the First Man on the earth is the gardener and caretaker of all he surveyed.

Widengren reports that Near Eastern kings were actually given the name of Gardener, which was considered a sacred title.[25] Images of the king guarding the Tree of Life are universal in the art of Mesopotamia (Fig. VI.1) and symbolized the king's service to the gods and his role as a giver of the gods' blessings to his people.[26]

Kings in the Old World are often shown holding a scepter bearing leaves, branches, or flowers (Fig. VI.2). According to Widengren, this represents the twig Adam cut from a branch of the famed Tree in paradise. It was a tradition for Adam and the kings who came after him to

Fig. VI.1 Mesopotamian seal-impression with image of king on both sides of the Tree of Life. Staatliche Museen, Berlin (drawn after photograph in Gray 1969:55).

Fig. VI.2 Stela of Bar Rekubin Siheirli, Northern Syria
(redrawn after Widengren 1951: 28, Fig. 6).

carry this life-giving branch of the World Tree as a sign of their calling as Gardener.[27] In Mesoamerica we find the same theme of the Gardener/King among the Aztec. Every year a one-day ceremonial tilling of the land was performed specifically by the king. This was not done to put himself on the same level as commoners, but to make it clear that he was the caretaker, fructifier, and provider for his people.[28]

First Man/First Father

The First Man was the gardener in a paradisiacal setting and was responsible for taking care of it as instructed by God. He was the first of his race—the head of his lineage—he could even be considered a trunk of the genealogical tree. This was true of the Near Eastern king. Gray writes that in the king's role as the gardener who tended the Tree of Life: "We have surely the original of primordial man (Hebrew *'adam*), the image of God, in the Garden of Eden, with its Tree of Life."[29] Perry proposes that kings in Israel took upon themselves the image of the First Man.[30]

The Maya king often wears the costume of a male figure named Hun-Nal-Ye, literally the "first ear of corn revealed." Hun-Nal-Ye is sometimes referred to by many Mayanists as First Father, the maize god.[31] First Father was the progenitor of the human race which was believed to be made of corn.[32] It has already been established that the king was considered the guardian of ordered nature, especially in the context of the World Tree.[33] When the Maya king dressed as the maize god, he demonstrated his association with the First Man who had strong agricultural ties.[34]

Eliade writes: "In ancient times great monarchs considered themselves imitators of the primordial hero."[35] Even Sumerian governors took on the image of the First Man.[36] Therefore, it is not so unusual for rulers in both the Old and New Worlds to play the role of First Father. Having such an important position, ancient kings were considered the central figure of their community, even the *axis mundi,* the center of the world. A concept of the center was essential to these early cultures and had a close association with both the king and the World Tree.

King as Axis Mundi

According to Tate, Maya rulers represent the axis that connected their royal, ancestral bloodline with the heavens and the Underworld.[37] In the Old World we find the same axiom. Eliade, for example, states that royal Near Eastern cities were considered "the image of the Cosmos, and the King . . . was the Axis Mundi."[38] Ramesses II of Egypt was called the Pillar of the Sky and Beam of the Earth.[39] The ruler was the central being of all that he surveyed, the role model of his community, the stabilizing force to whom all looked for their continuance. But the most profound certainty in this study is that the king was the embodiment of the World Tree, the *axis mundi,* in both the Middle East and in Mesoamerica.

KING AS WORLD TREE

The Sumerians depict the Tree of Life as a god named Tammuz. He is associated with the Underworld and is an ever-dying, ever-resurrecting god.[40] In Sumerian literature he is sometimes called Shepherd and/or Gardener. These early texts speak of the king as a cedar and, in some cases, proclaimed to be the Tree of Life.[41] Widengren writes: "The idea of the Tree of Life . . . has been seen . . . [as] . . . nothing but a mythic ritual symbol of both god and king. . . . The king may be viewed . . . as being himself a twig from the Tree of Life."[42]

In Egypt after Osiris is killed by Seth, his arch enemy, his body is placed in a tree from which he is reborn. Budge maintains that Osiris was the great Sky Tree.[43] The most common symbol of Osiris was the *djed* (Figs. VI.3 and 4), interpreted as both a tree and the backbone of Osiris.[44] The Egyptian king used this symbol to portray stability and life in the kingdom. In earlier times this emblem was associated with Ptah, the god of creation.[45] Its design is possibly derived from the bound sheaf of the first grain of the harvest.[46] Moreover, *djed* amulets were usually green, denoting vegetation.[47] In Egypt grain was considered the tree of the center, so it is no wonder maize in Mesoamerica represented the same concept, even from earliest times. Various other plants and trees could also represent the World Tree. This interchangeable tradition was certainly common to the Middle East as well.[48]

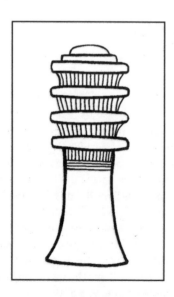

Fig. VI.3   Egyptian *Djed* amulet, symbol of Osiris (drawn after photograph in Andrews 1993: 83).

Fig. VI.4   *Djed* and Osiris combined, from Tomb of Nofretari, Egypt (redrawn after Hornung 1990: 118).

98

Bound sheaves of maize are portrayed with or on Olmec rulers (Fig. VI.5) who, together with the grain, represent the World Tree, the *axis mundi*.[49] In addition, Taube observes that the Olmec bundle of maize was bound and coupled with feathers, also a symbol of vegetation and fertility.[50] It is likely the feathers used were the green plumes of the quetzal, which represent the growing leaves and stalks of maize from very early times.[51] Whether or not this has any relation to the Egyptian *djed,* which was often displayed with feathers ceremonially placed at the top (Fig. VI.4 and 6), cannot be determined at this time. However, the similarities are striking.[52]

Pillars of the Cosmos

Reilly notes that if one views the incised design on the jade celt from Arroyo Pesquero (Fig. VI.7) in a three-dimensional format, the personified ruler/tree and four maize seeds may be regarded as the four trees/pillars of the earth, with the fifth tree as the central World Tree.[53] Stross agrees that groupings of four maize seeds may represent the four corners of structures, which in themselves is a metaphor for pillars of the cosmos.[54] This concept is also part of Old World traditions. A pillar altar at Hagar Qim in Malta has four trees sculpted on it, one on each of the four-sided pillar. It is one of the earliest known portrayals of the Tree of Life theme at the four quadrants of the earth.[55] The *djed* of Egypt may also personify the idea of four trees at the corners with one at the center. By contrast to the idea of the *djed* as bound grain, but following the same theme, Saad interprets some ivory symbols of the *djed* as Osiris, carved to represent cypress trees with tied branches.[56] Andrews suggests the four horizontal lines on the column may represent the branches of a tree,

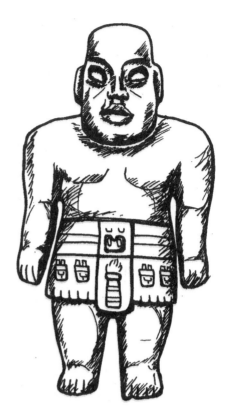

Fig. VI.5 Olmec ruler with bound maize on apron, Puebla, Mexico (drawn after photograph, Museo del Estado de Puebla).

which are now sawed off.[57] Legend has it that these four branches were originally turned to the four cardinal directions, the *djed* itself representing a pillar of the sky.[58]

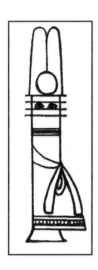

Fig. VI.6 Personified *Djed* topped with feathers (redrawn after Clark 1959: 237).

Fig. VI.7 Incised Olmec celt from Arroyo Pesquero, Veracruz, Mexico (redrawn after Reilly 1996: 38, Fig. 25).

The symbolism of maize representing the World Tree, also symbolized the ruler at the center of the world. This ideology was known from Olmec times and permeated Mesoamerican traditions for two thousand years. Long after the Olmec, a maize stalk was portrayed as the World Tree among the Maya in Palenque (Fig. VI.8). Following this, in the *Codex Borgia* the fifth and central World Tree is illustrated as a maize plant. The World Tree could be many other varieties of trees and plants in Mesoamerica. Tree iconography was often part of a ruler's regalia.

Fig. VI.8   Temple of the Foliated Cross, Palenque, Chiapas, Mexico (drawn by Linda Schele, © David Schele, in Schele and Miller 1986: 195, Fig. IIV.4).

King and Tree Parts

The Bible makes reference to king and tree symbolism. For example, the king of Judah is likened to a vine planted beside many waters. Other verses compare a foreign king to a mighty cedar.[59] The Hebrew king is also equated with a mighty tree. Just as a tree gives comfort and protection in its shade, the king is a guardian to his people (Dan. 4:22). In Mesoamerica we find identical meaning for their kings. The Quiché Maya in their *Popol Vuh* text show a clear association of the ruler with a Tree.

> You lord, you are our mother
> You are our father
> You are like the ceiba [the ceiba is a tree in Central America]
> Like the Temple pyramid
> Over our heads
> We find shelter at your roots
> You are our protection
> You are our shadow.[60]

The *axis mundi* was not located at any one place on earth but could be created through ritual as noted in Chapter III. More importantly, the World Tree was materialized in the person of the king at the center of the Mesoamerican world.[61] One of the titles of the Maya kings, *Yahau te*, "Tree Lord," reflect their role as a representative of the World Tree.[62] In fact, the text of a Maya vase reads, "his becoming the tree," which Reents-Budet suggests may refer to the king's role as the World Tree.[63] Other vases describe rulers as the "standing one tree person" and "holy tree person."[64] The supernatural world of the Mesoamerican community was a living reality, so it is no surprise that the king was believed to personify the World Tree in the flesh.[65]

World Tree Costume

The early Olmec in Mesoamerica give us the root of this tradition. According to Freidel, Schele, and Parker, the Olmec are the first to associate the reigning ruler with the World Tree.[66] A pectoral now at Dumbarton Oaks in Washington D.C., which dates back between 1000–600 B.C. (Fig. VI.9), was reworked by the Maya around 1–200 A.D.[67] It portrays a god or an early ruler wearing a personified World Tree growing from a U- shaped cleft in his headdress. Clothed in this costume the individual proclaims himself to be not only the Tree, but the *axis mundi* of the world. Stross supports Reilly's hypothesis that this individual was the forerunner of the Maya maize god known in the *Popol Vuh* as Hun Hunahpu.[68] A similar theme is seen on a ruler's headdress from Kaminaljuyu, Guatemala (Fig. VI.10). This ruler also wears an image of the World Tree, proclaiming himself as the center of the Maya cosmos as well as an imitator of First Father, the maize god.[69]

On a limestone tablet on Temple 14 at Palenque, King Kan-B'alam dances his way out of Xibalba, the Maya Underworld. This is after he posthumously defeated the evil Lords of Death as did the Hero Twins of the *Popol Vuh*. Like Osiris of Egypt, who represents the

Fig. VI.9 Olmec jade pectoral dated between 1000-600 B.C., housed at Dumbarton Oaks (drawn by Linda Schele, © by David Schele, in Schele and Miller 1986: 119, with emphasis of leaves by author).

sun as it travels through the Underworld, this Maya king wears the accouterments of the *kin* "sun" sign (the small x) on his headdress along with a personified tree (Fig. VI.11). According to Schele and M. Miller, this tree represents the road the king followed in his journey into and out of the Underworld.[70] This pathway is the conduit to the gods. To reiterate, both the Tree and the king are seen as a channel to the supernatural world. On Stela 10 at Seibal, Guatemala (Fig. VI.12), a Maya king is portrayed in full regalia as the World Tree. This costume will be explained in a discussion of the Tree.

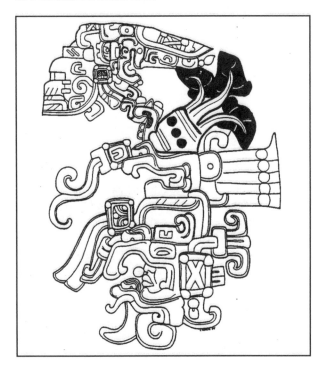

Fig. VI 10   Stela 11, Kaminaljuyu, Guatemala, dated between 100 B.C. - A.D. 100 (drawn by Linda Schele, © by David Schele, in Schele and Miller 1986: 109, Fig. II.2, with emphasis on leaves by author).

Fig. VI.11   Kan-Balam detail from limestone tablet, Temple 14, Palenque, Chiapas, Mexico, dated to A.D. 705 (redrawn after Schele and Miller 1986: 272, Fig. VII.2).

Key factors were assimilated in the function of the king in both the Middle East and Mesoamerica. The king was considered a divine/sacred being through lineage, or at least was called of God or gods to be the mediator between the earth and the supernatural realm. Vicarious sacrifice was performed in lieu of the king followed by a symbolic rebirth of the kingdom. Often this came at the time of the king's accession to the throne. The king was considered a gardener and protector of his people as was the ancestral First Man of creation. The *axis mundi* was centered in the king's presence. And last, the most important feature of this study—the king represented the World Tree.

THE WORLD TREE

The World Tree incorporates the same attributes as the king. The close association between the king and the World Tree in both the Middle East and Mesoamerica is no doubt more than coincidental.

Tree as Axis Mundi

In Mesoamerica some of the earliest representations of the World Tree as the axis of the earth were utilized by the Olmec. An inscribed stone tablet from Ahuelican, Guerrero, Mexico, illustrates many of the elements one would expect to find in a world center theme of the Near East (Fig. VI.13).[71] The crossed bands within an enclosure at the top of the tablet is an Olmec sky glyph. This motif is surrounded by thirteen squared and rounded scallops that may represent the thirteen heavens of the Mesoamerican world. Under the sky sign, and with its branches touching the heavens, is the World Tree or plant with four oval seeds signifying life, which are probably the four tree/pillars of the cosmos. The foundation for the World Tree is a stepped pyramid, temple, or sacred mountain, with an inner symbol representing the cosmic center, the navel of the earth or primordial hill from which life springs. Below this formation is a U-shaped entrance to the cave, the womb of the Underworld, where men go to complete the cycle of life, death, and rebirth. The entire cosmic scenario of the Sacred Tree is at the center that binds the heavens to the earth. The tablet is edged with representations of the four directions and corners of the universe, a concept mirrored in ancient cultures across the sea.

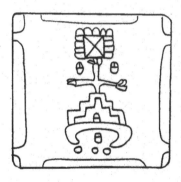

Fig. VI.13 Dallas Plaque at Dumbarton Oaks, from Ahuelican, Guerrero, Mexico, dated between 1000-400 B.C. (redrawn after Pratt in Gay 1973).

Fig. VI.12 Stela 10, Seibal, Guatemala, dated to A.D. 849 (from Turner 1980, courtesy of Dover Publications).

Raising the World Tree

We turn our attention to the role the king and the World Tree played in the creation and organization of the earth. Throughout the Middle East, festivals were performed involving the lifting of a tree. For example, there was a ceremonial raising of the *djed* pillar in Egypt at the time of a new king's accession or renewal to the throne (Fig. VI.14). Patai notes: "The setting up of the [sic] *Dd* column, [has its] parallels both in modern Africa and among the ancient Hebrews."[72] Raising this pole at the commencement of the king's reign or during New Year festivities marked the particular time as one of stability for the king's world and the cosmos, crops, new life, and rebirth in general.[73] Many

Fig. VI.14 Seti I erects *Djed* pillar, Abydos, Egypt
(redrawn after Budge 1961: Vol. I, 56).

Egyptian rituals, Moret observes, were only the imitation of the rites of the First Time.[74] More will be said regarding the raising of the Tree in the Old World, maypole style, in the discussion of the Tree and sacrifice.

With the Maya on the Western Hemisphere, the king in his role as the central pillar and/or Tree of Life symbolically represents First Father who, at the beginning of time, sets up the World Tree, the so-called *Wakah Kan*. It is First Father who raises the sky separating it from the earth upon which it rested.[75] The myth of a previously lying-down sky was not only a tradition among the Maya but the Sumerians and Egyptians as well.[76] It is significant that in the Egyptian Pyramid Texts, Shu, the god of air, raises up the sky from the earth, which was positioned directly under it (see Fig. IX.2).[77] In Mesoamerica we find a legend in the *Historia de los Mexicanos Por Sus Pinturas*. Quetzalcoatl, in his guise as the wind god, changes into a Tree of Sustenance in order to separate the sky from the earth at the time of the creation (see Fig. IX.1).[78]

At the Maya *Origins* Meeting held at the University of Texas in Austin in 1992, Reilly showed an Olmec sculpture from San Martin Pajapan, Veracruz, in the Tuxtlas of Mexico. The piece depicts an individual (probably the king) with his legs positioned as though he is about to stand. One leg is in a kneeling position while the other leg is raised in a stooping position (Fig. VI.15). Reilly explained that this individual, with

Fig. VI.15 A view of both sides of monument from San Martin Pajapan, Veracruz, Mexico
(redrawn after photographs, Museum of Anthropology, University of Veracruz).

his hands on a bar containing the central axis sky glyph carved at one end, is about to raise up the World Tree. From his headdress sprouts vegetation in a stylized form. Reilly proposed this sculpture is one of the earliest representations of creation found to date in the New World.[79] According to Maya cosmology, this act happened at the moment the earth and sky were separated whereupon the current cycle of time began. When a new king came to the throne it was considered a new era for the kingdom, bringing all the power, control, and order of the original one established by First Father. For this reason the king's costume, whether of First Father (the maize god) or the World Tree itself, is important as he re-creates the world.

Sacrifice of Tree

The sacrifice of the king, mentioned earlier, was deemed necessary to maintain order in the kingdom. It was also to ensure fertility and the well-being of the people. This sacrifice was also expressed in another profound manner. Trees were ceremonially sacrificed, not unlike bloodletting rituals performed by the king or a victim standing in vicariously for the king. In essence, when a tree was ceremonially felled, it became a sacrificial representative of the king.

Examining similar rituals in the Old World, there is an interesting tradition from Greece, which may come from Egypt. Attis, the god associated with vegetation and referred to as *Papas* meaning Father,[80] was killed by a jealous god. Rituals were performed in his honor in Greece and Rome every year in March. A cut tree was brought to a designated sacred spot where it was bedecked with woollen bands, ribbons, and violets (Fig. VI.16). Tied to the tree was an effigy of the sacrificed Attis, while bloodletting ceremonies and dances took place around the tree. On the next day the resurrection of Attis was celebrated.[81] Cutting down the tree represented the death of the old cycle, while decorating the tree with ribbons and flowers represented the hoped for rebirth. This renewal encompassed the cosmos, agriculture, and/or political governments.

The Book of Daniel in the Old Testament speaks of a tree cut down representing king Nebuchadnezzar in a humiliating manner. It was not until a seven-year period passed that he resumed his kingship, but this time with great aplomb. This scenario is in similitude of death and rebirth. The Bible contains numerous examples of the number seven representing a period of waiting before renewal.[82] In the case of king Nebuchadnezzar, his seven-year period of ostracism and waiting was followed by the renewal of his position in the kingdom. The act of splitting the tree represented the substitute royal sacrifice and, like everything in nature, it was believed that through death comes life.

Fig. VI.16 Attis on a drinking cup from Vulci, Rome, Bibliotheque National, Paris (redrawn after Henderson & Oakes 1990: 119).

Probably the best way to understand these rituals is to look to the familiar maypole ceremony still performed in Europe. When the ritual tree is stripped of its branches and foliage, which represent life, the barren pole becomes the center of the world at the end of a cycle. In May, the time of the year when vegetation is renewed as it rises out of death, dancing around the maypole with flowers and ribbons figuratively allows the human race to have an active part in the rebirth of nature.[83]

Perhaps this concept goes back to Egypt where a similar ritual was performed. A pole representing a tree at the center was set in place (Fig. VI.17). Ropes were attached to the top and along the length of the pole while men held the ends of the ropes and walked around the pole/tree. The men represented the constellations rotating around the Pole Star, appearing to reach the top via the cosmic tree that represented the path to the center of the Otherworld.[84] This too is identical in Maya thought.[85]

The tradition of bedecking a cut tree with ribbons and flowers and then placing the tree in a hole at a designated sacred spot continues among many Mesoamerican descendants today. One example was seen in an Aztec festival recorded by Bancroft. Describing this rite held at harvest time, Bancroft explains the following ritual.[86] A very tall tree was taken down from the mountains and carefully dragged on rollers to the temple courtyard. When the tree was cut, it was considered sacrificed—it died. It was then decorated with streamers representing vegetation. Sacrificial rites were performed at the site, which involved stripping victims of their dress just as the tree was stripped of its leaves and branches. Then, like the Egyptian and European maypole ceremony, many youths took hold of ropes that hung from the top of the tree, making a grand circle as they danced around the pole.

Fig. VI.17 Egyptian Pole of Min, Dendera (redrawn after Anderson 1987: Pl. 40).

World Tree and King

In the ancient Near East the World Tree is portrayed with either god(s), guardians of the god(s), or with the king (sometimes in duplicate) (Figs. VI.1, 18, 19, and 20). In addition, there was often a bird-like element at the top of the Tree designating its celestial and divine nature. In Mesoamerica we once again find the same iconographic elements. Whether the Tree is at the center of the world, or individual trees set at the corners of the earth, there is often a bird perched at the top of the Tree as well as humans or supernaturals beings standing next to the Tree (Figs. VI.8, 21 and 22).

Maya kings are considered holy lords, and wearing a costume of the World Tree made the sacred quality of the Tree real (Figs. VI.12 and VI.23). The thin appendages falling to the sides of the apron represent the branches of the Tree.[87] What this costume means is that both the Tree and the king are not only divine, but the *axis mundi* is the sacred channel to the gods and the stabilizer of the cosmos.[88] This view was held in many parts of Mesoamerica. At Cerro de las Mesas in Veracruz (a site that incorporated artistic styles from Mexico as well as the lands of the Maya and the earlier Olmec) we find the branch and leaf of the World Tree worn by rulers on their aprons (Fig. VI.24). Even the late great Aztec empire considered their rulers as representing the World Tree.[89] The same enduring tradition existed in the Old World. For example, Charlemagne (742–814 A.D.) is portrayed with the World Tree on his apron, a tradition that carried from ancient times (Fig. VI.25). Even Pharaohs of Egypt sometimes wore a collar of greenery to indicate their function as a tree.[90]

Tree as Milky Way Path

In addition to the above, the World Tree is considered the road to the supernatural world—the path deceased souls take in the hereafter. Freidel, Schele, and Parker explain the cosmology behind the Maya belief that the World Tree is not only the road to and from the Otherworld, but also the Milky Way when it appears perpendicular to the path of the Ecliptic as is the case in early February.[91] Many ancient accounts from the Old and New World refer to the Milky Way as the path of star/souls to the supernatural world beyond.[92] Zehren finds that in the Middle East, the Milky Way is also considered the sacred tree of the heavens.[93]

Fig. VI.18   Ruler grasping a vine of the Tree of Life. Ivory plaque from Nimrod, 8th century B.C. (drawn after photograph).

Fig. VI.19 Phoenician ivory plaque from Assyrian Palace of Nimrod. British Museum (drawn after photograph).

Fig. VI.20 Assyrian Tree of Life with attendant guardians (redrawn after Layard 1853).

Fig. VI.21 Mixtec World Tree (redrawn after *Codex Fejervary-Mayer*).

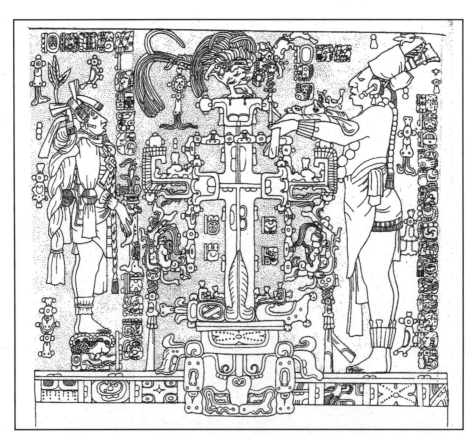

Fig. VI.22 Tree of Life, Tablet of the Cross, Palenque, Chiapas, Mexico (drawn by
Linda Schele, © by David Schele, in Schele and Miller 1986: 115, Fig. II.6).

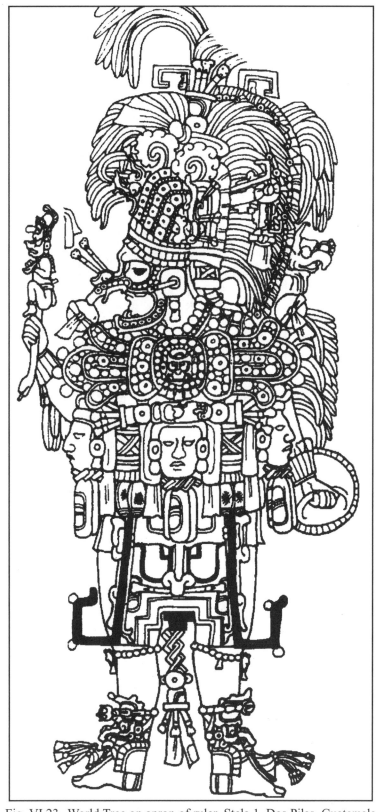

Fig. VI.23 World Tree on apron of ruler, Stela 1, Dos Pilas, Guatemala
(drawn by Linda Schele, © by David Schele, in Schele and
Miller 1986: 77, Fig. I.4e, with emphasis by author).

Fig. VI.24 Branches on apron of ruler, Stela 6
Cerro de las Mesas, Veracruz,
Mexico (redrawn after Winfield
Capitaine 1990: Fig. 27).

Fig. VI.25 Charlemagne wears apron of Tree
of Life (redrawn after Smith and
Cheetham 1968: 2: 1307).

Fig. VI.26   Sarcophagus lid of King Pakal, Palenque, Chiapas,
Mexico (drawn by Tom Weller in Bruhns and Weller
1971).

    All the elements of the king and the World Tree come together on the sarcophagus lid of Pakal at Palenque
(Fig. VI.26). This magnificent design carved in stone depicts the deceased elderly king in his youth. His dress is not
the garb of a king, but that of First Father in a simple net loincloth as the young maize god. Although he is at the
moment of death, from his body springs the Tree of Life—the World Tree—which is the pathway both into and out
of the Underworld. Stuart shows that the Maya death verb *och bih* on this sarcophagus lid translates as "he entered
the road."[94] And Schele comments that the Maya phrase "entered the road," is a metaphor for death.[95] King Pakal is
shown just within the skeletal open jaws of the Underworld, which contains glyphs of returning life, giving us an
interpretation of duality—death and rebirth.

The Tree springing from his chest declares that both Pakal and the Tree are the *axis mundi,* the center of the earth. Like the sun, and Osiris of Egypt, Pakal will rise triumphant over death. The celestial bird indicates the presence of the heavenly realm. It is poised at the top of the World Tree giving sanctification to the whole scenario below—just as a bird element is found in Middle Eastern Tree of Life themes. This sarcophagus lid encompasses all of the elements of one of the more sacred traditions in Mesoamerica.

SUMMARY

Myths of the World Tree were found throughout the ancient world. Most scholars are in agreement that those so-called independent inventions, which may turn out to be identical in differing cultures, are coincidental and a result of the common element that binds the human psyche.[96] Such scholars would argue that corresponding objects or ideas come about by some innate human quality that causes men to replicate certain behavioral patterns and practices. However, more than in any other culture, it is in the ancient Middle East and Mesoamerica where we find a close and detailed complex of traditions revolving around kings and the World Tree with its coinciding iconography and mythology. Granted, mankind embraces certain needs, and independent inventions created to fulfill those requirements of life may result in similar tools and ideas throughout the world. Man's quest for God is also surely an inherent quality of human nature. However, it is not plausible for traditions and belief systems among such diverse peoples to be identical solely on the basis of human qualities. Defining them as the collective unconscious, the human psyche, telepathy, random chance, or any other similar phenomenon is not an adequate explanation.

Land travel made cultural diffusion possible. Therefore, this accounts for many likenesses among individual cultures who live on the same continent. Perhaps it is time to give these ancient civilizations credit for having the capability to navigate the seas and spread their traditions. Iconography and literature surrounding the king and the theme of the World Tree are very relevant to this hypothesis.

NOTES - Chapter VI

1. Frankfort, "Kingship and the Gods," 1978.
2. Gray, 13.
3. 2 Sam. 7:14.
4. Patai, *On Jewish Folklore*, 126.
5. Gray, 130.
6. Lam. 4:20; 1 Sam. 16:6; 24:6, 10; 26:9, 11, 16, 23; 2 Sam. 1:14, 16; 19:21.
7. Gray, 53.
8. Siegfried Morenz, *Egyptian Religion*, trans. Anne E. Keep. (Stuttgart: Kolhammer, 1960; reprint, Ithaca, New York: Cornell University Press, 1990), 35, 37, 168.
9. Marcus, "Royal Families, Royal Texts," 224-25.
10. Schele and Freidel, *A Forest of Kings*, 218.
11. Linda Schele and Peter Mathews, *The Code of Kings: The Language of Seven Sacred Maya Temples and Tombs* (New York: Scribner, 1998), 108.
12. Michael D. Coe, *The Maya Scribe and His World* (New York: Grolier Club, 1973), 7.
13. Stephen Houston and David Stuart, "Of gods, glyphs and kings: divinity and rulership among the Classic Maya," *Antiquity* 70 (1996), 291.
14. Gray, 99.
15. Rosenberg; T. O Beidelman, "Swazi Royal Ritual," *Africa* 36 (1966): 542, cited in Jonathan Kaplan, "Monument 65: A great emblematic depiction of throned rule and royal sacrifice at Late Preclassic Kaminaljuyu," *Ancient Mesoamerica* 11/2 (Fall 2000), 193.
16. Reeder.
17. Eliade, *The Myth of the Eternal Return*, xiv.
18. Schele and Freidel, *A Forest of Kings*, 239.
19. Ibid., 469-70.
20. Schele and Freidel, "The Courts of Creation," 291.
21. Schele and Miller, 111.
22. Schele and Mathews, *The Code of Kings*, 93.
23. Margaret Mead and Nicholas Cales, eds., *Primitive Heritage* (New York: Randon House, 1953), 466-67.
24. Patai, *On Jewish Folklore*, 143.
25. Widengren, 11, 15-19, 35, 48.
26. Gray, 133.
27. Widengren, 38.
28. C. A. Burland, *Montezuma: Lord of the Aztecs* (New York: G. P. Putnam's Sons, 1973), 124.
29. Gray, 63.
30. Perry, 99.
31. Schele, *Workbook for the XVIth Maya Hieroglyphic at Texas*, 127-28.
32. Karl A. Taube, "The Classic Maya Maize God: A Reappraisal," in *Fifth Palenque Round Table, 1983*, gen. ed. Merle Greene-Robertson, vol. ed. Virginia M. Fields, vol. VII (San Francisco: The Pre- Columbian Art Research Institute, 1985), 181.
33. Schele and Freidel, *A Forest of Kings*, 407.
34. Freidel, 112.
35. Eliade, *The Myth of the Eternal Return*, 37.
36. Perry, 60.
37. Carolyn E. Tate, "The Period-Ending Stelae of Yaxchilan," in *Sixth Palenque Round Table, 1986,* gen. ed. Merle Greene-Robertson, vol. ed. Virginia M. Fields, vol. 8 (Norman: University of Oklahoma Press, 1991), 105.
38. Eliade, *Symbolism, the Sacred, and the Arts*, 111.
39. Reeder, 60.
40. Joseph Campbell, *The Masks of God: Oriental Mythology*, vol. 2 (New York: Viking, 1976), 14.
41. Widengren, 43; Perry, 69.
42. Widengren, 42, 56. See also the Genesis Apocryphon 19:14-17 of the Dead Sea Scrolls. Abraham describes a vision in which he saw himself as a cedar and Sarah, his wife, as a palm tree, in Michael Wise, Martin Abegg,

Jr., and Edward Cook, *The Dead Sea Scrolls: A New Translation* (San Francisco: Harper Collins, 1996), 79.

43. Budge, *From Fetish to God*, 183.
44. Carol Andrews, "Ancient Egyptian Funerary Amulets: Protection, Power and Patronage," (paper presented at The Annual American Research Center in Egyptian Symposium, jointly sponsored by the Brooklyn Museum, December 4, 1993); Sellers, 144.
45. Wilkinson, *Reading Egyptian Art*, 165.
46. Hornung, *Idea into Image*, 31.
47. Andrews, "Ancient Egyptian Funerary Amulets."
48. For examples of a variety of trees that may represent the World Tree in the Middle East, see Cook.
49. Kent Reilly, "Art, Ritual, and Rulership in the Olmec World," in *The Olmec World: Ritual and Rulership* (Princeton: The Art Museum, Princeton University, 1996).
50. Karl A. Taube, "The Rainmakers: The Olmec and Their Contribution to Mesoamerican Belief and Ritual," in *The Olmec World: Ritual and Rulership* (Princeton: The Art Museum, Princeton University, 1996), 88-89, 106, 163.
51. Ibid., 7l.
52. Clark, 236.
53. Reilly, "Art, Ritual, and Rulership," 39.
54. Stross, "Maize and Blood," 93.
55. Baring and Cashford, 103.
56. Zaki Y. Saad, *The Excavations at Helwan* (Norman: University of Oklahoma Press, 1969), Plate 109.
57. Andrews, "Ancient Egyptian Funerary Amulets."
58. E. A. Wallis Budge, *The Gods of the Egyptians*, 2 vols. (London: Methuen & Company, 1904; reprint, New York: Dover Publications, 1969), 125; J. W. Helck, "Bemerkungen zum Ritual des Dramatischen Ramesseums-papyrus," *Orientalia* 23 (1954), 408-09.
59. Ezek. 31:2-9.
60. Fray Thomás de Coto, *Vocabviario de la lengua Cakchquel v Guatemalteca, nueuamente hecho y recopilado con summo estudio, trauajo y erudicion*, ed. René Acuña (Mexico: Universidad Nacional Autonoma de Mexico, 1983), 385.
61. Schele and Freidel, *A Forest of Kings*, 67.
62. Schele, *Workbook for the XVth Maya Hieroglyphic Workshop*, 46.
63. Reents-Budet, 141.
64. Ibid., 150, 167.
65. Schele and Freidel, *A Forest of Kings*, 418.
66. Freidel, Schele, and Parker, 196.
67. Personal Communication from Allen Christenson to Diane Wirth, October 26, 1998.
68. Stross, "Maize and Blood."
69. Schele and Miller, 108-09.
70. Ibid., 274
71. Carlo T. E. Gay, "Olmec Hieroglyphic Writing," *Archaeology* 26/4 (1973).
72. Patai, *On Jewish Folklore*, 142.
73. Wilkinson, *Reading Egyptian Art*, 117, 165.
74. A. Moret, *Mysteres Egyptiens* (Paris: A. Colin, 1913), 97.
75. Schele and Freidel, *A Forest of Kings*, 129, 472.
76. Jeremy Black and Anthony Green, *Gods, Demons and Symbols of Ancient Mesopotamia* (Austin: University of Texas Press, 1992), 30, 52; Krupp, *Beyond the Blue Horizon*, 141.
77. Morenz, 174; Patrick Boyland, *Thoth: The Hermes of Egypt* (London, 1922; reprint, Chicago: Ares Publishers, Inc., 1987), 157.
78. R. A. M. van Zantwijk, *Handel en Wandel van de Azteken de Sociale geschiedenis van voor-Spaans* (Assen/Amsterdam: Van Gorcum, 1977), 179.
79. Kent Reilly, "Cosmology and Rulership at the Olmec Site of La Venta, 900-500 B.C.," (paper presented at *Origins: Creation and Continuity: Mythology and History in Mesoamerica*, The Maya Meetings at Texas, March 12-13, 1992, VIIIth Texas Symposium. Austin: University of Texas, 1992); Reilly, "Art, Ritual, and Rulership," 141.
80. *New Larousse Encyclopedia of Mythology*, s.v. "prehistoric archaeology," (New York: Paul Hamlyn, 1972), 150.

81. *Standard Dictionary of Folklore, Mythology and Legend*, vol. 1 (New York: Funk and Wagnalls Co., 1949), 90.

82. Maureen Tilley, "Typological Numbers: Taking a Count of the Bible," *Bible Review* (June 1992), 48.

83. Cook, 91.

84. Clark, 58, 163-64.

85. Freidel, Schele, and Parker, 76.

86. Hubert Howe Bancroft, *The Native Races*, vols. II and III (San Francisco: Bancroft & Co., 1883), II: 329- 30; III: 385-89.

87. Schele and Miller, 72, 77.

88. Tate, "The Period-Ending Stela of Yaxchilan," 105; Tate, *Yaxchilan*, 59.

89. Sahagún, *Florentine Codex*, Bk. 6: 58, 252; Heyden, "Metaphors, Nahualtocaitl, and Other," 35.

90. J. Tondrian, "Le tatouage sacre et la relig. de dionysiaque," *Aegyptus* 30 (1950), 62.

91. Freidel, Schele, and Parker, 86.

92. Walter Wili, "The Orphic Mysteries of the Green Spirit," in *The Mysteries: Papers from the Eranos Yearbooks*, ed. Joseph Campbell (Princeton: Princeton University Press, 1990), 89; Black Elk, *The Sacred Pipe*, rec. and ed. Joseph Epes Brown (Norman: University of Oklahoma Press, 1967), 29.

93. Zehren, 113, 153, 257.

94. Noted in Schele, *Workbook for the XVIth Maya Hieroglyphic Workshop*, 43.

95. Ibid., 254.

96. Joseph Campbell, *The Way of the Seeded Earth, Part 1: The Sacrifice*, Historical Atlas of World Mythology, vol. II (New York: Harper & Row, Pub., 1988), 28.

CHAPTER VII

MESOAMERICAN AND EGYPTIAN SCRIBES

Throughout this book many similarities between the Egyptian and Mesoamerican cultures present an obscure riddle. One of the more unusual parallels is found in a study of the scribes of the two civilizations.

SUPERNATURAL EGYPTIAN AND MAYA SCRIBES

The Egyptians believed the god Thoth, the scribe par excellence, was not only the creator of writing but played a prominent role in the arts and sciences (arithmetic, geometry, computing time, surveying, astronomy, prophecy, magic, medicine, surgery, art, and music). He was also the keeper of books and a patron of history. Research and accumulated information on the attributes of the Egyptian scribe are extensive, and it will be demonstrated here that some of his characteristics are common to the Mesoamerican scribe as well.

As one of the primary rulers of the Underworld, Thoth is usually portrayed either in human form with the head of an ibis (Fig. VII.1) or as a baboon (Fig. VII.2). Both the ibis and baboon are affiliated with the moon. However, in Egypt, the baboon is also connected in some way with the rising sun. In fact, it is not until the New Kingdom (1570–1070 B.C.) that Thoth is associated with the baboon/moon combination.[1] The moon is often considered a substitute for the sun and sometimes referred to as the sun of the Underworld, i.e., the 'sun shining at night.'[2] In some respects, what is true of sun symbolism is also true of the moon.

Fig. VII.1   Egyptian Ibis-Scribe (redrawn after Greenfield Papyrus, British Museum)

Fig. VII.2   Typical Egyptian Baboon Scribe

Among the Maya, the vulture is the only supernatural bird scribe.[3] Therefore, to say the vulture may be equated with the ibis scribe just because it is a bird is not justifiable. Supernatural scribes are also portrayed as various other animals of the Underworld realm but, more often than not, as a monkey-headed anthropomorphic being. This is the most commonly depicted patron of writing and time-keeping among the Maya (Fig. VII.3).[4] One of the animal forms of the sun in Mesoamerica is the monkey.[5] The fact that both the Egyptian and Mesoamerican scribes are frequently shown as divine monkey scribes is probably the most signifiant feature they both share.

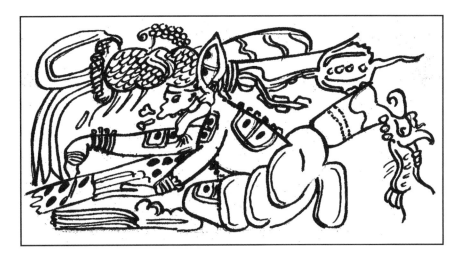

Fig. VII.3 Monkey-Scribe on Maya cylindrical pot from Guatemala, housed
at New Orleans Museum of Art (redrawn after M. Coe 1977: Fig. 10).

Nets

In Mesoamerica we also find scribe-like attributes associated with the Maya god Pawahtun (a.k.a. God N), with the calendar name of One Monkey (Hun Chuen) who, like Thoth, is also one of the principal lords of the Underworld.[6] A possible parallel should be considered in that Pawahtun means Net/Stone, and it is the net (pawah) that this god wore as a headdress (Fig. VII.4).[7]

Thoth, the Egyptian scribe, is also associated with a net. According to Budge, among many titles for Thoth is "great god in Het-Abitit," which means "House of the Net," i.e., the temple where a net was preserved and venerated.[8] The two existing versions of Chapter CLIII of *The Book of the Dead* present evidence that a net exists in the Underworld. Those who pass through the Egyptian Underworld attempt to avoid the net at all costs—it is the net that ensnares the fiends of the Underworld. *The Book of the Dead* depicts a scene that takes place at the Ninth Gate of the Underworld. Along with a series of other figures, four baboons ritualistically hold nets over their heads. The meaning of this ceremony, however, is obscure.[9] Perhaps further study will yet reveal the role of the Pawahtun scribe's net headdress in Mesoamerica, as well as the use of a net by baboons in Egyptian myth.

Fig. VII.4 Pawahtun-scribe with slight simian features, Copan, Honduras (redrawn after Fash 1991b: 75, Fig. 8).

Cardinal Points

In Mesoamerica it has been established that Pawahtuns were also associated with the four corners of the world. They were frequently depicted holding up the sky like an Atlantean figure (Fig. VII.5).[10] Thoth was also connected with the cardinal points, which makes the function of the Maya Pawahtun and the Egyptian Thoth quite similar.[11]

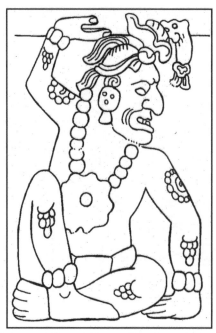

Fig. VII.5   Pawahtun as an Atlantean figure, Copan, Honduras (redrawn after Fash 1991a: 165, Fig. 101).

The Number Tree

The so-called Number Tree, often compared to a computer printout, is an unusual feature of the Maya maize god, which grows out of the side of this particular scribe (Fig. VII.6). It appears to be a sheet of paper with bar-and-dot numbers and usually ends with a vegetal motif of branches, leaves, or flowers.[12]

In conjunction with the paper Number Tree, we may be able to make a parallel to the Middle East. In both Mesopotamia and Egypt there was a tendency to write on leaves, connecting the writing to the annals. The Egyptian king often had his name including the number of his reign written on leaves of the Ished tree. This was especially popular in Ramesside times.[13] In addition, the Sumerians wrote their years with a year sign *mu,* which is actually a type of plant.[14]

Fig. VII.6 Maize god writes in a codex, from Nakbe-style vase (drawn after photograph in Coe and Kerr 1998: 108).

HUMAN SCRIBES

The respective scribes of the ancient world are frequently portrayed in realistic roles as men of noble class. Maya scribes were under the patronage of the monkey-man scribe and other sacred scribes of the Underworld. Therefore, we must differentiate between human scribes and supernatural scribes portrayed in their art. The same holds true for Egyptian supernatural scribes (primarily Thoth) and their servants, the human Egyptian scribes.

Scribes—Court Officials

As an official of the court, the Egyptian scribe usually sits in a crossed-legged position, is bare-chested, wears a short kilt ending at the knees, and holds a scroll in his lap with a two-hole ink pot nearby (Fig. VII.7). Portraits of the Mesoamerican scribe are very similar. Supernatural scribes often wear a kilt or breech cloth. However, many human scribes wear a kilt or a sarong which is a longer version of the kilt (Fig. VII.8). Egyptian and Maya scribes also carry pens on their heads. In Egypt their writing implements are placed over the ear (Fig. VII.9), whereas the Maya scribe wears his pens tucked into and protruding from his headdress (Fig. VII.10).

Scribes of both Egypt and Mesoamerica were highly esteemed in their respective cultures and it was not uncommon for buildings to be dedicated to them in recognition of their craft and role in this privileged class of professionals.[15] In Mesoamerica, the sites of Copan, Honduras and Pomona, Tabasco have excellent examples of artistic tribute to the scribe.[16] At Copan, lavish living quarters were built for the polity's scribe, who may have been second in power to the great king Yax Pas.[17]

Literacy was also important to both Egyptian and Mesoamerican royalty. The titles of some of the Maya kings attest to the fact that they were important in Mesoamerica. For example, at Copan two rulers were called *itz'at,* meaning "learned man," "sage," and/or "man of letters."[18]

Fig. VII.7 Egyptian scribe Amenophis, son of Hapu, Thebes (drawn after photograph, Egyptian Museum, Cairo).

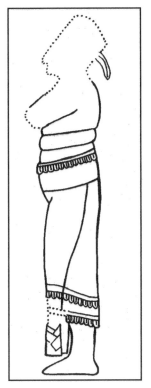

Fig. VII.8 Maya scribe wearing a sarong, Lintel 3, Piedras Negras, Guatemala (redrawn after Coe and Kerr 1998: 94).

Fig. VII.9 Egyptian scribe with pens worn tucked behind his ear on mastaba of Kan-ni-Nesut, Giza (drawn after photograph in Pritchard 1969: Fig. 52).

Fig. VII.10   Seated Maya scribe with pen in his headdress. Detail of a Late-Classic polychrome vase (drawn after photograph in Coe and Kerr 1998: 96, Fig. 56).

Black and Red

Although oceans apart, a parallel custom of human scribes was the use of black and red inks. Coe finds that "writing" in the Aztec language is *tlilli tlapalli,* which translates as "black and red."[19] To the Mesoamerican native, these two colors represent knowledge. The Aztecs called the Maya lowlands the Land of the Black and the Red, a direct reference to their books, which were the codices where glyphic texts were painted with black and red inks.[20] For the Egyptian scribe, the palette of black and red inks also became a symbol of their expertise.[21]

Anointing Books

Anointing was a common practice in both Mesoamerica and Egypt. Therefore, the ritual of pouring liquids over a scribe's books is not surprising. The Maya used sacred, virgin water to anoint tablets for the purpose of purification.[22] Egyptian scribes also used water to wash their texts that were sometimes made of stone. This procedure was often followed by drinking the liquid to symbolically absorb the contents of the text. In Egyptian, the verbs "to swallow" and "to know" are the same.[23]

Hieroglyphics

Mesoamerican hieroglyphs are not identical to Egyptian hieroglyphs. Nevertheless, Marcus demonstrates there are some conceptual similarities between the two writing styles. She finds that Mesoamerican writing can be compared to Egyptian hieroglyphic writing in both its format and in its function.[24] This is an indication that the basic logic of both systems is similar.

Summary

Another significant parallel between the scribes of Egypt and those of Mesoamerica are the roles they fulfilled in the arts and sciences. If they were both portrayed solely as monkeys and considered the inventors of writing, that would be cause enough to take note of a significant correlation possibly resulting from early transoceanic voyages. Kroeber, an early authority on anthropological theory and method, postulates that:

> A complex device used in two or more parts of the world suggests a connection between them in very proportion to its complexity. A combination of two or even three elements might conceivably have been repeated independently. . . . A combination of five or ten parts serving an identical purpose in an identical manner must necessarily appeal as impossible of having been hit upon more than once. One thinks almost under compulsion, in such a case, of historical connection.[25]

Mesoamerican and ancient Egyptian cultures hold a very similar set of symbols with regard to the scribe and his many attributes. Even so, where the symbolism is prolific, the Egyptian scribe's culture dates back much earlier than the scribe's in Mesoamerica. And yet, the gap in time may be bridged by what many believe to be a scribe portrayed on Stela 5, Izapa. This one dates to around 200 B.C. (Fig. VII.11).[26] We can only speculate about the Egyptian and Mesoamerican scribes' corresponding attributes as a result of cultural diffusion.

Fig. VII.11 Earliest portrait of a Mesoamerican scribe, detail from Stela 5, Izapa, Chiapas, Mexico (redrawn after Norman 1976: Part 2, 165, Fig. 4.1).

NOTES - Chapter VII

1. Boyland, 76.
2. Budge, "From Fetish to God," 182.
3. Coe and Kerr, *The Art of the Maya Scribe*, 109.
4. Miller and Taube, 148.
5. Tate, "The Period-Ending Stelae of Yaxchilan," 105.
6. Schele and Miller, 141.
7. Michael D. Coe, "Supernatural Patrons of Scribes and Artists," in *Social Process in Maya Prehistory*, Norman Hammond, ed. (London: Academic Press, 1977), 337.
8. Budge, *The Gods of the Egyptians*, I: 405-06.
9. Budge, *From Fetish to God*, 374.
10. Miller and Taube, 133.
11. Edouard Naville, "Le dieu Thoth et les points cardinaux," *Zeitschrift fuer Aegyptische Sprache und Altertumskunde* 15 (1877), 28-31.
12. Coe and Kerr, *The Art of the Maya Scribe*, 105.
13. Wilkinson, *Reading Egyptian Art*, 117.
14. Personal Communication from John Gee to Diane Wirth, April 13, 2000.
15. William Fash, *Scribes, Warriors and Kings: The City of Copan and the Ancient Maya* (New Work: Thames and Hudson, 1991), 120.
16. Schele and Miller, 140, 142.
17. Coe and Kerr, *The Art of the Maya Scribe*, 101.
18. Fash, *Scribes, Warriors and Kings*, 87.
19. Coe, "Supernatural Patrons of Scribes and Artists," 327.
20. Coe and Kerr, *The Art of the Maya Scribe*, 151.
21. Gordon Brotherston, *The Image of the New World* (London: Thames and Hudson, 1979), 270; Hart, *A Dictionary of Egyptian Gods*, 216.
22. Coe, "Supernatural Patrons of Scribes and Artists," 330; Diego de Landa, *Yucatan Before and After the Conquest*, William Gates, trans. (Baltimore: The Maya Society, 1937; reprint, New York: Dover Publications, Inc., 1978), 71.
23. Robert Ritner, "Horus on the Crocodiles: A Juncture of Religion and Magic in Late Dynastic Egypt," in *Religion and Philosophy in Ancient Egypt*, Yale Egyptological Studies 3, William K. Simpson, ed. (New Haven: Yale University, 1989), 106-08.
24. Joyce Marcus, *Mesoamerican Writing Systems: Propaganda, Myth, and History in Four Ancient Civilizations* (Princeton: Princeton University Press, 1992), 19, 21, 26.
25. A. L. Kroeber, *Anthropology* (New York: Harcourt, Brace & Co., 1923), 216.
26. Schele and Miller, 140; Norman, 172-73.

CHAPTER VIII

WOMB OF EARTH—WOMB OF SKY

The mother goddess cult and her associated attributes can be traced in rites, myths, and symbols throughout history. However, there are certain elements associated with her that are more particularly common to both Mesoamerica and the Near East. Traditions and iconography from these two settings will be addressed in this chapter with a special emphasis on the dichotomous nature of the goddess's life/death association and her womb-of-earth-and-sky imagery.

WOMB OF THE EARTH

In the Old Testament, several verses indicate a belief in mother earth; not in the sense that the earth was worshiped, but that the earth was female in gender. For example, in Psalms there is reference to the human body being wrought in the depths of the earth.[1]

> Thou hast covered me in my mother's womb. . . . My substance [frame] was not hid from thee, when I was made in secret, and curiously [intricately] wrought in the lowest parts [depths] of the earth (Ps. 139:13, 15).

In Mesoamerica there is a similar connotation. Mayan Tzeltal and Tzotzil languages sometimes refer to one's child as "earth" or "mud."[2] For them, the earth is female and the body is wrought in the depths of the earth. In his study of the highland Maya, Vogt translates the words of a marriage petitioner who said to the prospective bride's father, "Today I speak because of your mud, your earth." This metaphor refers to the father's daughter who came from Mother Earth.[3]

Dahood's translation of Psalm 139:15 reads: "Since I was nipped off in the Secret Place, kneaded in the depths of the nether world."[4] Whether the phrasing is "depths of the earth," "Nether World," "Otherworld," or "Underworld," the meaning is the same. This is the womb of the earth, which in some respects was equated with the night sky.

Giver of Life—Taker in Death

During Neolithic times, figures of pregnant females were abundant and this was the beginning of a visual manifestation of the mother goddess. Things associated with fertility, growth, water, and birth, were identified with the mother goddess. She also exhibited a dark side—a denizen of the Underworld waiting to receive the dead in her tomb-like womb. The goddess could do a turnabout and figuratively give birth to the deceased as they were reborn in the next cycle of their journey. Many of her traits were universal. However, we find certain elements of the mother goddess common to Mesoamerica and the Middle East that are not seen elsewhere.

Fertility

Fertility is the number-one aspect of the mother goddess in the Near East and Mesoamerica. In ancient times the goddess was considered to control fertility by wearing leaves and stalks emanating from her person (see for example Fig. VIII.45). Writings from Sumeria confirm what we know to be true from the prehistoric archaeological record. Early agriculturists conceived of the earth in the form of a female goddess and the most popular aspect of the great goddess was her power over vegetation—the well-being of all mankind.[5] This is not far removed from concepts held today among Pueblo cultures. Cultivation of the soil is one of the prime concerns of this particular society. In fact, Mother Earth is still of paramount importance to all Native Americans. On this subject, Waters states:

> The Mother Goddess is expressed in Pueblo cultures as the Earth Mother. In the winter she is considered to be asleep, whereas in the spring she emerges triumphant bringing a rebirth and renewal of nature.[6]

U-shaped Elements

Throughout the Near East, a U-shaped element was a major symbol of the mother goddess. Sometimes the U was made with curls at the ends similar to the shape of the Greek letter Omega. Representations of U-shaped markings are on Mesopotamian boundary stones dating from very early times to as late as the seventh century B.C. (Fig. VIII.1). The Sumerian goddess Inanna (or Ishtar) sometimes holds a U-shaped mace with feline heads. A beautiful example of this symbolism is on a Babylonian terracotta. Elongated wombs (which are representations of the Mother goddess Nin-hursag, the goddess of mankind) are portrayed on both sides of the goddess who proudly stands in the center nursing a child (Fig. VIII.2). Below each womb are individuals whom are surmised to be either infants or, perhaps, aborted fetuses.[7] We can readily associate the U-shaped designs on this plaque with a woman's womb. Frankfort aptly demonstrates that the U-shaped element was one of the major emblems of the Sumerian goddess Nin-hursag and stated that this symbol indeed represented the womb or uterus.[8]

Fig. VIII.1 Mesopotamian boundary stone containing U-shaped element (redrawn after Keel 1987: 52).

Fig. VIII.2 Goddess Nin-hursag, 19th century B.C. Mesopotamian terracotta (redrawn after Keel 1987: 50).

In Egyptian symbolism we again see the U-shaped element associated with goddesses—primarily with Hathor who, in Figure VIII.3, is depicted with the ears of a cow (her animal form). Hathor often wears a headdress of horns, making the U-shaped design of the womb (Fig. VIII.4). Sjöö and Mor comment, "the symbolic attribute of the goddess of birth was the bicornate uterus of a heifer; i.e., the cow-headed horns were echoed in the 'horned' cow womb."[9] The maternal waters of the heavens (the Milky Way) was comparable to a mother's milk, thus comes the cow symbolism for Hathor.[10] As a celestial cow, Hathor is portrayed with stars on her body (Fig. VIII.4). Cows, in and of themselves, were considered a symbol of vitality and immortal life.[11]

Fig. VIII.3 Egyptian goddess Hathor, tomb ceiling, Thebes, 13th Dynasty (redrawn after Sibbett, Jr. 1978: 3).

Fig. VIII.4   Hathor's celestial cow form (redawn after Budge 1988: 58).

U-Shaped Hairstyles and Headdresses

During early periods of ancient history it became fashionable for women to wear their hair styled like Hathor's, representing the birth symbol (Fig. VIII.5). Patai gives an excellent account of ancient mother goddess cults in the Near East in his book *The Hebrew Goddess*. Descriptions of Astarte terracotta figures are presented. Patai states that Astarte's hair is worn exactly the same with Egyptian Hathor ringlets (Fig. VIII.6).[12] He also interprets the original name for Astarte (Ashtoreth), to mean "womb," or "that which issues from the womb."[13]

These ringlets, or end curls, are significant. According to Cirlot, a spiral or curl is symbolic of growth or elements in motion and power. He also finds that hair represents physical and spiritual energy and fertility.[14] Hair, particularly curled hair, designates a springing forth or a thrusting out of life and energy, even creative power, which is seen in the birth process. If the curls at the tips of

Fig. VIII.5 Female member of the family of Ukh-hotep II, Meir, Egypt (drawn after photograph, D'Auria et. al. 1988: 121).

Fig. VIII.6 Hathor hairstyle on Astarte, gold
pendant, Ras Shamra, Syria (drawn
after photograph in Patai 1978).

Fig. VIII.7 Hathor-style U-shaped, horned crown
(with emphasis by author), detail from
Stela 5, Izapa (redrawn after Norman
1976: Part 2, 165).

the U stand for the generative power of nature, the U itself must represent the womb. It is interesting to note that a lock of hair among the Maya is found to be a distinguishing mark of the goddess.[15]

An early Mesoamerican woman's headdress on Stela 5 from Izapa, created about 400–200 B.C., has a possible U-shaped, horned design similar to those worn by mother goddesses in Egypt (Fig. VIII.7). As noted in Chapter VI, many archaeologists consider this Mesoamerican figure to be the ancestral mother of her people. However, far more universal in Mesoamerica are inverted U-shaped elements incorporated in headdresses, many made to look like the upper mouth of a monster (Figs. VIII.8 and 9). It will be demonstrated in our discussion of the U-shaped, mouth-like entrance to the Underworld, that this visual representation is of significance.

U-Shape and Womb

The feminine U design was frequently used as the symbol of life and childbirth in ancient Middle East cultures including Sumerian, Babylonian, Assyrian, Egyptian, Palestinian, and Hittite. Form, associated symbols, and meaning, are identical to those of Mesoamerica. From Mesoamerica, a wide variety of examples exist that show the multifaceted nature of this design, all associated with fertility and birth. From the *Codex Vindobonensis* we find the unmistakable representation of an infant in a U-shaped enclosure representing the womb (Fig. VIII.10). Another from the *Codex Nuttall* gives the definitive answer regarding the connotation of this symbol—it is a mother's womb (Fig. VIII.11). Here we have not only the birth of a child with umbilical cord still attached, but several U-shaped womb elements, both large and small, on a mountain. Continuing controversy exists as to what exactly is happening on this page of the Codex Nuttall. What is apparent is that Lady 3 Flint Feathered Serpent Tail gives birth to a child. In front of her is another image of this same noble woman entering (diving into) a cave from which flowing waters issue. This enclosure with a womb-like, U-shaped portal may be a steam bath, which is associated with childbirth.

Fig. VIII.8 Figure wearing U-shaped headdress in front of U-shaped jaws of the Underworld, jade plaque, Tula, Hidalgo, Mexico (redrawn after Acosta in Nicholson and Berger 1968:20).

Fig. VIII.9 Headdress exhibiting upper jaw of Earth Monster, Chalco, Mexico (redrawn after Spinden 1975: 221).

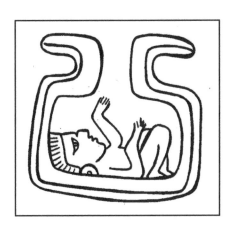

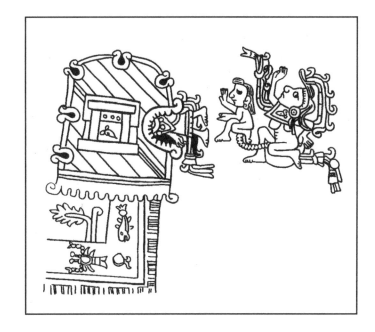

Fig. VIII.10 Child in U-shaped womb (redrawn after *Codex Vindobonensis*).

Fig. VIII.11 Birth of a child and U-shaped womb symbols (redrawn after *Codex Nuttall*, page 16).

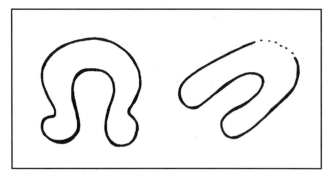

Fig. VIII.12 Stone headrests on burial benches of
St. Etienne cave tombs, Jerusalem, 7th
century B.C. (drawn after photographs
in Barkay and Kloner 1986: 36).

In the Near East, two articles were published in *Biblical Archaeology Review* containing photographs of stone headrests recently discovered in a burial chamber in Jerusalem, which date to the seventh century B.C. (Fig. VIII.12).[16] Some of these headrests are a straight U shaped design, while others incorporate the end curl (omega style), both typical of the design portrayed in hairstyles of the goddesses Hathor and Astarte. Hathor appears on ivories from an Israelite palace in Samaria in the eighth century B.C.[17] In this particular burial chamber in Jerusalem, it was customary for the head of the deceased to lie within the U-shaped stone, symbolizing what some scholars believe to be a return to the comfort of the mother. No doubt it meant a rebirth and resurrection of the deceased.[18]

Stone Yokes

The U-shaped design of the stone yoke in Mesoamerica has mystified scholars ever since they were discovered (Figs. VIII.13 and14). Archaeologists are aware that a leather and wood, U-shaped yoke was worn around the waist of ballplayers as a physical and spiritual shield, but the heavy stone yokes remain, to some extent, an enigma.[19] The ballgame was a religious act—the ballcourt representing the cosmic realms of the Underworld. Stone yokes contain images of various kinds of animals that were associated with either the sky or the Underworld. Some are designed after the U-shaped, monster mouth, which was considered a portal to the Otherworld. Others are double-headed serpents. In fact, when the yoke in Figure VIII.14 is viewed from the top, it appears as the double-headed sky serpent. In Mayan, the word *kaan* means "sky." *Kan,* a near homophone, means "serpent." Often both the sky and serpent are portrayed in the shape of a U (Fig. VIII.15). From Colima, western Mexico, there is a wonderful depiction of a man within the U-shaped double serpent looking very much like a yoke (Fig. VIII.16). Eric Thompson makes a statement on a burial find in Mexico, which I believe may clarify the purpose of the stone yoke-type headrests in Jerusalem:

A burial was described in which the body lay full length with the head placed inside the yoke, which lay flat. The open ends of the yoke reached to the person's shoulders. Joyce has suggested that the yokes represent the gaping jaws of the earth monster ready to receive the dead, and this is a feasible suggestion since such scenes are frequently depicted in the codices.[20]

Heyden had these funerary yokes in mind when she wrote that yokes were symbols of the jaw of the earth into which the wearer descended after death.[21] Jill and Peter Furst carry this theme even further and explain that these yokes had a symbolic function, clearly extending beyond the ballgame. In addition, they write that many of the remarkable objects depict Underworld symbolism and that their uterine shape suggests an entrance to a cave. This was traditionally conceived of as the passage into the maternal cave.[22]

The yoke worn by ballplayers was made of lightweight materials as opposed to the ceremonial stone yokes placed with the deceased. Both were associated with life forces, and especially the womb or point of emergence for life.[23]

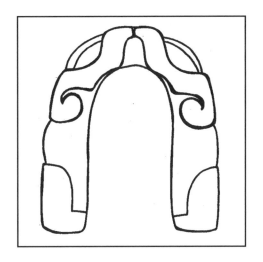

Fig. VIII.13 Stone yoke with monster mouth design on typical Veracruz-style yoke (drawn after photograph in Shook and Marquis 1996: 51).

Fig. VIII.14 Double-headed serpent yoke from Guatemala (drawn after photograph in Shook and Marquis 1996: 36).

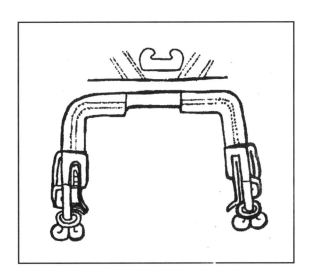

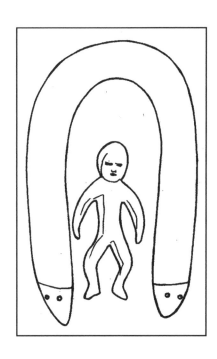

Fig. VIII.15 Double-headed sky serpent on Stela 23, Izapa, Chiapas, Mexico (redrawn after Norman 1976: Part 2, 27).

Fig. VIII.16 Double-headed U-shaped serpent surrounds man on Colima vessel, Mexico (drawn after photograph in P. Furst 1973: 106).

In Mesoamerican art the earth monster represents the womb of Mother Earth—the Underworld—where all men return when life on earth ceases (Fig. VIII.17). The open mouth of this monster (usually a serpent or jaguar)is symbolic of the portal where men pass either into this world or into the Otherworld, from whence they came.[24] These mouth openings are often viewed as the entrance to caves. Krickeberg notes that the yoke, as seen from above, resembles a cave, a symbol of the entrance to the womb of the Underworld. As already mentioned, many stone yokes contain carvings of the gaping open mouth of a monster.[25]

U-Shaped Burial Chambers

The Mesoamerican yoke is also styled exactly like burial chambers drawn in the codices. Examples are shown below, one from the *Codex Magliabecchi* and the other from the *Codex Laud* (Figs. VIII.18 and19). In the first illustration, a U-shaped burial place holds the skull of the same individual at the right wrapped in a death bundle. The latter example shows the underground U-shaped tomb with skull and protruding bones. The head of the deceased is represented above ground.

Fig. VIII.17 Monster-mouth cave entrance (redrawn after *Codex Durán*).

Fig. VIII.18 Left: Mictlan, the place of the dead. Right: People grieving over death of loved one in death bundle (redrawn after *Codex Magliabecchi*).

Fig. VIII.19 Decapitated head marks location of a tomb (redrawn after *Codex Laud*).

Emerging from Caves

Discussion of the Earth Mother leads to an interesting subject. To many in the ancient Mesoamerican community, the earth is considered the primeval home where mankind once crawled from a hole, i.e., the womb. This hole is often referred to as a dark cave from which mankind emerged. Caves are of great significance in Mesoamerican symbology and must be understood in order to fully comprehend origin myths regarding the emergence of peoples. From Mesoamerican antiquity it appears caves were closely associated with birth and creation. The darkness of a cave is similar to the darkness of the womb—the place of emergence. Waters seeping from caves are comparable to life-sustaining waters or, more technically, embryonic fluids that flow from the womb. In Chapter V we saw that both the Tutul Xiu leader and his genealogical tree emerge (born) from the mouth of a mountain's cave (see Fig. V.5).[26]

U-shaped elements appear in the early Olmec culture of Mesoamerica.[27] Persons emerging from caves is a very common theme among Olmec sculpture (Fig. VIII.20). This tradition held sway in Mesoamerica for more than 1,000 years and has the same implication to this day. Monument 1 at Chalcatzingo, Morelos, Mexico, depicts an Olmec individual in a monster mouth cave (Fig. VIII.21). The eye of the monster is portrayed at the top of the mouth/cave opening with an X. The ruler or shaman inside the cave holds and sits on S-curved cloud symbols. Droplets of rain fall from the sky. A similar scene in Egypt shows a deity of the Nile in a serpent cave while waters flow from vases (Fig. VIII.22). In Egypt, caverns and crevices were linked to goddess imagery.

Lurker notes that caverns in Egypt had special significance and explains, "the female image of the hollow space was the seat of birth and death."[28] The cave is a dark, mysterious, and damp enclosure not unlike the womb. Among the Hebrews, when Abraham purchased the cave at Machpelah for a tomb, he was aware of the burial practices in the Near East.[29] Caves were considered a type of womb where death and rebirth would take place.[30]

Fig. VIII.20 Olmec figure emerges from cave on Altar 4, La Venta, Veracruz, Mexico (drawn after photograph).

Fig. VIII.21 Ruler or shaman sits in a monster-mouth cave at Chalcatzingo, Morelos, Mexico (drawn after photograph).

Fig. VIII.22 Serpent cave encloses a deity of the Nile (redrawn after Neurath 1964: 7).

There was a belief that was prevalent of seven caves of origin throughout Mesoamerica. The *Popol Vuh* (the historical portion of the Quiché Maya of Guatemala) speaks of this people's origins as being in the East. The world was dark while they lived in seven caves, but during that time they received guidance from the gods. They crossed the sea, using stepping stones, and finally arrived in the new land.[31] Tulan Zuyua or *vukub pek, vukub zivan* ("seven caves" or "seven canyons") was the name of their place of origin in the *Popol Vuh*.[32] This leads to a discussion of Mesoamerican origin myths that describe an emergence from caves. In Mesoamerica caves were associated with beginnings and, more particularly, with birth in general.

According to some traditions the seven central Mexican Nahua speaking tribes came from a place known as Chicomoztoc ("Seven Caves"), their legendary point of origin (Fig. VIII.23). This implies that like many other American peoples, the Aztec believed their origin to be from the womb of Mother Earth.[33] Each petal of the U- shaped flowered Chicomoztoc design represents a cave, or womb, from which each of the tribes emerged. According to Heyden,

Fig. VIII.23 Chicomoztoc, the place of emergence (redrawn after *Historia Tolteca-Chichimeca* 1978: F.16r Ms. 51-53, p. 28).

xochitl, meaning "flower," represents the womb, origin, and paradise of Mexican mythologies. It is no surprise that the Chicomoztoc design is shaped like a flower.[34] Another example from the *Historia Tolteca-Chichimeca* depicts actual flowers representing the seven caves (Fig. VIII.24).

Underneath some Sumerian temples is a hollow sanctuary/tomb that represented the womb of the goddess—the realm of the Underworld.[35] Several such structures, natural or manmade, were found in the depths of Mesoamerican pyramids. The Temple of the Sun at Teotihuacan, in particular, contains a natural tunnel that leads to a cave of four chambers.[36] To the Teotihuacanos this represented the place of emergence for mankind.

Throughout the Old World, caves were considered to be the womb of the Great Mother as well as the place of origin for whole tribes of people.[37] Therefore, caves were and are a place for ritual initiation, where a symbolic return to the womb followed by a spiritual rebirth continues as a tradition among many peoples today.[38]

Fig. VIII.24 Tlachihualtepetl, with seven flowers representing seven caves (redrawn after *Historia Tolteca-Chichimeca* 1978: F. 14r MS 54-58, p. 40).

Seven Caves of Origin

An elaborate, stylized version of a U-shaped element can be seen on depictions of mountains in Maya art (Fig. VIII.25). In this illustration from Palenque, we see a monster-mountain sprouting maize from the top of a U-shaped crevice. This is the crack in the Mountain of Sustenance, the Mountain of Creation from which all life springs. Perhaps the end curls were meant to express the fallopian tubes of the earth monster or at least the spiraling force of energy equated with fertility and life. Cracks, crevices, and caves all have a similar connotation in Mesoamerican art. To reiterate, the dark, moist interior of the cave was the embodiment of the great womb of mother—of life, death, and emergence.

Fig. VIII.25 Vegetation grows from a crack in mountain, Temple of the Foliated Cross, Palenque (drawn by Linda Schele, © by David Schele, in Freidel, Schele, and Parker 1993, Fig. 3.8a).

WOMB OF THE SKY

Most of the U-shaped elements thus far discussed are associated with the womb of the earth. To a lesser degree there is another important facet of this ideology. It is the womb of the sky. Mesoamerican art depicts this in various U-shaped forms. The sky band from the *Codex Nuttall* not only contains the scalloped fleshy texture of the womb of the sky, but the sun, moon, and stars indicate this is the night sky of the Underworld through which the sun travels (Fig. VIII.26). The double serpent in U-shape form (see Fig. VIII.15) is a celestial sky band. The nighttime brings an aura of mystery akin to the darkness of a womb, whereas the dawning sun symbolizes rebirth from the womb of the dark Underworld sky.

Fig. VIII.26 Sky band with U-shaped womb at center (redrawn after *Codex Nuttall*, Plate 19).

Christenson, who lived among and studied the Quiché Maya, translates the legendary beginning of creation in the *Popol Vuh.* "This is the account of when all is yet silent and placid. All is silent and calm. Hushed and empty is the womb of the sky. . . . Alone lies the expanse of the sea, along with the womb of all the sky."[39] This moment, just before creation, is expressed very beautifully by these people.

In Egypt the goddess Nut, whose starry U-shaped body stretches across the night sky (Fig. VIII.27), is a representation of the womb of the sky.[40] Once again, the night sky represents the Underworld.[41] In this respect Nut becomes the womb of the dead from which rebirth is anticipated. Tower Hollis notes that Nut was more than just the vault of the night sky; her nature was multifarious. She includes other functions associated with the coffin, sarcophagus, and tomb.[42] All of these facets are considered the womb of Nut. A deceased Pharaoh was metaphorically viewed as being swallowed by Nut in the west, where the sun entered her mouth, and the king was then reborn with the new sun at dawn in the east from Nut's womb.[43]

Other cultures of the Middle East also exhibit womb-of-the-sky imagery. For example, winged sun discs often incorporate the U-shaped emblem of the mother goddess (Fig. VIII.28; see also Fig. VI.19). A Hittite state seal shows their version of the winged sun disc (Fig. VIII.29) with the sun directly positioned in the womb of the sky.[44]

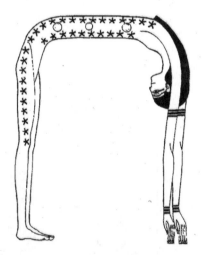

Fig. VIII.27 Nut, the Egyptian sky goddess, ceiling of Ramesses VI, Thebes, 20th Dynasty (drawn after photograph).

The Moon

An important symbol of the Underworld is the moon. Most mother goddesses of the ancient world are associated with the moon. According to Neumann, who did extensive research on the mother goddess of the Old World, the favored spiritual symbol of the matriarchal sphere is the moon in its relation to the night and the great mother of this realm.[45] During the day the moon is believed to pass through the waters of the Underworld—the abode of Mother Earth. In addition, the moon's waxing and waning from crescent to full crescent and to new moon, is widely considered a metaphor of life, death, and rebirth.[46]

Fig. VIII.28 Womb of the sky in winged-sun disc from Sakjegozu, Syria, 850-650 B.C. (redrawn after Frankfort 1970: 303).

Fig. VIII.29 Womb of the sky in winged-sun disk on Hittite state seal (redrawn after Kitchen 1982: 81).

In Mesoamerica the moon symbol is portrayed in glyphic form as a U (Fig. VIII.30). Imagery of the moon is often in the shape of a womb filled with water sometimes containing a rabbit, which is also a symbol for the moon (Fig. VIII.31). A more elegant portrait of the mother goddess sitting in the U-shaped moon element cannot be found than that from Yaxchilan (Fig. VIII.32). Sometimes the moon is even incorporated directly into the face of the goddess (Fig. VIII.33). At Rio Azul in Guatemala, there is a tomb glyph composed of a moon sign and a skull (Fig. VIII.34). M. Miller proposes that this glyph indicates birth—perhaps rebirth in the Underworld.[47] When a rabbit is portrayed with the Maya goddess, it is the moon/rabbit—her symbolic partner (Fig. VIII.35). Oddly, the rabbit is also associated with the moon in Mesopotamia and Egypt.[48]

Fig. VIII.30 Typical Maya moon glyph.

Fig. VIII.31 Rabbit in the womb of the moon (redrawn after *Codex Borgia*).

Fig. VIII.32 Ix Chel sits within U-shaped moon emblem, wall relief, Yaxchilan,
Chiapas, Mexico (drawn after photograph in Dütting 1978: 187).

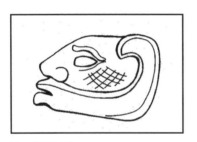

Fig. VIII.33

Fig. VIII.34

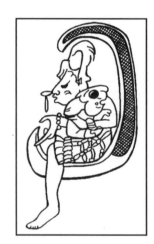

Fig. VIII.35

Fig. VIII.33 Moon goddess with infixed moon glyph (drawn after photograph in Kerr 1990:
Vol. 2, 181).
Fig. VIII.34 Glyph from tomb, Rio Azul, Guatemala (redrawn after photograph in M. E. Miller
1986: 115).
Fig. VIII.35 Maya goddess sitting in the moon with rabbit. Detail from a Late-Classic cylindrical
vase (redrawn after Schele and Miller 1986: 55).

Throughout the Middle East, goddesses were connected with the moon. However, it is in Egypt where the moon
and the U shape are more specifically linked. It is Hathor's cow horns that carry a symbolic identification with the
crescent moon.[49] In Israel, although not associated with cow horns of a goddess, three-year-old heifers were equated
with the moon as their horns resembled a new moon.[50]

VESSELS AND CONTAINERS

Another popular U design is the vase, which is considered sacred in that it symbolized the womb/vessel of the Earth Mother. Jars overflowing with streams of water were fertility symbols in Egypt from the beginning of their civilization.[51] It was the same in Mesopotamia, where Sumerian mother goddess figures are often portrayed holding the popular motif of a flowing vase (Fig. VIII.36).

The vase as a hallowed container was believed to hold the waters of the terrestrial center. Filled with rain water it nourishes or even floods the earth as is portrayed in the Maya *Dresden Codex* (Fig. VIII.37). All manner of things are seen emerging from pots in Mesoamerica. The womb shape of the vessel is clearly understood. Mathews states that the inverted vase had been interpreted to be a glyph expressing the relationship between child and mother.[52] No doubt this is due to the womb-like quality of the vase. In fact, an image of an inverted jar is often incorporated in Maya glyphs of women's names.[53]

Fig. VIII.36 Mesopotamian goddess with flowing vase, Iraq.

Fig. VIII.37 Old mother goddess Chak Chel, assists in flooding the previous creation of the world (redrawn after *Dresden Codex*).

In Egypt the meaning is the same. Speaking of Nut, Sjöö and Mor observe: "As [a] uterus, she is a vessel that breaks with childbirth, pouring forth water like a wellspring."[54] In fact, Nut is often depicted bearing a vase on her head, and the hieroglyph for her name includes a vase.[55] Budge proposes that this vessel symbolized a human uterus,[56] as did Ions who notes: "The hieroglyph for her name [Nut], which she wore on her head when depicted as a woman, is thought to be a womb as well as a waterpot."[57] As Gimbutas concludes, water containers are sacred to the goddess, in whose power is the source of the water of life.[58] Like the mother's womb containing the waters of life, the waters of the earth may be readily identified with the goddess. Vessels are a natural—even utilitarian—symbol of the womb.

Burials in Urn/Womb

Within the vase or bowl the contents remain sheltered from the world, as does a child in its mother's womb. Vessels in the ancient world were usually made of clay, which comes from Mother Earth.[59] In Babylonian and Assyrian cultures as well as other areas of the Near East, large earthen jars were often used to bury the deceased (Fig. VIII.38). In order to accommodate the interior structure of these urns, knees were drawn up, placing the body in the desired fetal position. This is emblematic of a future rebirth when the individual is born anew from the womb-like enclosure.[60]

In Mesoamerica the custom of burying the dead in urns was not as widespread as in the Middle East, but it did take place on occasion. For these burials, skeletal remains were placed in jars that were then interred. The space inside the urn was considered to be like a cave that was viewed as a uterus.[61] Another Mesoamerican practice was to place the ashes of the deceased directly into a hole that was referred to as a "cave." This was considered the mouth of the earth.[62] Butterworth explains that the mouth of funerary vessels from the Old World (especially those protruding from the ground) were symbolic of both the entrance and exit of the Underworld.[63] This is consistent with Mesoamerican thought.

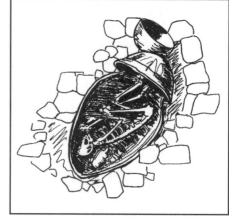

Fig. VIII.38 Deceased in earthen jar. Excavated near Nazareth, Palestine (redrawn after Neumann 1974: Fig. 37).

U-Shaped Sweat Baths, Cenotes, and Wells

The last item that falls into the category of U-shaped, womb containers in Mesoamerica is the sweat bath called the House of Flowers. Flowers in Mexico may symbolize both the womb and cave as previously noted.[64] Examples of U-shaped sweat baths exist at Xochicalco, Morelos, Mexico (Fig. VIII.39a). The waters of the sweat bath were associated with the embryonic fluid of the womb.[65] The Maya also depicted a U-shaped glyph full of water to designate a *cenote*, a natural well of water (Fig. VIII.39b). The largest and most well-known *cenote* is at Chichen Itza and is believed to perform a miraculous thing in the future. It is still believed by many Maya that the cosmic umbilicus that once connected the earth with the sky will once again emerge from this *cenote*.[66] In Egypt the hieroglyph for well is also a U-shaped element. To further substantiate the concept of a well with a mother's womb, the Egyptian well symbol was used as a substitute for this female organ.

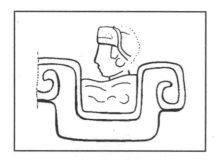
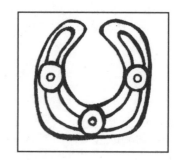

a.   b.

Fig. VIII.39 U-shaped water containers: a. Sweat bath design, Xochicalco, Morelos, Mexico (drawn after photograph). b. Cenote glyph (redrawn after J. E. S. Thompson 1962: 219).

SERPENTS AND BIRTH

In Mesoamerica a serpent is often worn or carried by the mother goddess. The Maya goddess Ix Chel frequently wears a twisted serpent on her head (Fig. VIII.40; see also Fig. VIII.37). Serpents are also occasionally positioned around the waist of goddesses. However, the most impressive accouterment perhaps is the snake skirt worn by Mexican goddesses, especially the Aztec goddess Coatlicue (Fig. VIII.41). The serpent's periodic rebirth through the shedding of its skin was associated with the cyclic changes of the moon. It embodied the regenerative powers of the waters, ruled by the moon, and the energies contained within the body of the earth.

Fig. VIII.40 Goddess with twisted serpent headdress (redrawn after *Dresden Codex*).

Fig. VIII.41 Aztec goddess, Coatlicue, housed at National Museum of Anthropology, Mexico City (drawn after photograph in Séjourné 1956: Plate 20).

Similar serpent symbolism on or near mother-goddess figures existed from very early to late times among the Canaanite, Egyptian, Minoan, and Roman cultures. In Figure VIII.6 (shown earlier in this chapter) Astarte is portrayed with snakes coming from her sides not unlike her Mesoamerican counterpart. Yadin excavated a plaque dating to around 1300 B.C. at Hazor, north of modern-day Israel, that depicts the torso of a goddess holding two snakes, while an omega-shaped U symbol was placed in the sky and another below her torso.[67]

Besides the regenerative quality of the snake, mother goddess figures are also known for their association with death in that the place of interment was comparable to her womb. Sjöö and Mor posit that the Underworld aspect of the serpent glided in and out of crevices of the earth, the place where the dead repose, awaiting rebirth. This enigmatic aspect of the serpent was both feared and respected, its demeanor being reflected in the goddesses who wore this creature of the earth.[68]

NET PATTERN AND EARTH

Net designs on goddess figures are another important feature relating to fertility and earth patterns. In both Mesoamerica and Egypt, women of royal lineage and their goddesses wore beaded net costumes (Figs. VIII.42 and

Fig. VIII.42 Net and bead outfit worn by elite Maya woman,
Altar I, La Corona, Guatemala, Dallas Museum of Art
(emphasis of darkened area by author, redrawn
after Jones and Spetzler 1992: 114).

Fig. VIII.43 Net beaded Egyptian dress
worn by Isis (redrawn after
Casson 1965: 184).

43). It is not clear if the net fabric design worn by Egyptian goddesses carried any significance, yet in light of this study, the likelihood that it carried the same symbolism as held in Mesoamerica should be considered.

Among the Maya this netting or beaded lattice garment most likely represents an image of the earth's surface.[69] Cross-dressing was not unusual among the people of Maya and Egyptian cultures. Maya males occasionally wore the net skirt of fertility. In fact, it was often worn on depictions of the maize god or maize god impersonators. The reasoning behind this iconography is that maize was born of the earth, which the net pattern represented. When Pakal was portrayed as the maize god on his sarcophagus (see Fig. VI.26), it was as though he fell into the jaws of the Underworld. Then, with the World Tree, he rose from the earth and was reborn. Male rulers who wore netted clothing took on the persona of the maize god, or First Father.

The Seeded Earth

The beads between the netting appear to represent the seeds that are planted in the earth. In Maya Yucatec the word for bead, *inah,* can also be read as "seed for planting." In a letter to *Archaeology* magazine, Frisbie notes that among the Pueblo peoples a dot in a square represents an individual kernel of life-sustaining maize.[70] The diamond or square shapes may indicate cultivated fields of the earth while the dots or beads, as the case may be, were the seeds. Perhaps the bead in the net pattern in ancient Egypt has a similar connotation.

Above all, the net pattern represents Mother Earth. Clear imagery of this concept appears on designs of hills and mountains (Figs. VIII.44 a and b). When drawn as a monster-earth mountain, the mouth represents the cave entrance to the Underworld as previously noted. When drawn more realistically, the cave entrance appears below in an elongated U shape. The net pattern designates the hill/mountain as a sacred earth location. Other net patterns appear on animals associated with fertility and the earth, such as the crocodile and turtle (Figs. VIII.44 c and d). The turtle is especially interesting in that the maize god emerges from the crack in its carapace, i.e., the earth (see Fig. II.10).

Pakal, who in death takes on the form of the maize god, wears a necklace/pendant of a turtle (see Fig. VI.26). At Copan, Waxaklahun-Ubah-K'awil, commonly referred to as 18 Rabbit, is portrayed on Stela C. This monument stands separate and behind a stone sculpture of a turtle. Viewing these two pieces from a short distance the ruler appears to emerge from the back of the turtle, just as the maize god did in Maya creation mythology.

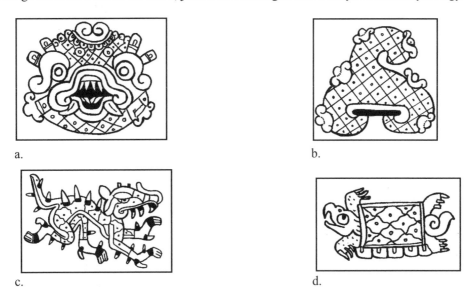

a.

b.

c.

d.

Fig. VIII.44 a. and b. from Huitzuco, Guerrero, Mexico. a. Net patterened anthropomorphic mountain, b. Mountain with net pattern and cave below (redrawn after Klein 1976: 352), c. Crocodile with net pattern (redrawn after *Borgia Codex*), d. Turtle with net pattern (redrawn after *Codex Trocortesianus*).

In the Middle East and other nearby locations of the Old World mother goddesses are also portrayed with net-like apparel. In Greece, Hera was known as a wife of Zeus, although her origins are far older than myths of Zeus. Baring and Cashford demonstrate that Hera was originally an earth goddess. She is beautifully portrayed in a clay relief from Thebes, Egypt, around 680–670 B.C. Vegetation grows from her head, or headdress, declaring her a goddess of fertility (Fig. VIII.45).[71] More importantly, she wears a net-like robe comparable to that worn by Isis, which, according to Baring and Cashford, may represent the seeded fields as well as the stars of the heavens.[72] In this case, a dot (which replaces the bead at the corner of the netting), is marked at the center of each diamond net pattern. In Mexico, a mold form of a goddess contains the identical pattern on her skirt, denoting exactly the same symbolic imagery (Fig. VIII.46).

As Baring and Cashford note, the net/bead combination may represent both seeds in fields and stars of the sky. This is most interesting when examining the practice in Egypt of plac-ing a sheet of beadwork over the deceased, which Budge believed typified the blue sky of night.[73] In their book, *Mummies & Magic,* the Boston Museum of Fine Arts write that such a covering would simulate a garment of life.[74] The beads in this funerary net/bead covering may represented the stars of the night sky. In Mesoamerica, stars are equated with seeds.

Fig. VIII.45 Greek goddess Hera wearing net-patterened dress, Thebes, Egypt (drawn after photograph in Baring amd Casjfprd 1991: 314).

Fig. VIII.46 Mold-made earth goddess with net skirt, Tenochtitlan, Mexico (drawn after photograph in Day 1992b: 44).

Fig. VIII.47 Osiris with beaded robe (redrawn after Lanzone 1881-85: Vol. 2, Plate CCXCIII, Fig. 4).

Fig. VIII.48 Osiris sprouting vegetation lying on a crocodile, bas-relief at Philae (redrawn after Budge 1961: Vol. I. 21).

More particularly, when the Pleiades appear to fall in the sky, it is imagined that a handful of seeds is planted.[75]

Osiris is the personification of vegetal life that came from the earth. Perhaps this is the reason he sometimes wears a net-like tunic (Fig. VIII.47). In Figure II.11, the dead Osiris is shown with grain germinating from his body. Another striking illustration of this theme shows the same symbolism coupled with the net pattern of the crocodile (Fig. VIII.48). This animal was also portrayed in Mesoamerica with the net pattern of the earth (see Fig. VIII.44).

A small patch of the net pattern in Sumeria is a pictograph for plant.[76] This is in keeping with the motif in other areas of the ancient world having to do with the earth and fertility. This concept commenced at a very early date. According to Johnson, the net pattern in the Old World represents the life cycle and death, having an Underworld connotation.[77]

Fig. VIII.49 Minoan ring with temple on net-patterned ground (redrawn after Johnson 1990: 295).

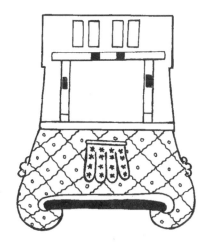

Fig. VIII.50 Temple built on top of net-patterned hill/mountain (redrawn after *Codex Borbonicus*).

Engraved on a gold Minoan ring is a temple built atop the crisscrossed-net pattern of holy ground (Fig. VIII.49).[78] Grain grows from the earth of this example, while two female figures wearing net skirts stand on either side. The same concept was held to be true in Mesoamerica and examples from the Mexican codices in particular verify this ideology. From the *Codex Borbonicus* a temple is built on top of a net-patterned hill/mountain with a small sprig of vegetation at each side (also note the cave underneath) (Fig. VIII.50).

Together, the various net motifs share in the ideology of earth, fertility, and rebirth. The Egyptian goddess Nut, takes us to another level of the multilayered symbolism incorporated in goddess imagery. From a bronze vessel made around 633–525 B.C., she is portrayed not only with her net skirt, but in front of the World Tree (Fig. VIII.51). Nut is also often seen leaning from a tree, giving food and drink to the deceased.[79] The Tree of the Center was popular from very early times, and as in Chapter VI, was a key element in ancient world mythology especially in the Middle East and Mesoamerica.

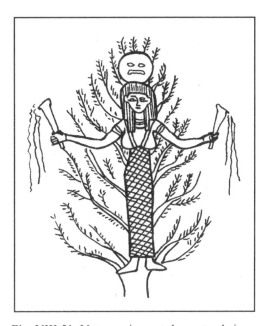

Fig. VIII.51 Nut wearing net dress stands in front of Tree. Detail from bronze vessel (drawn after photograph in Sjöö and Mor 1987: 154).

Fig. VIII.52 Sumerian earth-vase flows with water and sprouts Tree of Life (drawn after photograph in Wolkstein and Kramer 1983: 102).

THE TREE AND MOTHER

An early Sumerian representation of this Tree may be seen on a cylinder seal. An earth vase overflows with omega-womb style libations from which springs the sacred date palm (Fig. VIII.52). The Tree of Life is the embodiment of the great Earth Mother, for both the tree and womankind are visible manifestations of fruitfulness. The roots of the Tree spread deep into the depths of Mother Earth from the place they draw up the vital sap of life. In Egypt, the sap or fruit of the tree is likened to milk from the breast of the great goddess herself (Fig. VIII.53). Among the Maya, unweaned children of the Tzotzil of Chamula, who died, went to a paradise where there was a tree in the sky. This tree had many women's breasts from which the children were nursed.[80]

When Osiris is encased within the sycamore tree, as in Chapter II, he is considered to be in the womb of Nut,[81] where he would eventually be reborn. Wilkinson notes that when the deceased was buried in a wooden coffin, it symbolized the return into the womb of the mother tree goddess.[82] Even more so than Nut, Hathor is the tree goddess supreme in Egypt. It is she who accompanies the dead under her tree where they could rest from the cares of the mortal world.[83]

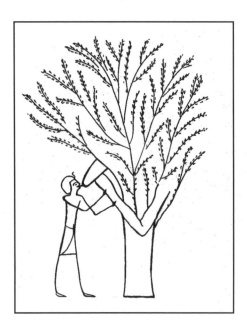

Fig. VIII.53 Breast of tree goddess nourishes the deceased in an Egyptian scene of the afterlife (drawn after photograph in Cook 1974: Fig. 11).

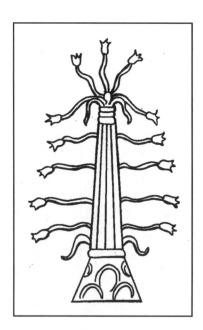

Fig. VIII.54 The Asherah Tree (redrawn after Walker 1988: 197).

In the Old Testament trees are often considered feminine, although the Hebrew word for tree is masculine (see Jeremiah 17:8 and Joel 2:22). Referring to the World Tree in general, Golan notes that it may be presumed that the World Tree is thought to be an incarnation of the great goddess.[84] It is well known that to the western Semites the sacred tree or pillar is also called an *asherah*. This is the name of the Canaanite goddess who was adopted by the ancient Hebrews for a time (Fig. VIII.54). For example, "You shall not plant any tree as an asherah beside the altar of the Lord " (Deuteronomy 16:21); and Gideon is commanded to cut down the *asherah* that stood next to an altar of Baal (Judges 6:25).[85] The Israelites were admonished not to worship the foreign tree goddess *Asherah*. While the Canaanites were in Egypt, the cult of Hathor penetrated their culture and became known by several names: Qudshu, Athirat, Elat, Astarte, Anat, and so on. Most of these, but not all, are one and the same with the biblical *Asherah*.[86]

In Mesoamerica the tree was often visualized as having both male and female attributes or, at least, a male and a female side. For example, at Teotihuacan on the Tepantitla murals, a great tree grows from the goddess where she represents the earth or primordial hill. Two trunks of the World Tree intertwine as they grow from the headdress of the goddess. One depicts butterfly designs (a symbol for dead warriors) and is considered the male side of the tree. The other trunk contains spiders, which is the popular weaving aspect of the goddess and women in general.

Another example of a tree growing from the head of a goddess is in the *Codex Vindobonensis* (Fig. VIII.55).[87] According to J. Furst, the left side of the tree with jade circles (a water symbol) is female, while the right side containing arrows is male.[88] Another option for the circles would be that they are spindle whorls used by women for weaving and the arrows (probably atlatl javelins) used by men at war.[89] At the top an individual is born from a V-shaped cleft in the tree, which, like the U-shaped element, is also a uterine symbol.[90] The Mixtec of southern Mexico (of which this drawing is an example) believed their ancestors were born from Mother Earth (the head at the base of the tree), via the trunk of the World Tree.[91] Although some of the Mesoamerican trees indicate a dual nature of male and female, trees in general are referred to as female throughout the Maya area.[92]

Sometimes Mesoamerican trees are pregnant as is the case of the bulging portion of our example from the *Vindobonensis*. Another example is found on a Mixteca vessel known as the Nochixtlan Vase. This pot depicts

Fig. VIII.55 Tree grows out of head of earth goddess (redrawn after *Codex Vindobonensis*).

a swollen hill topped by a maize plant repreenting the World Tree. Referring to this object and others, Byland and Pohl remark that the birth tree is often depicted as swollen with pregnancy.[93] Moving our attention to South America for a moment, the Milky Way as the World Tree was viewed by peoples of the Amazon Basin as a womb filled with fish. The fish represented the first humans to people the world.[94]

Neumann sums up the relation between the goddess and the World Tree quite nicely when he writes, "The Great Earth Mother who brings forth all life from herself is eminently the mother of all vegetation. . . . The center of this vegetative symbolism is the tree."[95]

Summary

The Mesoamerican and Middle Eastern tree, together with the moon, the vase, the net pattern, and various U-shaped elements, present a symbolic composite picture of all that is associated with life, death, and rebirth.

NOTES - Chapter VIII

1. See also Prov. 30:16, Eccles. 5:15, and Job 1:21.
2. Personal communication from Brian Stross to Diane Wirth, March 23, 1998.
3. Evon Z. Vogt, "The Zinacantecos of Mexico: A Modern Maya Way of Life," *Case Studies in Cultural Anthropology* (New York: Holt, Rinnehart and Winston, 1970), 69. Traditionally in Mesoamerica, the human race was made of maize as already noted.
4. Mitchell Dahood, *Psalms III: 101-150* (New York: The Anchor Bible, Doubleday, 1970), 284.
5. Pamela Berger, *The Goddess Obscured* (Boston: Beacon Press, 1985), 12.
6. Frank Waters, *Masked Gods: Navaho and Pueblo Ceremonialism* (Chicago: Swallow Press, Inc., 1950).
7. Othmar Keel, "The Peculiar Headrests for the Dead in First Temple Times," *Biblical Archaeology Review* 13/4 (1987), 50.
8. Henri Frankfort, "A Note on the Lady of Birth," *Journal of Near Eastern Studies* 3 (1944): 198-200.
9. Monica Sjöö and Barbara Mor, *The Great Cosmic Mother* (San Francisco: Harper & Row, Publishers, 1987), 161.
10. Neumann, 47-48, 218.
11. Bleeker, 41.
12. Raphael Patai, *The Hebrew Goddess* (New York: A Discus Book, Avon Books, 1978), 49.
13. Ibid., 46, 286 n.25.
14. J. E. Cirlot, *A Dictionary of Symbols*, trans. Jake Sage (New York: Philosophical Library, Inc., 1971), 135.
15. J. Eric S. Thompson, *Maya Hieroglyphic Writing*, 131.
16. Gabriel Barkay and Amos Kloner, "Jerusalem Tombs from the Days of the First Temple," *Biblical Archaeology Review* 12/2 (1986), 22-39; Keel, 50-53.
17. Keel, 50.
18. Ibid., 52.
19. Walter Krickeberg, et. al., *Pre-Columbian American Religions* (Great Britain: George Weidenfeld and Nicolson, Ltd., 1968), 25-26.
20. J. Eric S. Thompson, *Mexico Before Cortez* (New York: Charles Scribners, 1937), 278. See also Krickeberg, 25.
21. Doris Heyden, "Mesoamerican Religions: Classic Cultures," in *The Encyclopedia of Religion*, Mircea Eliade, ed., vol. 9 (New York: Macmillan Publishing Company, 1987), 417.
22. Jill Furst and Peter R. Furst, *Pre-Columbian Art of Mexico* (New York: Abberville Press, 1980), 49.
23. Armand J. Labbé, *Man and Cosmos in Prehispanic Mesoamerica* (Santa Ana, California: Bowers Museum Foundation, 1982), 28.
24. Norman, 179.
25. Krickeberg, 25.
26. Bassie-Sweet, 168.
27. Jacinto Quirarte, "Early Art Styles of Mesoamerican and Early Classic Maya Art," in *The Origins of Maya Civilization*, SAR, Richard E. W. Adams, ed. (Albuquerque: University of New Mexico Press, 1977), 261. Both the U-shaped and V-shaped elements denote a place of emergence. The earliest form was the V-shaped cleft incorporated by the Olmec, followed by the U-shape cave motive. See Tim Laughton, "Izapa: A Preclassic Codex in Stone," *Indiana Journal of Hispanic Literatures*, No. 13 (Bloomington: Indiana University, 1998), 17.
28. Lurker, 39.
29. Jon Davies, *Death, Burial and Rebirth in the Religions of Antiquity* (New York: Routledge, 1999), 72-74, 76.
30. For a belief in a resurrection among the Israelites, see Job 19:25-26; Isa. 26:19; Ps. 30:3; Ezek. 37.
31. Recinos, Goetz, and Morley, 63-64.
32. Dennis Tedlock, *Popol Vuh* (1985), 360.
33. Ake Hultkrantz, *The Religions of the American Indians* (Los Angeles: University of California Press, 1980), 244.
34. Doris Heyden, *Mitologia y simbolismo de la flora en el Mexico prehispanico* (Mexico City: Universidad Nacional Autonoma de Mexico, 1983).
35. Baring and Cashford, 185.
36. Doris Heyden, "An Interpretation of the Cave Underneath the Pyramid of the Sun in Teotihuacan," *American Antiquity* 40/2 (1975), 131.
37. Sjöö and Mor, 73, 77.

38. Nancy E. Auer Falk, "Feminine Sacrality," *The Encyclopedia of Religion*, Mircea Eliade, ed., vol. 5 (New York: Macmillan Publishing Co., 1985), 304.

39. Allen Christenson, "Prehistory of the K'ichean People," *Texas Notes on Precolumbian Art, Writing and Culture* 75 (Austin: The Center for the History and Art of Ancient American Culture, Art Department, 1997), 2.

40. E. A. Wallis Budge, *The Egyptian Heaven and Hell* (London, 1925; reprint, La Salle, Illinois: Open Court, 1989), 192; Donald Alexander Makenzie, *Myths of Pre-Columbian America* (London: Gresham Publishing Co., Ltd., n.d.), 169.

41. Bleeker, 44.

42. Tower Hollis, "5 Egyptian Goddesses," *KMT* 5/4 (1994-5).

43. Hart, *A Dictionary of Egyptian Gods*, 145.

44. Ariel Golan, *Myth and Symbol: Symbolism in Prehistoric Religions*, trans. Rita Schneider-Teteruk (Jerusalem: Ariel Golan, 1991), 81.

45. Neumann, 55.

46. Ibid.

47. Mary Ellen Miller, 115.

48. Robert Briffault, *The Mothers*, vol. 2 (New York: Johnson Corporation, 1969), 782; J. Saul. "As it is Above, so shall it be Below," *Archaeoastronomy* XI (1989-93), 105.

49. Allison Coudert, "Horns," *The Encyclopedia of Religion*, Mircea Eliade, ed., vol. 6 (New York: Macmillan Publishing Company, 1987), 462.

50. Graves and Patai, 43.

51. Barbara G. Walker, *The Woman's Dictionary of Symbols and Sacred Objects* (San Francisco: Harper and Row, Publishers, 1988), 40.

52. Peter Mathews, "Notes on the Dynastic Sequence of Bonampak, Part 1," in *Third Palenque Round Table, 1978/Part 2*, Merle Greene-Robertson, ed., vol. V (Austin: University of Texas Press, 1980), 61.

53. Genevieve LeFort, *Lady Alligator Foot Emerges From the Past: Maize God Iconography at Yomop* (Paris: Galerie Memorz, 1995), 21.

54. Sjöö and Mor, 52.

55. Budge, *The Book of the Dead*, 246.

56. Budge, *From Fetish to God*, 239.

57. Ions, 50.

58. Gimbutas, *The Language of the Goddess*, 22.

59. Zelia Nuttall, *The Fundamental Principles of Old and New World Civilizations: A Comparative Research Based on a Study of the Ancient Mexican Religious, Sociological and Calendrical Systems*, vol. II, Archaeological and Ethnological Papers of the Peabody Museum (Cambridge, Massachusetts: Harvard University, 1901), 100-01, 283.

60. Morris Jastrow, *The Civilization of Babylonia and Assyria* (Philadelphia: J. P. Lippincott, Co., 1915), 280, 380.

61. Heyden, "Caves, Gods, and Myths," 22; Eduardo Matos Moctezuma, *Life and Death in the Templo Mayor*, trans. Bernard R. and Thelma Ortiz Montellano (Niwot, Colorado: University Press of Colorado, 1995), 32.

62. Heyden, Ibid.

63. Butterworth, 30.

64. Heyden, "Mesoamerican Religions,"132.

65. Koontz, *The Iconography of El Tajin,* 77, 79, 82.

66. Freidel, Schele, and Parker, 157.

67. Keel, 53.

68. Sjöö and Mor, 59.

69. Information display, Peabody Museum, Harvard University, 1994.

70. *Archaeology* (Jul/Aug 1993), 11.

71. Baring and Cashford, 310-12.

72. Ibid., 312.

73. E. A. Wallis Budge, *The Mummy: A Handbook of Egyptian Funerary Archaeology* (1893; reprint, London: KPI, 1987), 222.

74. d'Auria, Lacovara, and Roehrig, 79.

75. Freidel, Schele, and Parker, 92.

76. Diane Wolkstein and Samuel Noah Kramer, *Inanna: Queen of Heaven and Earth* (New York: Harper & Row, Publishers, 1983), 144.

77. Johnson, 40, 160.

78. Ibid., 295.

79. Bleeker, 42.

80. J. Eric S. Thompson, *Maya History and Religion* (Norman: University of Oklahoma Press, 1970), 301.

81. T. Hopfner, *Plutarch über Isis u. Osiris* (Prague: I. Tiel, Orientalisches Institute, Die Sage, 1941), I: 159.

82. Wilkinson, *Reading Egyptian Art*, 117.

83. Bleeker, 43.

84. Golan, 227.

85. Ruth Hestrin, "Understanding Asherah," *Biblical Archaeology Review* 17/5 (1991), 50.

86. Ibid., 55.

87. Esther Pasztory, *Teotihuacan: An Experiment in Living* (Norman: University of Oklahoma Press, 1997), 86.

88. Jill Leslie Furst, *Codex Vindobonenis Mexicanus 1:A commentary* (Albany: Institute for Mesoamerican Studies, State University of New York, 1978), 134.

89. Linda Schele, "The Olmec Mountain and Tree of Creation in Mesoamerican Cosmology," in *The Olmec World: Ritual and Rulership* (Princeton: The Art Museum, Princeton University, 1996), 113.

90. Jill Leslie Furst, *Codex Vindobonensis*, 137.

91. Cecelia F. Klein, *The Face of the Earth* (New York: Garland Publishing, Inc., 1976), 144.

92. Ibid., 145.

93. Bruce E. Byland and John M. D. Pohl, *In the Realm of 8 Deer* (Norman: University of Oklahoma Press, 1994), 79, 115.

94. Peter G. Roe, *The Cosmic Zygote: Cosmology in the Amazon Basin* (New Brunswick, New Jersey: Rutgers University Press, 1982), 137, 158. See also Chapter II for discussion of fish symbolism.

95. Neumann, 48.

CHAPTER IX

Mountain of Creation

Contained in the texts of Sumerian mythology is the Myth of the Pickax, wherein Enlil, the god of storm and Air, performs an act of creation that is amazingly similar to that of storm gods in Mesoamerican creation stories. According to Jacobsen, Enlil's first act of creation was to separate heaven from the earth, which were originally united. The text says this was performed "in order to make the creature grow that came forth." Enlil proceeded to crack open the earth, to split or to cleave it with his gold pickax. In fact, the ground in which he thrust his ax is called *U zu-mú-a,* "the (place where) flesh sprouted forth." Jacobsen concludes that this happened in primeval times and this is where the earth produced mankind, which grew from the earth like plants. Also, the word *a-ri-a* used in these texts means "engendered things," "seed," or "offspring."[1] This line of reasoning is not unlike that of Mesoamerican cultures.

Earth Separated from Sky

Unlike the god Enlil of Mesopotamia, in Mesoamerica there is a distinction between the two supernatural forces of rain and air. At the hour of creation in Mesoamerica we find the lying-down sky that needs to be separated from the earth.[2] Among Nahua speakers of Mexico it is Quetzalcoatl who is known in his role as Ehecatl, the god of air, who separates the sky from the earth (Fig. IX.1). Among the Maya it is First Father, the maize god, who is called "Stand up, Sky Lord" in hieroglyphic texts. This title specifically refers to the moment in creation when the maize god is reborn and sets up the World Tree at the center. That action separates the sky from the earth.[3] In another myth, Quetzalcoatl was said to turn into a tree and accomplished the same task, allowing light to come into a darkened world.[4] Is some ways, the Mexican god Quetzalcoatl and the maize god of the Maya have an affinity to one another in their respective roles.

Fig. IX.1 Ehecatl-Quetzalcoatl, Mexican god of air, lifts the sky
(redrawn after *Codex Vindobonensis*).

In Egypt the sky is lifted from the earth by Shu, the god of air, (Fig. IX.2).[5] However, this role is not confined solely to Shu. Sometimes it is ascribed to Ptah, the creator god, in his close association with Osiris, the grain god.[6]

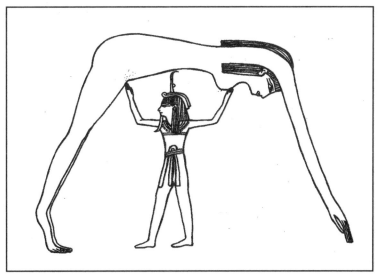

Fig. IX.2   Shu, Egyptian god of air lifts the sky (detail, redrawn
after Greenfield Papyrus, British Museum, London).

Among the Hebrews, the Bible speaks of the waters of creation that were divided by the firmament that in Hebrew is *raqiac,* meaning "expanse" (Genesis. 1:6–8). As a result the waters above (in the clouds) are separated from the waters below (on the earth).[7] In a succeeding act of creation, man and woman are formed.

THE PRIMORDIAL MOUND

In the legends of Mesopotamia and Mesoamerica it is the storm/rain god who cracks open the earth with his lightning ax, having the prime objective of allowing men to spring forth like vegetation. According to Taube, both the inhabitants of central Mexico and the southern Maya believe in myths of lightning explicitly breaking open the maize-enclosing rock. Taube maintains that the emergence of mankind and maize are associated. In fact, they may be the result of a single event occurring at the time of creation.[8]

Jacobsen describes the crack in the earth in Near Eastern art as a cavity shaped like an inverted truncated pyramid.[9] This would be a V shape identical to that used in Mesoamerica since Olmec times and a popular motif used until the arrival of the Spanish in the sixteenth century (see for example, Fig. VIII.55). The V-shaped crack in the earth is an iconographic insignia of the earth goddess—it denotes the entrance to her womb from which all are born, much as the previously discussed U-shaped element.

Fig. IX.3   Mesopotamian sun god, Shamash,
emerges from crack between
mountains (redrawn after Black and
Green 1993: Fig. 152).

Referring to the Primordial Mound in Near Eastern myths, Frankfort writes, "The plot of ground from which creation proceeded was obviously a depository of creative energy powerful enough to carry anyone who might be buried there through the crises of death to rebirth."[10] Frankfort also notes that in the sacred area, *Dur- anki* (the bond of heaven and earth), is the place where flesh sprouts forth. It is where Enlil split the crust of the earth with his pickax to allow mankind to break through and populate the earth.[11] From the Akkadian period in Mesopotamia, gods emerge from this crack between two mountain peaks (Fig. IX.3). This is comparable to the imagery portrayed in

Fig. II.20 where the Maya maize god emerges from the crack of Creation Mountain.

Temple and Mound of Creation

The crack made in the earth became the Primordial Mound or the first bit of earth that arose at the moment of creation. All life sprang from this spot. It became a central theme upon which sacred mountain lore is based. Perhaps more importantly, it is the core of the symbolism for temples and pyramids, which are often one and the same. The temple is the manmade mountain from which the waters of creation flow. Brandon states that in both Egypt and Mesopotamia the founding of an important temple is associated with the creation of the world. The Temple of Atum-Re at Heliopolis, for example, is said to have been built on the Primeval Hill that appeared out of the watery abyss of Nun.[12]

The well-known omphalos of the Greeks typifies the Primordial Mound (Fig. IX.4). To those at Delphi, their omphalos represented the navel of the world, which is an important symbol of Mother Earth.[13] Kristensen explains that the Egyptian texts declare the day of creation was the day of the elevation of the earth.[14] Among the Egyptians, Osiris is shown as buried in the Primeval Mound in the hieroglyph for the his tomb from which he is expected to arise (Fig. IX.5).

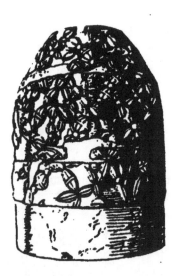

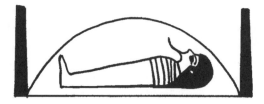

Fig. IX.4 Omphalos (drawn after photograph, Delphi Museum, Greece).

Fig. IX.5 Osiris mound, British Museum Papyrus 1008 (redrawn after Niwinski 1989: Plate 19a).

Serpents and Primordial Hill of Creation

Occasionally the omphalos is topped with a pillar, which represents the World Tree. At other times it is covered with a net pattern as in Figure IX.4. The creature that is associated with the omphalos, especially in the Mediterranean, is the serpent that coils its body around the mound.[15] An example of a winged serpent around a mound is depicted on an Orphic bowl. According to Leisegang, the winged serpent of Orphic theology represents the Creator of the world.[16] The serpent is also clearly associated with creation mountains in Mesoamerica, which will be discussed shortly.[17] However, there is not yet sufficient evidence to warrant this tradition as a cultural connection with the Mediterranean even though the parallel symbolism is noteworthy.

Split or Double Mountain

Ceremonies in Yucatan were recorded in the sixteenth century by Diego de Landa. He found that several towns were ritually laid out as a counterpart to their view of the cosmos. Four roads radiated from the center while at each entrance two heaps of stones represented the mythological Mountain of Creation.[18] The space between these mounds represented the crack in the mountain—the visual imagery being quite similar to the dual mountains on the horizon of Egypt (Fig. IX.6). The single mound of the omphalos or the split mountain (which appeared as a double mountain) was the same Mountain of Creation. They represented two different stages of the first parcel of earth to emerge from the Primordial Sea.

Both designs (the single or the double motif) were eventually transferred to architecture. The Olmec site of Chalcatzingo, Morelos, Mexico, dates back to as early as 1200 B.C.[19] This remote center of rituals was chosen by the inhabitants for a specific reason. For them, the Sacred Mountain of Creation was visibly there. Two natural mountains created the illusion of the crack or the place of emergence of Creation Mountain (Fig. IX.7).[20] This sacred site was filled with monuments depicting various scenes that took place before the creation of the world.

Fig. IX.6   Egyptian hieroglyph for horizon.

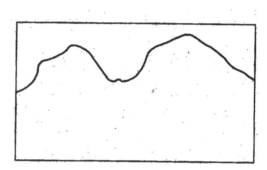

Fig. IX.7   Silhouette of Cerro de Gado and Cerro Chalcatzingo, Morelos, Mexico.

This tradition still continued in Mesoamerican ideology 2,000 years later as demonstrated by the Aztec in their Templo Mayor (Fig. IX.8). The Templo Mayor in Tenochtitlan (in today's Mexico city) has two parts to it representing the two mountains in our discussion. One was built to honor Huitzilopochtli and represents the mountain of Coatepec, which has long been recognized as a re-creation of the mythical Serpent Mountain. The other portion denotes a Mountain of Sustenance and was built to honor the rain god, Tlaloc.[21] The two parts of the temple together left the visual impression of two mountains alongside each other, or one mountain with a cleft at the center. Either way, it would fulfill the criteria for this perception. The power of an ancient tradition was made manifest, which deeply influenced the understanding of cosmology and the concept of the center to the people at that time. The Aztecs were able to take part in the beginning of creation—the place where it all began. At this temple they stood on sacred ground.

People in Egypt, like Chalcatzingo and other Mesoamerican sites, also have their split-mountain imagery in a natural setting. The hills on the east bank of the Nile at Amarna were celebrated in myth as the mountain of the east—a portal to the Otherworld (Fig. IX.9).[22] One is also tempted to look at the entrance pylons

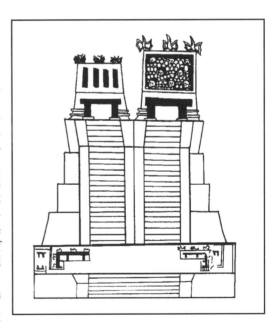

Fig. IX.8   The Templo Mayor (redrawn after *Codex Ixtlilxochitl* 1976: 112v).

of the Temple of Luxor in Egypt as portrayed on the temple wall (Fig. IX.10). Here also are two mountain-like structures that represent the mountains on the horizon. There is a great difference in time between the Aztec Templo Mayor and the Egyptian pylons. The similar architecture is not so much the consideration; rather, it is the importance of the parallel concept that was timeless in the ancient world. For both, it was the belief in a primordial, cleft mountain.

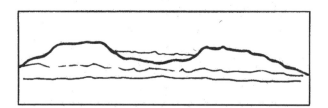

Fig. IX.9   Silhouette of hills at Amarna, Egypt (redrawn after Wilkinson 1994: 167).

Fig. IX.10   Entrance pylon of the Temple of Luxor as depicted on temple wall, Egypt (redrawn after Wilkinson 1994: 76).

Fig. IX.11   Portal of eternity at the Eastern Horizon (redrawn after Hornung 1990: 72).

Portal of Return

Not only did all things in nature emerge from the crack in Creation Mountain—this is the place where all things returned. In various representations of Egypt, the sun is often shown between these two mountains of the horizon (see Fig. IX.6). According to Goelet, this is the *Akhet*, which is the place where the gods and spirits came into being.[23] Like the sun that dies and is reborn through the passage, men followed the same course after death.[24] In *The Book of the Dead of Neferrenpet*, the deceased is portrayed going through the door that leads to eternity (Fig. IX.11). The doors stand between the split-mountain horizon on the bottom and the sky at the top.[25] Much like the Egyptian after-death tradition, the Mexican deceased had to cross two mountains to go to the Underworld, where many trials would be faced.[26] Matos Moctezuma thinks it is possible that the space between the double-temple hill of the Templo Mayor was the access to the world of the dead.[27]

House of God(s)

Many temples in Mesoamerica are patterned after a single mountain, as are the pyramids of Mesopotamia and Egypt.[28] Lundquist observes that in Egypt all temples are seen as representing the primeval hillock.[29] Sometimes a site's Creation Mountain in Mesoamerica was nearby, but it was replicated by man's hand for the purpose of performing rituals. This was true of the Pyramid of the Sun in Teotihuacan, which represents Cerro Gordo, the natural

Primordial Mound behind the structure. According to Miller and Taube, Houston and other epigraphers demonstrate that the Maya referred to both pyramids and mountains as *uitz*.[30] Temples and mountains were places where rulers were able to communicate with the gods. This was due to the fact that mountains were the residence of the gods,[31] the same as in Egypt.[32] Carmack states that the temples of the Quiché Maya were houses of the gods.[33] One is reminded of the Hebrew phrases, "the mountain of the Lord" and "the temple of the Lord" (Isaiah 2:2; 1 Kings 9:1). A Sumerian hymn describes the Temple of Enlil in Nippur as "the house of Enlil—it is a mountain great."[34] Creation Mountain became the true archetype of the temple.

In Judaism there is a passage in *Midrash Tanhuma* stating that a temple was built in the center of Jerusalem and the Holy of Holies was built at the center. In front of the Ark of the Covenant, which was at the center of the Holy of Holies, the Foundation Stone rested over the foundation of the world.[35] This was the Primordial Mound. In Mesopotamia at Sumer, the innermost portion of the temple sanctuary was called the Holy Mound. Once again this refers to the first mound of creation. The same was true in Egypt where the inner sanctum represented this mythical mound.[36] In Mesoamerica, at Tikal in Guatemala, a pit was cut through the floor of a temple. This was located in a room at the rear and represented a portal into the waters of the Underworld.[37]

The dedication of temples in the Middle East and in Mesoamerica often took place during the New Year festival, which was symbolic of the day of creation. The people believed that by doing this, both the Primordial Hill and the sacred manmade temple/mountain complex would arise simultaneously. The past was brought into the present and the temple rested on sacred ground charged with supernatural power.

Serpent Mountain

The theme of Snake Mountain associated with creation was prevalent in the Mediterranean and Mesoamerica. This may or may not be a valid connection between the two cultures. However, examining some Mesoamerican temples as a Serpent Mountain, a possible tie-in with the Near East may be found in Solomon's Temple which incorporated sculpted serpents patterned after the one fashioned by Moses.[38] They remained on it until its destruction in 586 B.C.[39]

In Mesoamerica serpent symbolism is widespread on pyramids and facades that portray mountains. One of the earliest is found on a Late Pre-Classic relief at Uaxactun, Guatemala, where the Mountain of Creation with watery fish imagery is topped by a manmade replica of a Creation Mountain—a pyramid Snake Mountain.[40] Well known temples where snakes are exhibited include the Pyramid of Quetzalcoatl at Teotihuacan and the High Priest's Grave and Castillo at Chichen Itza. Page six of the *Codex Azcatitlan* clearly shows this theme (Fig. IX.12). In this codex a manmade temple appears above Serpent Mountain together with another small temple including a serpent gliding down the stairs. Serpents are also on the balustrades of the Serpent Mountain side of the Temple Mayor in Tenochtitlan.

Fig. IX.12 Coatepec, Snake Mountain (redrawn after the *Codex Azcatitlan*, p. 6).

The Primordial Waters of Creation

Unique to both mountain and temple settings were the nearby waters of creation (the Primordial Sea). In Mesopotamian, Egyptian, Israelite, and Mesoamerican tradition, sacred water flowed under the temple from these waters of the Underworld. To ancient peoples, these streams of water were thought to once cover the earth during the creative process. They were chaotic waters before this great event and life-giving waters after all things were set in order on the day of creation. For Mesoamericans, waters, mist, clouds, springs, lakes, and caves were all associated with mountains. According to Broda, the Templo Mayor at Tenochtitlan was founded "over two rocks that arose above two caves filled with water . . . the temple itself was a sacred mountain covering the subterranean waters like a cave."[41]

Fig. IX.13 Tula toponym (redrawn after Manuscript *Tovar*, in Lafaye 1972: Plate 11).

In Mesoamerica, the traditional site of the creation was known among Nahua speakers from the valley of Mexico as Tula or Tollan, and by the Maya as Puh. Stuart identifies the word *puh* as "cattail." Tula and Tollan have the same meaning. These are the Place of Cattails or Bulrushes and refer to the Primordial Sea where creation took place, as well as to sites that re-created this creation complex in their architecture and landscape.[42] This ideology was popular in Mesoamerica for more than 1,500 years, and perhaps even longer.[43] Many examples of this imagery exist in the codices. Present are the mountain and/or the manmade temple mountain and creation waters with cattails (Fig. IX.13).

Funerary vessels from both Egypt and Mesoamerica carry the theme of the Primordial Sea. As Miller and Taube note, the water lily may serve as a model for the creation of the earth.[44] It is a given fact in Egypt that the lotus (a type of water lily) was associated with rebirth. This flower closes at night and opens with the dawn's first sun. Egyptian bowls portray the Primordial Sea at the center, sometimes decorated with a pinwheel surrounded by lotus flowers, fish, and occasionally birds (Fig. IX.14).[45] In Mesoamerica a lid from an Early-Classic Maya vessel depicts the the same theme—a circular action at the center of the Primeval Waters, water lilies, birds, and fish (Fig. IX.15). These objects were placed with the deceased in hope of rebirth in the waters of life.

Fig. IX.14 Primordial pond, lotus, and fish, funerary bowl from Egypt (redrawn after Wilson 1987: Fig. 83).

Fig. IX.15 Early-Classic Maya vessel lid depicting the primordial center, lilies, fish, and birds (redrawn after Miller and Taube 1993: 185).

When natural water was not available in a geographical setting in Mesoamerica, the courtyard of a temple often represented the watery surface of the Underworld.[46] Other places were viewed metaphorically as Creation Waters. At Palenque, Stuart and Schele identify a glyph phonetically read as *pib na*. Stuart suggests that the inner sanctuary of the temples served as a sweat bath.[47] Houston finds in his study of these sweat baths that, within the internal layout of a temple, an inner sanctuary was often constructed. It was separate and contained the water and creation-myth iconography. Although Houston does not believe that all sweat baths in temples were ever actually used, he proposes that their purpose was symbolic rather than functional and may represent the natal steam baths of the gods or possibly the rulers.[48] These, then, were the waters of creation. As Miller and Taube explain, "when a person emerged from a sweat bath, that person was 'reborn' from the womb of the earth."[49]

Another place where water was envisioned was on the ballcourt, and sometimes water was intentionally routed to fill these courts. A case in point is at Tenochtitlan where a dam was constructed at the ballcourt. Periodically the cleft that allowed the water to enter was unblocked in order to fill the court with water.[50] This action symbolically made a place of cattails, a Tula, and the Primordial Waters in duplicate. These were not only the waters of creation, but the watery surface of the Underworld through which the deceased traveled.

Typical of the Old World tradition that the four waters of Paradise issued from beneath the temple[51] is a parallel tradition found at Teotihuacan under the Pyramid of the Sun. Near the center of the pyramid is found a cave with a passageway that led to four distinct petal-like appendages as noted previously in the discussion of caves. These chambers have been interpreted as representative of the Underworld.[52] More significant is the presence of a stone drainage system that allowed water to ceremonially pour into the four cave chambers.[53]

The grand stepped ziggurat of Ur in Mesopotamia had a wide courtyard with a pool of water that probably exemplified the Primordial Waters.[54] Even Ezekiel's temple to be constructed in the future includes a river flowing under the threshold.[55] In Egypt an even greater presentation of this theme is made. Was the Egyptian paradise called the Field of Reeds comparable to Tollan or Tula of Mesoamerica? Descriptions of the Field of Reeds from Egyptian texts and their interpretation by Egyptologists is significant. The reeds are papyrus reeds while the Mesoamerican counterpart was made of cattails or bulrushes. Enormous pillars with designs of aquatic plants support the ceilings of Egyptian temples. These columns with plant motifs gave the people a visual image of the surrounding Primeval Waters, whereas the temple shrine was the Mound of Creation.[56]

The Field of Reeds in Egypt was a place where the spirits of the deceased went to live in abundance and happiness. This is made clear in books buried with the deceased. One of the more famous was written for a scribe named Ani. In an introductory hymn to the god Osiris, a vignette from the *Egyptian Book of the Dead* reads, "May there be given to me bread from the House of Cool Water and a table of offerings from Heliopolis, my toes being firm-planted in the Field of Reeds."[57]

Goelet states that the Field of Reeds was thought to lie in the world of the dead, in the "regions near the horizon, a transition point before one entered the celestial sphere."[58] It represented a kind of paradise. Among the Egyptians the papyrus reed was not only a symbol of life but of the primeval marsh from which all life emerged. Again, papyrus pillars were often part of a building's structure implying a setting of the Field of Reeds.[59] This is the same concept as in Mesoamerica. These Primordial Waters are a place of birth, death, and rebirth.

Summary

The Egyptian model of the cosmos is built into their ceremonial centers just as it is among Mesoamerican peoples. The specific details are amazing as they appear to parallel each other in an unprecedented manner. The Egyptian temple is a symbolic model of the universe and Wilkinson suggests that they constituted a working model that formalized the actual running of the cosmos.[60] The roof of the temple represents the sky, while the floor is the great marsh (Field of Reeds) from which the primeval world rose. Wilkinson also finds that "the lower sections of the temple walls were often decorated with representations of marsh plants . . . where the outer courts and pillared hall were actually flooded in the annual inundation of the Nile."[61] Many sites in Egypt were built close to the Nile in order to be partly submerged during the rainy season. This was to emphasize the watery creation of the world.[62] It is a theme that is identical to many sites in Mesoamerica.[63]

The Old Testament states that a precious cornerstone as a sure foundation was laid in the temple (Isaiah 28:16). This stone was known to hold back the chaotic waters of the abyss.[64] These were not waters of death but were life-giving and possessed the power to overcome death.[65] In addition, Josephus reported that the courtyard of the Temple of Jerusalem represented the sea. Eliade remarked that these waters referred to the waters of the inferior regions or the abyss, in other words, Primordial Waters.[66] The tradition is significantly the same throughout the Middle East and in Mesoamerica.

Regarding this central theme, Lundquist argues that in the Middle East there was a "remarkable interlocking inter-relationship, symbolic and cultic within the temple, around the issues of cosmic mountain, primordial hillock, primordial waters, and sacred tree."[67] The Sacred Tree brings us full circle in the complex related traditions that are also found in Mesoamerica.

In the ancient Middle East, the tree in temple courtyards, or even a sacred grove of trees, represents the World Tree in a paradisiacal setting. We find this theme in Mexico as well. According to Durán, a forest was established in the courtyard of the temple. One large tree was singled out, brought to this manmade forest, and given the name *Tota*, which means "Our Father."[68] First Father was the maize god who, with the World Tree, separated the sky from the earth after he was born from the crack in the Primordial Mound around which existed the Primordial Sea.

NOTES - Chapter IX

1. Thorkild Jacobsen, "Sumerian Mythology: A Review Article," *Journal of Near Eastern Studies* V (1946).
2. Schele and Freidel, *A Forest of Kings*, 255.
3. Lynn Foster and Linnea Wren, "World Creator and World Sustainer: God N at Chichén Itzá," in *Eighth Palenque Round Table, 1993*, gen. ed. Merle Greene-Robertson, vol. eds. Martha J. Macri and Jan McHargue, vol. X (San Francisco: The Pre-Columbian Art Research Institute, 1996), 261.
4. H. Nicholson, 399.
5. Boyland, 157.
6. Morenz, 173.
7. Personal communication from John Tvedtnes to Diane Wirth, April 7, 1999.
8. Taube, "The Teotihuacan Cave of Origin," 56.
9. Jacobsen.
10. Frankfort, *Kingship and the Gods*, 152-53.
11. Ibid., 217.
12. Brandon, 92.
13. Lundquist, *The Temple*, 22.
14. W. Brede Kristensen, *The Meaning of Religion* (The Hague: Martinus Nijhoff, 1960), 106.
15. Hugh Nibley, *Temple and Cosmos* (Salt Lake City: Deseret Book Company, and Provo, Utah: F.A.R.M.S, 1992), 160.
16. Hans Leisegang, "The Mystery of the Serpent," in *The Mysteries: Papers from the Eranos Yearbooks*, ed. Joseph Campbell, Bollingen Series XXX/2 (Princeton: Princeton University Press, 1978), 195, 232.
17. Schele, "The Olmec Mountain and Tree," 109.
18. Bassie-Sweet, 134, 219 n.4.
19. Personal communication from Linda Schele to Diane Wirth, January 1998. See also David C. Grove, *Chalcatzingo: Excavations on the Olmec Frontier* (New York: Thames and Hudson, 1984), 40.
20. María Elena Bernal-García, "La Venta's Pyramid: The First Successful Representation of the Mesoamerican Sacred Mountain," (Cambridge: England, a preliminary paper for Spring Seminar at the Center for Latin American Studies, 1988), 14.
21. Eduardo Matos Moctezuma, "Symbolism of the Templo Mayor," in *The Aztec Templo Mayor*, Elizabeth Hill Boone, ed. (Washington, D.C.: Dumbarton Oaks Research Library and Collection, 1987).
22. Wilkinson, *Symbol & Magic in Egyptian Art*, 167.
23. *Egyptian Book of the Dead*, 143.
24. Ibid., 174.
25. Hornung, *The Valley of the Kings*, 72.
26. Sahagún, *Florentine Codex*, Bk. 1: 294.
27. Eduardo Matos Moctezuma, "The Templo Mayor of Tenochtitlan History and Interpretation," in *The Great Temple of Tenochtitlan: Center and Periphery in the Aztec World* (Berkeley: University of California Press), 57.
28. Wilkinson, *Reading Egyptian Art*, 219.
29. Lundquist, "What is a Temple?," 86.
30. Miller and Taube, 120.
31. Bernal-García, 9.
32. *Egyptian Book of the Dead*, 121, 143.
33. Carmack, 186.
34. James B. Pritchard, *Ancient Near Eastern Texts Relating to the Old Testament*, 3rd. ed. (Princeton: Princeton University, 1969), 582.
35. Lundquist, *The Temple*, 7.
36. Ibid., 7-8.
37. Schele and Freidel, *A Forest of Kings*, 199.
38. Num. 11:9.
39. Maurice H. Farbridge, *Studies in Biblical and Semitic Symbolism* (Hartford, England: Stephen Austin and Sons., Ltd., 1923), 75; Lindon Joseph Smith, *Tombs, Temples, and Ancient Art* (Norman: University of Oklahoma Press, 1956), 40.

40. Schele, "The Olmec Mountain and Tree," 109.

41. Johanna Broda, "The Provenience of the Offerings: Tribute and Cosmovision," in *The Aztec Templo Mayor*, Elizabeth Hill Boone, ed. (Washington, D.C.: Dumbarton Oaks Research Library and Collection, 1987), 231-32.

42. Verbal communication from David Stuart to Diane Wirth, March 1998.

43. Schele and Mathews, *The Code of Kings*, 337.

44. Miller and Taube, 184.

45. d'Auria, Lacovara, and Roehrig, 138.

46. Schele and Miller, 113; Stross, "Maize and Blood," 103.

47. Bassie-Sweet, 257 n.4.

48. Stephen D. Houston, "Symbolic Sweatbaths of the Maya: Architectural Meaning in the Cross Group at Palenque, Mexico," *Latin American Antiquity* 7/2 (1996).

49. Miller and Taube, 159.

50. Rex Ashley Koontz, "Cosmology and Natural Modeling Among Aboriginal American Peoples: Mesoamerica" (paper presented at Second D. J. Sibley Conference on World Traditions of Culture and Art, Austin: University of Texas), 2.

51. Hugh Nibley, "The Hierocentric State," *Western Political Quarterly* 4 (1951), 235.

52. Taube, "The Teotihuacan Cave of Origin," 54.

53. René Millon, "Teotihuacan: City, State and Civilization," in *Supplement to the Handbook of Middle American Indians, Vol. I*, Victoria R. Bricker and Jeremy A. Sabloff, eds. (Austin: University of Texas Press, 1981), 234.

54. Zehren, 112.

55. Ezek. 47:1, 12.

56. Lundquist, "What is a Temple?," 87.

57. *Egyptian Book of the Dead*, Plate 2.

58. Ibid., 169.

59. Wilkinson, *Reading Egyptian Art*, 123.

60. Wilkinson, *Symbol & Magic*, 27.

61. Ibid.

62. Ibid., 66.

63. Schele and Miller, 113, 122.

64. Lundquist, *The Temple*, 10.

65. Ibid., 31.

66. Eliade, *Symbolism, the Sacred, and the Arts*, 15.

67. John M. Lundquist, "The Common Temple Ideology of the Ancient Near East," in *The Temple in Antiquity*, ed. Truman Madsen, vol. 9 (Provo, Utah: Religious Studies Center, Brigham Young University, 1984), 71.

68. Fray Diego Durán, *Historia de las Indias de Nueva España e Islas de la Tierra Firme*, ed. Angel Maria Garibay K., 2 vols. (reprint, Mexico: Editorial Porrúa, 1984), 1: 86.

CHAPTER X

MISCELLANEOUS PARALLELS

This chapter contains individual similarities between Mesoamerica and the Near East that are not always part of a larger complex. As with other seemingly plausible connections, they may have developed in isolation, been the result of the human psyche, or brought to the New World via the process of cultural diffusion. These traditions are presented here in hope that further study and/or discoveries will determine the answers. Some parallels are more definite than others, yet all must be considered in light of the vast number of coinciding traditions that have already been presented in previous chapters.

Most of the following traditions are linked to death and the afterlife—concepts that intrigued ancient cultures around the world. Things in nature were used to visualize and explain these mysteries and, more often than not, the ideas set forth included multilayered meanings in order to understand an individual principle. Let us proceed and examine some of the lesser known traditions common to the ancient Middle East and Mesoamerica.

Nine Lords of the Underworld

A fragment of a Babylonian text mentions Nine Gods of the Night. Their names were pronounced by priests and nine incense-burning censers were placed in their honor.[1] An important Egyptian classification of gods mentioned in the early Pyramid Texts is the Ennead, which is comprised of nine gods who preside in the Underworld.[2] To the Egyptians the number nine encompassed the meaning of totality.[3] In a scene referred to as the Judgment Hall of Osiris, according to *The Book of Gates,* these nine deities ascended nine stairs as they approached Osiris (Fig. X.1). This represented the rule of Osiris over the nine gods of the Underworld.[4] In a rubric to Chapter 72 of the *Egyptian Book of the Dead,* the deceased is told that in the Field of Reeds he will receive barley and emmer and will become as strong as when he lived on the earth. More particularly, the deceased will be able to do what he wishes like the nine gods of the Duat (the Underworld).[5]

Fig. X.1 Egypt's Nine Gods of the Underworld (redrawn after Budge 1989: 161).

The same concept is found in Mesoamerica. However, instead of calling these nine supernatural beings gods, scholars frequently refer to them as Nine Lords of the Night.[6] Nine, in and of itself, can represent the number of the Earth Lord and/or the Underworld.[7] In Maya cosmology there were thirteen layers to the heavens and nine layers in the Underworld, with some variation at times depending on the locale. Not only are many Mesoamerican pyramids constructed with nine levels, but Coggins suggests the nine doorway structures on a pyramid at Tikal represents this Underworld link.[8]

The Maya glyph for Nine-God Place often appears inside *ol* portal signs. This portal is the entrance to the Underworld.[9] The ballcourt also represents this portal, and the court at Yaxchilan notably includes nine steps leading up to it.[10] Therefore, it is quite appropriate for the Nine Lords of the Night to be modeled in stucco on the walls of Pakal's tomb at Palenque, as well as at a tomb found at Comalcalco in Tabasco, Mexico.[11]

Atlantean Figures

In both Mesoamerican and Middle Eastern traditions, there are gods of the four cardinal directions. There are also gods of the four sides who specifically hold up the sky. These are the so-called Atlantean figures. The Pharaoh of Egypt was equated with Horus and, therefore, was likened to the father of the four sons of Horus. These four offspring are the gods of the canopic jars involved in mummification. However, they are also the four Atlantean type gods who support the sky.[12] In some cases goddesses support the sky, but the important fact is that there are usually four, which correspond to the four cardinal directions (Fig. X.2). These Egyptian Atlantean figures may be compared to the four Bacabs of Maya mythology, which concept goes back to Olmec times.

Fig. X.2 Four deities hold up the symbol of the sky, main hall Dendera, Egypt (redrawn after Budge 1969, Vol. 2: 311).

Fig. X.3 Olmec Skybearers hold up four quarters of the sky, Monument 2, Potrero Nuevo, Veracruz, Mexico (drawn after photograph in Bernal 1969: Plate 15).

One of the earliest Olmec portrayals of deities holding up the sky comes from Potrero Nuevo near San Lorenzo in Veracruz (Fig. X.3). The sky element of the Olmec is nearly identical to the Egyptian sky glyph in the preceding illustration. However, although only two figures hold the sky, in this case four sky motifs indicate the four sides of the cosmos. In the later Maya tradition, four supernaturals deities called Bacabs are represented supporting the sky above the earth at Chichen Itza in the Yucatan (Fig. X.4). Scholars understand that this concept in Mesoamerica survived from very early to late times.[13] On occasion these four world sky bearers are substituted with four pillars or trees in both Egypt and Mesoamerica. The symbolism being the same—the sky was conceptualized as needing support to keep it separated from the earth.[14]

Fig. X.4 Four Skybearers from columns in the Castillo, Chichen Itza, Yucatan, Mexico (redrawn after J. E. S. Thompson 1954: 115).

Dog as Guide for the Dead

Much more is known about the Underworld role of the dog in Mesoamerica than in the Old World. However, what we know of Anubis in Egypt is significant. Anubis was not only the guardian of the door that led to the Underworld, it was his responsibility to lead the souls of the dead to the Place of the Reeds—a place of abundance and rest for the deceased.[15] Anubis's connection with the dead is reflected in the fact that priests wore his mask in embalming scenes.[16] The animal portrayed by Anubis is either a dog or a jackal and is sometimes shown lying on a tomb-like structure indicating his role as guardian of the dead (Fig. X.5).[17] The Greeks borrowed the Egyptian Anubis and his name became Cerberus. This ferocious dog guards the entrance to the Underworld, Hades, and is clearly associated with the deceased.[18]

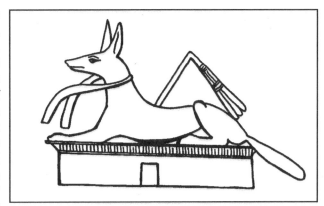

Fig. X.5 The Egyptian dog-headed god Anubis (redrawn after Wilkinson 1992: 64).

The Egyptians also had the jackal-headed Wepwawet (a.k.a. Upwawet or Ap-uat), which was often equated with Anubis.[19] Apparently Anubis and Wepwawet occasionally worked together as they guided the souls of the dead through the Underworld.[20] According to Hart, in non-royal mortuary texts, Wepwawet is the opener of ways in terms of guiding the deceased onto a good path in the Underworld.[21]

There are numerous examples from Mesoamerica of the dog and its relation to the deceased. Here, too, it is the dog's role to accompany the dead through the dangerous realm of the Underworld. His first task was to take his deceased master through the waters of the Underworld. Not unlike the maize god's trip through these waters in his canoe on the Tikal Bones (see Fig. II.8), there is a ceramic vessel where a dog is portrayed at the stern of a canoe accompanying an individual. The boat's downward tipping signified its descent into the waters of the Underworld.[22]

Mesoamericans are sometimes buried with an actual dog or a substitute ceramic one, which was expected to accompany their soul through treacherous waters to their final destination in the Underworld.[23] These dogs are guardians of the tomb as is the dog Anubis, the Egyptian god. Among the Lacandon Maya, small palm figures of dogs were placed at each corner of the burial mound to guard the soul during its netherworld journey.[24] Some painted designs on ceramic vessels show the dog with the deceased in a funeral procession (Fig. X.6). The man's trip is his last journey—the one to the Underworld. It is apropos, therefore, that a dog should accompany the deceased in this funerary promenade.[25]

Fig. X.6 Dog accompanies a Maya ruler at his funeral, vase from Ratinlinxul, Guatemala (redrawn after J. Eric S. Thompson 194: 38).

The Deer, the Sun, and the Tortoise

The Hittites in the Near East (a people who lived in Syria and Anatolia) had a tradition involving an anthropomorphic creature with deer antlers pushing the sun before it shows itself.[26] Writing on this theme in a museum collection, Borowski describes ceremonial standards that were widely used in the ancient Near East. Some had stags surrounding the rim of an openwork disc, which Borowski suggests is the sun.[27] It is easy to assimilate the branching antlers of a buck with rays of the sun.[28] In the Old World this type of deer symbolism is often interchanged with the horse, such as in Greek mythology where the sun chariot is pulled by horses.[29]

The animal most commonly associated with the day sun in Mesoamerica is the deer (the monkey would be a close second). In Maya calendrical distance numbers, it is the deer that personified the sign of *kin*, "sun."[30] Junell and Stross demonstrate a strong relationship between the Mayan Yucatec and the Mayan Cholan words for deer and west. In fact, for a time the Yucatec term for west was literally "deer sun."[31]

Fig. X.7 Deer and sun combination (redrawn after *Borgia Codex*).

A vivid example of this theme appears in the Central Mexican *Borgia Codex,* as the deer carries the sun on its back (Fig. X.7). The Huichol Indians of northern Mexico revered the deer as a major deity. The deer god played an important role at the beginning of the world when he lifted the newborn sun in his horns, making life possible on earth. He became regarded as a solar deity.[32] In Mayan *ceh* means "deer" and is associated with the number seven. The number seven among the Maya is connected to the earth's surface and, by extension, of the sun at horizon.[33] But, as we will see, the deer is not the only animal associated with the sun.

Lions and Jaguars

The two most magnificent felines of the Old and New Worlds were, respectively, the lion and the jaguar. These two large cats played a similar role in their geographical areas. There are several corresponding concepts with these animals, yet their association with the sun is preeminent. In Egypt one of the prime representations of the sun was the lion. Wilkinson surmises:

> Under the name *Hor-em-akhet* the god Horus assumed leonine form as the deity of the appearing sun, and although the identification of this god with the human-headed sphinx is a late one, it is possible that this composite animal originally had solar significance. The great Sphinx of Giza may thus represent its builder, Chephren, as the sun god.[34]

The famous Sphinx is anthropomorphic as it is a combination of lion and man. In the *Egyptian Book of the Dead,* lion is referred to as "bright of mouth and shining of head."[35] This refers to its sun-like qualities. The Egyptian cat could also represent the night sun—that is, the day sun as it travels through the Underworld.[36]

In Sumeria the lion represented the god Nergal, who was associated with the Underworld when, as the sun, he traveled through this realm. For this reason, the lion was connected to concepts of kingship in Mesopotamia,[37] similar to close ties of the sun with the Pharaoh in Egypt. Like the sun, the Sumerian deceased king was expected to be reborn after his sojourn through the Underworld.

In Mesoamerica we find no animal with greater strength than the jaguar. In the heavens nothing was more powerful than the sun. The ruler was frequently associated with this beast in light of its relationship to the sun, which could be either the day sun or the night sun.[38]

Another curious aspect of the lion and jaguar is their unusual depiction in a back-to-back arrangement. In Egypt this posture is related to the sun, where the lions guard the gates of the horizon through which the sun passes twice a day (Fig. X.8). The lions are sometimes labeled "yesterday" and "tomorrow," or "yesterday" and "today."[39] In Mesoamerica jaguars are occasionally positioned in like manner, although this is not necessarily interpreted as having the same expression as it did in Egypt. The sculpture of significance to this topic is located in Uxmal in the Yucatan (Fig. X.9). It is very much like its Egyptian counterpart in design. As to its meaning, one cannot be certain if there is a solar connotation, yet we do know this particular sculpture is a throne. Jaguar thrones among the Maya were often portrayed within a temple complex (see for example Fig. III.9). The one at Uxmal, on the other hand, is clearly out in the open.

Fig. X.8 Egyptian lion gods, back to back (redrawn after Budge 1969, Vol. 2: 98f).

Fig. X.9 Back to back jaguars, Uxmal, Yucatan, Mexico (redrawn after Baldwin 1872: Fig. 38).

Fig. X.10 Horus (Nerfertun) emerges from lotus (redrawn after Budge 1969: Vol. 1, 484).

In both Egypt and Mesoamerica gods were sometimes portrayed as born from flowers. In Egypt the flower associated with birth and resurrection is the lotus, particularly as seen in examples of the young Horus (Nefertum) rising as a child from the center of a water lily (Fig. X.10). Equally important among the Lacandon Maya who still live in Chiapas, Mexico, the Creator made the water lily from which gods are born.[40] A common theme found in clay sculptures from Jaina, an island off the Yucatan Peninsula in Mexico, is a figure rising from the center of a flower (Fig. X.11). M. Coe's interpretation is that the persons emerging from these Jaina flowers become deities at the moment of birth.[41]

Fig. X.11 Birth of a god from a flower, Jaina, Campeche, Mexico (redrawn after Kurbjuhn 1985a: 232).

In Egypt the flower most connected with the creation is surely the lotus, a type of water lily, which lived in the Primordial Waters.[42] In Mesoamerica it could be the water lily or a number of other flowers such as the Plumeria. For both the Mesoamericans and the Egyptians the water lily is frequently associated with ancestry, the Underworld, and with life and death.[43] As these flowers opened to catch the sun's rays in the morning light, so too were men and gods thought to be born as visualized in this beautiful metaphor for birth.

The Day of the Dead

Ancient Egyptians celebrated a special night of the year called the Feast of All Souls. This particular night was a time when dead ancestors were believed to visit their previous homes. The descendants of the deceased prepared food and drink for them and provided light to illuminate their dark path from the grave.[44]

To both the Egyptian and Mesoamerican communities, death was not regarded as the end of existence but was a step to the next level of continued life. It is not surprising that a similar rite was performed in Mesoamerica in honor of ancestors. This tradition originated in pre-Columbian times and is still held on the first of November. In many ways it is similar to present-day Halloween. The difference between Halloween and the Day of the Dead is perhaps the macabre aura of the western celebration as opposed to a joyous festival in Mesoamerican tradition. The Day of the Dead is considered a festival of welcome for the souls of the dead.[45] Both in Mesoamerica and Egypt, altars full of flowers, lights, and offerings of food are prepared for the ancestors.

Bones and Seeds

Tvedtnes states that for the ancient inhabitants of the Near East, the burial of the human body was paralleled by the planting of seeds.[46] In Jewish tradition there is a small bone called *luz,* or the almond bone in the spine. It was believed to never decay and became the seed from which the human body would grow for the resurrection.[47] This teaching may derive from the Egyptian concept of the sacrum at the base of the spine as the seat of Osiris's resurrection and the source of seed (semen), which carried the magic of new life.[48]

Conceptualizing bones as seeds awaiting rebirth is true of Mesoamerican cultures as well. In Mesoamerica the bones of the dead (particularly the skull) are considered seeds. For example, in Santiago Atitlan, Guatemala, maize seeds set aside for planting are called *muk,* meaning "interred ones," or even *jolooma,* indicating "little skulls."[49] The Maya word *bak* is also the word for "bone," while a similar pronunciation (but with a glottalized k) is the word for "seed."[50] J. Furst notes that the use of skulls by Mesoamerican peoples should not be interpreted as symbols of death but of life.[51] Bones are looked upon as seeds—something that, although appearing dead, would again regenerate new life.[52]

The Deceased as Stars

Although several ancient cultures viewed the stars as deceased souls, Gundel claims this idea is Egyptian in origin.[53] The concept of the deceased becoming stars in ancient Egypt is expressed in their Pyramid Texts which call the dead "Imperishable Ones."[54] Stars represent the souls of the dead.[55] These stars are thought of as eternal entities as they circle endlessly about the celestial pole.[56] From in the sky, the deceased are thought to visit the earth from time to time.[57] This concept is echoed in the Old Testament.

> [2]And many of them that sleep in the dust of the earth shall awake, some to everlasting life, and some to shame and everlasting contempt. [3]And they that be wise shall shine as the brightness of the firmament; and they that turn many to righteousness as the stars for ever and ever (Dan. 12:2–3).

In the *Egyptian Book of the Dead* the gods shout praises with the stars.[58] We are reminded of the biblical Hebrew text which states: "When the morning stars sang together, and all the sons of God shouted for joy " (Job 38:7). And in Jewish Merkabah mysticism, going back to the second century A.D., texts express the concept of astral immortality for those who lived wise and righteous lives while on earth.[59]

In Mesoamerica, the Quiché Maya also believe their ancestors become stars after death.[60] Moreover, Sol Tax informed Eric Thompson that there was a clear notion among the Maya that when a person died he becomes a star—the better the person, the bigger the star.[61]

Funerary Goods and Sacrifices

It is well known that numerous ancient cultures buried goods with their dead. Perhaps no one did it with more aplomb than the Egyptians. Pharaohs were buried with food and lavish objects they would consider necessary for their post-mortal journey into the "beyond." Such items included wine, honey, fruits, bread, fish, and fowl. For royal women even cosmetics were supplied for their beautification in the hereafter. Fine linen and clothing were also displayed for the deceased. From the eloquent furnishings of King Tutankhamun's tomb we know deceased kings were equipped with all types of furniture. Implements of war were also supplied so the king could defend himself on his journey against the denizens of the Underworld.[62]

The first Pharaohs of Egypt were accompanied by their servants in death. These individuals were sacrificed to serve the king in the hereafter as they had done while he lived. The custom was apparently also practiced in Mesopotamia.[63] In addition to slaves, dwarves and dogs were buried with the dead Egyptian king. This may be of special significance as will be pointed out later.

In Mesoamerica we find a similar situation. For example, at Tikal, Guatemala, M. Miller reports: "When Maya kings were prepared for interment, they were splendidly equipped for their journey and transformation in the underworld, and funerary furniture often reflected these concerns in its iconography."[64] The king's war implements were also laid about for his use in battling his enemies in the Underworld.[65] Vessels containing food were frequently buried with the dead in Mesoamerica. Human remains of the sacrificed were sometimes found interred with the dead king.[66] According to Bancroft, the purpose of this practice in Mesoamerica was to provide slaves to serve their master in the other world.[67]

The significance of dogs buried with royalty in both Egypt and Mesoamerica has been mentioned, as the dog was considered a guide to the dead in both locales. However, the fact that dwarves were also buried with the deceased in both Egypt and Mesoamerica is an unusual parallel. Durán reports this custom in his research, which was completed in 1581 shortly after the Spanish Conquest. He notes that among the Indians of Mexico it was a custom to sacrifice and bury hunchbacks and dwarves who served the king, in order to continue their service in the afterlife.[68]

Wheeled Funerary Objects

In the ancient Near East funerary cult, objects on wheels were made, and this practice continued for thousands of years.[69] These miniature vehicles found in a burial context are a noted likeness to such objects found in Mesoamerica. Miniature clay vehicles in the form of animals were discovered in Mesopotamia, and they too are remarkably similar to those from Mexico and Central America (Fig. X.12).[70]

More than seventy wheeled terracotta figurines have been found in Mesoamerica, the earliest dating back to 100 B.C.[71] The Museum of Anthropology in Jalapa, Veracruz, displays several of these wheeled clay animals. The most significant are three placed in a funerary vessel along with the remains of a human skull. The geographical areas where most of the wheeled pieces were discovered are Western Central Mexico, Veracruz in Mexico, and El Salvador.[72]

Fig. X.12 Animal on wheels, Mesopotamia (drawn after photograph in Ferguson 1958: 103).

In Mesoamerica these clay objects can be described as standing animal effigies mounted on four solid, disk wheels attached with wooden axles. Due to the fragile organic nature of wood, no axles survived to our day. Scholars report that five ways to attach wheels were used.[73] This is significant and suggests that early Mesoamericans were not novices in the use of axles. What is noteworthy is that besides the typical full-bodied animals with attached wheels (Fig. X.13), at least one had a body that transformed into a flatbed or platform (Fig. X.14). Another animal (actually a monkey skin) rides on a wheeled platform (Fig. X.15). Wheeled objects with flatbeds carrying an animal were also popular in Mesopotamia (Fig. X.16).

As these Mesoamerican wheeled objects were buried with the dead it might be concluded that they are symbolic vehicles of transport for the dead, as similar pieces are in the Near East. Like the sun, the deceased would descend into the Underworld, pass through it, and be reborn in the morning. In Mesoamerican thought, the solar cycle, the calendar round, and the cyclic belief in life, all point to the shape of a sacred wheel.

Fig. X.13   Wheeled animal, Tres Zapotes, Veracruz, Mexico (drawn after artifact on display at Museum of Jalapa, Veracruz, Mexico).

Fig. X.14 Wheeled animal with flatbed back, Nahualac, Mexico (drawn after photograph in Boggs 1973: Fig. 1).

Fig. X.15   A monkey skin rides on a wheeled platform, Veracruz, Mexico (drawn after photograph in Sorenson 1998: 59).

Fig. X.16   Limestone lion on a platform wheeled cart, Susa, the capital of Elam in modern (drawn after photograph in *Biblical Archaeology Review* 1996, 22/5: 80).

F. Gibson, who lived among the Maya and studied their ways, finds religious importance behind the symbol of the wheel. Many of the Maya in remote areas of Guatemala still walk and choose to carry heavy loads rather than use a wheeled cart. Gibson asked the Maya why they still do this after having been exposed to wheels for over four hundred years. Their response was that the wheel was a symbol of the ancient sun god and was a sacred symbol.[74]

Although these figurines portray a variety of animals, the majority are dogs (see Fig. X.13). Dogs exhibit a special meaning in Old and New World mythologies having to do with the afterlife. Being closely associated with the sun, the dog knew the way through the foreboding Underworld. Other animals that are depicted on these wheeled figurines are deer, large cats, and monkeys—all associated with the sun in Mesoamerica and parts of the Middle East.

Incense and Horned Altars

Incense was employed in many areas of the ancient world and is still used today. However, there are some interesting similar conceptions incorporated in the significance of burning incense with its resulting smoke that exists between the ancient Middle East and Mesoamerica. When incense was burned before a Pharaoh, it had a cleansing and purifying quality. Incense was also offered to the gods and in a sense was a manifestation of the god when it was burned.[75] The rising smoke was the connecting link between man and his gods. The fumes were considered the words of power from the individual making the offering.[76]

Another interesting facet of incense smoke was its use in funerary rites. Budge explains that a passage in the Pyramid Text of Pepi II shows the soul of the deceased ascending into heaven by means of the incense that was burned on his behalf.[77] The fish ascending in incense smoke on Stela 5, Izapa (see Fig. IV:15), may represent the deceased ancestral couple as mentioned in Chapter IV.

In Mesoamerica there is a great variety of material used as incense. This includes tree resins such as copal, rubber, and chicle. Ceramic censers buried with the dead indicate that incense was important in a funerary context.[78] For example, a Zoquean group called the Sierra Popoluca from the area of the Isthmus of Tehuantepec, Mexico, used copal smoke to return souls of animals killed in a hunt.[79]

Incense was also a way of purification for native Mesoamericans. It seals the interaction between the object or purified individual and the gods.[80] Among the Lacandon Maya, incense burners called god-pots are used as tangible representations of deities rather than the carved images of the gods.[81] As in the Near East, prayers were offered to the gods as incense smoke billowed towards the heavens.[82] The smoke itself is a metaphor for speech.[83]

Many incensarios in Mesoamerica have three legs, but we note that one such cult stand with three legs from Megiddo made by the Israelites was reported in *Biblical Archaeology Review*, Jan/Feb 1998, page 46.

The horned altar of Israel presents another fascinating tradition. It is directly associated with the burning of incense (Fig. X.17).[84] Nielsen believes these horned altars may have supported a bowl of incense, and Haran notices that it is likely a little frankincense was added to bread cakes,[85] which were a popular offering on these altars.[86] This practice coincides with Mesoamerica where grain was often mixed with incense.[87]

Most incense burners in Mesoamerica do not have horned appendages at the top. However, a very interesting burner was found at Monte Alban, Oaxaca, Mexico. It fits the description of the four-horned motif of the Hebrews (Fig. X.18). A similar one found in Guatemala is reported by Borhegyi, which also has a horned stand for an incense burner.[88]

Fig. X.17 Limestone incense altar, Megiddo, about 1000 B.C. (drawn after photograph in Nielsen, June 1991: 28).

Banners and Sacredness

According to Hornung, the Egyptian hieroglyph for god, *ntr,* is a staff bound with cloth. The end consisted of two to four streamers. This banner did not represent the god itself, but where the staff was grounded is an indication of the presence of a deity. Anciently flagpoles stood at the entrance pylons of Egyptian temples, which designated the site as sanctified by the gods. Hornung explains that strips of cloth are also an important accouterment of a god's costume and are more than a decoration. The wrapping of cloth around a staff is clearly identified with the process of mummification when the deceased is prepared for the afterlife. This type of symbolism exists in modern times from North Africa through the Sudan. Flagpoles are set at the entrance to tombs, and according to Hornung, is evidently a tradition that went back to ancient Egyptian times.[89]

It is not known how early similar customs with banners took root in Mesoamerica. However, during the wanderings of the Aztec, certain objects represented the presence of a deity. These markers might have been a reed, arrow, or a staff to which was attached white bark paper. Sometimes banners were placed at the tops of temples to indicate a divine presence.[90] This concept is not much different than its counterpart in the Middle East. It should also be noted that banners were set alongside mummy bundles in Mesoamerica (Fig. X.19).

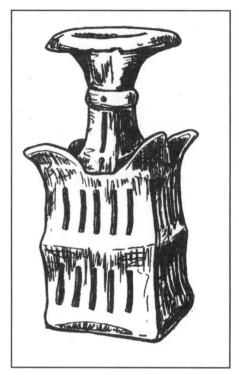

Fig. X.18 Horned incense burner, Monte Alban, Oaxaca, Mexico. Housed at National Museum of Anthropology, Mexico City.

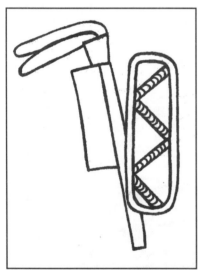

Fig. X.19 Funerary banner with mummy bundle (redrawn after *Borgia Codex*, Plate 70.

Traditions with Captives

Three practices pertaining to captives that are paralleled in both Egypt and Mesoamerica are important to this study.

Standing or Sitting on Captive

From artistic expression, we find rulers who sit or stand on prisoners. In Egypt, sitting or standing on one's enemy had special significance and several texts exist that describe such acts (Figure X.20).

King Tutankhamen's sandals depicted foreign enemies, so that whenever he walked he was treading on them. Enemies were sometimes pictured on the floors so members of the royal court could step on their bodies. Tutankhamen's canes portrayed foes in such a way that every time he grasped these implements he was crushing his enemies.[91]

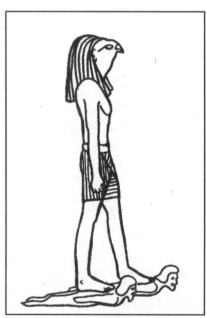

Fig. X.20 Horus stands on enemies (redrawn after Budge 1987: 357).

Seth was the enemy of Osiris and his son Horus. Referring to an Egyptian Pyramid Text, Budge explains that Osiris "made his seat." That is, he seated himself upon the body of Seth in triumph over him.[92] This was meant to humiliate the conquered and to establish supreme authority. Among the Hebrews, no visual imagery exists of them standing or sitting on their enemy as there is in Egypt; and yet there are numerous scriptures in the Old Testament that speak of treading on one's enemies or foes being put under one's feet.[93] We find an identical symbolic statement among the Maya.

Depictions of rulers seated on their enemy may be more widespread among the Maya than among the Egyptians (Fig. X.21). This act was often performed at the time of accession of a ruler to the throne where the text states: "he was seated."[94] This phrasing is similar to Egyptian statements of authority and rulership as noted above.

Fig. X.21   A Maya king, Tablet of the Slaves, Palenque, Mexico (drawn by Linda Schele, © by David Schele, in Freidel, Schele, and Parker 1993: 307, Fig. 7:14).

Grasping the Hair of Captive

The grasping of an enemy's hair is the second feature common to the cultures to consider. The famed green-stone ceremonial Palette of Narmer in Egypt shows a prime example of the practice (Fig. X.22). An Egyptian writing known as the Unas Text states: "Am-Rehau, who seizes the hair on top of the head, ropes [his enemies] together."[95] In Mesoamerica this tradition appears in the *Codex Nuttall* where the Mixtec ruler, 8 Deer, is capturing a man by the name of 4 Wind (Fig. X.23). The Maya use the same artistic expression to portray the capture of their enemies.

Fig. X.22 Narmer captures an enemy (redrawn after Budge 1987: 23).

Fig. X.23 Mixtec conqueror 8 Deer captures 4 Wind (redrawn after *Codex Nuttall*).

Jaw Removal of Captive

The last practice is the removal of the lower jaw of a victim in a sacrificial rite. This tradition is significant to both Egyptian and Mesoamerican cultures. The *Egyptian Book of the Dead* says that Horus smote the jawbone of his enemies. Budge maintains that his study of the modern tribes of West Africa brought meaning to this ancient practice. Horus destroyed the jawbones of his deceased enemies as illustrated by the custom in Ashantee and Dahomey. They wrenched the jawbones from the heads of dead foes and sent them to their kings.[96] Budge also makes it clear that Horus destroyed the jawbones of his father's enemies as the jawbone was in some special way the seat of the soul.[97]

Fig. X.24 Hand replaces jaw of sacrificial victim (redrawn after Schele and Miller 1986: 54).

According to Schele and Miller, the Maya actually removed the lower jaw from living victims.[98] A number of gods in the Maya pantheon are depicted with scrolls of blood coming from a missing lower jaw. In these cases a human hand is shown gripping the area of the lower jaw (Fig. X.24).

In addition, the practice of smoking the jawbones of animals by the Sierra Popoluca of Mexico is noteworthy. The custom enabled the soul of an animal to find its way to the hereafter.[99] This is the same ritual mentioned in the discussion of incense smoke in which animal souls were carried to heaven. It is a reminder of Budge's statement that to the Egyptians the jawbone represented the seat of the soul.

These three practices, world's apart, violated and humiliated the enemy. They were obviously visual symbols of power and a warning to those of the opposition that the rulers and their gods held the reigns of authority in the land.

Accessories for Clothing

Many similar accessories of the cultures considered have already been mentioned, such as the hair cloak covering, the scribes' wearing apparel, the U-shaped headdress, and garments containing the net pattern. There is another item that needs to be addressed, and that is the earflares worn in Mesoamerica and ear ornaments worn by the Egyptians.

Mesoamericans were noted for their large earflares, often made of jade or shell. This motif is comprised of a circular disc with a hole (Fig. X.25a). Protruding from the hole is a long tubular bead with a small round bead affixed to the end. The various pieces are held together by a string with a weight hung on the backside of the earlobe. There are many illustrations of this type of earflare worn by individuals in the previous chapters. It has been determined by Schele that the earflare, tubular bead, and small bead assemblage represent a flower.[100] The circular earflare is the calyx (from which petals and organs grow), and the long cylindrical bead is the pistil (the seed bearing organ of a flower).[101] An even more pronounced design of a hanging flower from an earflare can be seen on an Olmec pectoral dated between 1000—600 B.C. (see Fig. VI.9).

Interesting ear ornaments from Egypt bring to our attention a parallel concept of the earflare worn by Mesoamericans (Fig. 25b). These Egyptian earrings were made of glass, bone, ivory, gold, alabaster or wood. The most striking feature are the holes, which scholars suggest were stuffed with freshly cut flower in the center of the hole cavities.[102]

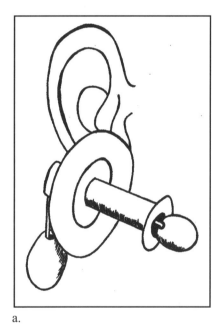

a.

b.

Fig. X.25   Flower ear ornaments. a. Maya earflare exhibiting a flower design with jade pieces (after Wagner 2000: 68). b. Egyptian glass ear ornament specifically made to hold flowers (after photograph in *Biblical Archaeology Review* Nov/Dec 2002: 22).

NOTES - Chapter X

1. Aylward M. Blackman, "The Rite of Opening the Mouth in Ancient Egypt and Babylonia," *Journal of Egyptian Archaeology* 10/Pt. I (1924), 48.
2. Hornung, *Conceptions of God*, 221-23.
3. Hornung, *Idea Into Image*, 45.
4. Wilkinson, *Symbol & Magic*, 137.
5. *Egyptian Book of the Dead*, Plate 6.
6. Miller and Taube, 53.
7. Stross, "Maize and Blood," 85.
8. Clemency Chase Coggins, "The Birth of the Baktun at Tikal and Seibal," in *Vision and Revision in Maya Studies*, Flora S. Clancy and Peter D. Harrison, eds. (Albuquerque: University of New Mexico Press, 1990), 89.
9. Schele and Mathews, *The Code of Kings*, 166, 350 n.36.
10. Gutierrez, 2-3.
11. Heinrich Berlin, "Nominal Glyphs of the Palenque Sarcophagus," *Texas Notes on Precolumbian Art, Writing, and Culture,* trans. Khristaan D. Villela, 37 (Austin: Center of the History and Art of Ancient American Culture of the Art Department, University of Texas, 1993), 11.
12. Samuel Alfred Brown Mercer, *The Pyramidi Texts*, vol. 4 (London: Longmans, Green, 1951), 214.
13. Schele and Miller, 61.
14. Budge, *The Gods of the Egyptians*, I: 466-67; Miller and Taube, 154-55.
15. Budge, Ibid., I: 418.
16. Personal communication from John Tvedtnes to Diane Wirth, April 9, 1999.
17. Wilkinson, *Reading Egyptian Art*, 65.
18. Bruce J. Long, "Underworld," in *The Encyclopedia of Religion*, Mircea Eliade, ed., vol. 15 (New York: Macmillan Publishing Co., 1987), 129.
19. Morenz, 271.
20. Spence, 105.
21. Hart, *A Dictionary of Egyptian Gods*, 223.
22. Reents-Budet, 352.
23. Burr Cartwright Brundage, *The Jade Steps: A Ritual Life of the Aztecs* (Salt Lake City: University of Utah Press, 1985), 196; Miller and Taube, 39, 178.
24. Peterson, 40.
25. MacLeod and Kerr, 70-71.
26. Golan, 52.
27. Elie Borowski, "Against All Odds," *Biblical Archaeology Review* 19/2 (1992), 53.
28. Goldsmith, 263.
29. Personal communication from John Tvedtnes to Diane Wirth, April 9, 1999.
30. Basie-Sweet, 183-84.
31. Cathy Junell and Brian Stross, "The Deer as Western Sun," in *U Mut Maya V*, Carolyn and Tom Jones, eds. (Arcata, California: U Mut Maya, 1994), 237.
32. Fernando Benitez, *The Magic Land of Peyote* (Austin: University of Austin Press, 1975), 90.
33. Marvin Cohodas, "The Iconography of the Panels of the Sun, Cross, and Foliated Cross at Palenque: Part II," in *Primera Mesa Redonda de Palenque, Part I*, Merle Greene-Robertson, ed. (Monterey, California: Robert Louis Stevenson School, 1974), 95.
34. Wilkinson, *Reading Egyptian Art*, 69.
35. *Egyptian Book of the Dead*, Plate 10.
36. M. Oldfield Howey, *The Cat in Magic, Mythology, and Religion* (New York: Crescent Books, 1989), 23.
37. Henry O. Thompson, "Tell el-Husn—Biblical Beth-shan," *Biblical Archaeologist* 30/4 (1967), 110-35.
38. Miller and Taube, 104.
39. Wilkinson, *Reading Egyptian Art*, 68.
40. Robert D. Bruce, "Jerarquia Maya Entre los Dioses Lacandons," in *Anales de I.N.A.H.* (Mexico: Instituto Nacional de Antropologia e Historia, 1967), 220.

41. Michael D. Coe, "Three Maya Figurines from Jaina Island," *Yale University Art Gallery Bulletin* 35 (New Haven: Yale University, 1975).

42. d'Auria, Lacovara, and Roehrig, 199.

43. Francis Robicsek, *The Maya Book of the Dead: The Ceramic Codex* (Charlottesville, Virginia: University of Virginia Art Museum, 1981), 149; Wilkinson, *Reading Egyptian Art*, 121. Also, in both Hebrew and Egyptian, some words suggest a tie between flowering and childbirth. For example, in Hebrew the root *p-r- h* (where *peri*, "fruit") means "be fruitful" for humans, animals, and plants. The Egyptian cognate *pry* ("come out") gives us *prw* ("motion, excess, surplus"), *pr.t* ("fruit, seed"), and *prw* ("sprout"). Information supplied by John Tvedtnes to Diane Wirth, April 9, 1999.

44. James G. Frazer, *The Golden Bough* (New York: Macmillan Company, 1942), 374.

45. Chloë Sayer, *The Skeleton at the Feast: The Day of the Dead in Mexico* (Austin: University of Texas Press, 1991), 9.

46. Tvedtnes, 5.

47. Louis Ginsberg, *The Legends of the Jews*, 7 vols. (1909; reprint, Philadelphia: The Jewish Publications Society of America, 1953), V: 81, 184, 363. In addition, John Tvedtnes has supplied the following information on the bone called *luz* from the Jewish Midrash Rabbah Genesis 28.3, "Hadrian (may his bones be ground) asked R. Yehoshua ben Hanania: 'From what will the Holy One, blessed be He, rebuild the bodies of the dead in the future to come?' He said to him: 'From the *luz* [a bone] of the spine.' He said to him: 'How do you know?' He said to him: 'Give me one, and I shall show you.' He cast it into the fire, and it did not burn. He put it into water, and it did not dissolve. He ground it between millstones, and it could not be ground. He put it on an anvil and hit it with a hammer—the anvil split in two and the hammer broke, but the *luz* was not damaged" (Midrash Rabbah 1961 [orig. 1939], 2:223).

48. Walker, 302.

49. Nathaniel Tarn and Martin Prechtel, "Metaphors of relative elevation, position and ranking in Popol Vuh," *Estud. Cult. Maya* 13 (1981).

50. Personal communication from Brian Stross to Diane Wirth, September 7, 1998.

51. Jill Leslie Furst, *Codex Vindobonensis Mexicanus*, 318.

52. Jill Leslie Furst, "Skeletonization in Mixtec Art: A re-evaluation," in *The Art and Iconography of Late Post-Classic Central Mexico*, E. H. Boone, ed. (Washington, D.C., Dumbarton Oaks, 1982), 221.

53. Ioan Petru Culianu, "Sky: The Heavens as Hierophany," in *The Encyclopedia of Religion*, vol. 13, ed. Mircea Eliade (New York: MacMillan Publishing Company, 1987), 345.

54. E. L. Highbarger, *The Gates of Dreams* (Baltimore, 1940), 10.

55. Wilkinson, *Reading Egyptian Art*, 131.

56. Hornung, *The Valley of the Kings*, 87.

57. Budge, *Osiris*, II, 155.

58. Budge, *The Gods of the Egyptians*, I: 201.

59. E. R. Goodenough, *Jewish Symbols in the Greco-Roman Period*, abridged edition, Jacob Neusner, ed. (Princeton: Princeton University Press, 1988), 155.

60. Michel Graulich, *Myths of Ancient Mexico* (Norman: University of Oklahoma, 1997), 111.

61. J. Eric S. Thompson, *Maya Hieroglyphic Writing*, 85.

62. Hornung, *The Valley of the Kings*, 168.

63. Ibid., 183.

64. Mary Ellen Miller, 116.

65. Fray Diego Durán, *The Aztecs: The History of the Indians of New Spain*, trans. Doris Heyden and Fernando Horcasites (New York: Orion Press, 1964), 177.

66. Mary Ellen Miller, 116.

67. Bancroft, II: 799.

68. Durán, "The Aztecs," 177.

69. M. A. Littauer and J. H. Crouwel, *Wheeled Vehicles and Ridden Animals in the Ancient Near East* (Leiden: Brill, 1979), 80.

70. Gordon F. Ekholm, "Wheeled Toys in Mexico," *American Antiquity* 11/3 (1946), 227.

71. Stanley H. Boggs, "Salvadoran Varieties of Wheeled Figurines," *Contributions to Mesoamerican Anthropology*, Pub. No. 1 (Miami: Institute of Maya Studies of the Museum of Science, 1973), 3.

72. Stephan F. Borhegyi, "Wheels and Man," *Archaeology* 23 (January 1970), 24.
73. Gordon F. Ekholm, 222-28.
74. Frances Gibson, *The Seafarers: Pre-Columbian Voyages to America* (Philadelphia: Dorrance & Co., 1974), 63.
75. Wilkinson, *Symbol & Magic*, 92.
76. Budge, *Osiris*, II: 175. An association of prayers and incense was also made in the Bible; e.g., in Psalms 141:2 it reads, "Let my prayer be set before thee as incense," and written later in Revelation 8:3-4 by John after offering incense, he saw the prayers of the saints rise before God.
77. Budge, *Osiris*, II: 255.
78. Michael D. Coe, "Ideology of the Maya Tomb," 231.
79. George Foster, "Sierra Popoluca Folklore and Beliefs," *University of California Publications on American Archaeology and Ethnology* 42/2 (Los Angeles: University of California, 1991), 186.
80. Miller and Taube, 99.
81. J. Eric S. Thompson, *Maya History and Religion*, 76.
82. Ibid., 191.
83. Heyden, "Metaphors, Nahualtocaitl," 37.
84. See Exod. 30:2
85. Kjeld Nielsen, "Ancient Aromas: Good and Bad," *Bible Review* (June 1991), 29.
86. Menahem Haran, "Altar-ed States," *Bible Review* (February 1995), 36.
87. Alfred M. Tozzer, "Landa's Relación de las Cosas de Yucatán," *Papers of the Peabody Museum of American Archaeology and Ethnology*, vol. 18 (Cambridge, Massachusetts: Harvard University, 1941), 104, 142.
88. Stephan F. Borhegyi, "El Incensario de 'Tres Asas' de Kaminaljuyu, Guatemala," *Historia de Guatemala*, 8(2) (1956).
89. Hornung, "Politische Planung," 34-38.
90. Brundage, 68.
91. Information from John Gee via John Tvedtnes to Diane Wirth, April 14, 1999.
92. Budge, *Osiris*, I: 27.
93. See for example 1 Kings 5:3; Psalms 18:37-38; Isaiah 10:6.
94. Schele and Miller, 121.
95. Budge, *Osiris*, I: 20.
96. Ibid., II: 91-93.
97. Ibid., Introduction: vii.
98. Schele and Miller, 54, 61.
99. George Foster.
100. Freidel, Schele, and Parker, 394.
101. Elizabeth Wagner, "Jade – the Green Gold of the Maya," in *Maya: Divine Kings of the Rain Forest*, Nicolai Grube, ed. (Cologne, Germany: Könemann Verlagsgesellschaft mbH, 2000), 68.
102. *Biblical Archaeology Review*, 28/6 (2002), 21-22.

EPILOGUE

Archaeologists dig into the refuse left by ancient cultures and only a minute fraction of the tangible things people used in their daily lives are left to be discovered. Belief systems are even more fragile and much is left to interpretation by scholars. The many diverse scientific disciplines such as linguistics, botany, archaeology, geology, genetics, anthropology, etc., all contribute to our understanding the relationship between various cultures. Each year with its technological advances brings new light to the field of Mesoamerican studies and to the more fully understood, the Middle East.

DENIAL OF TRANSOCEANIC VOYAGES

Mainstream isolationists demand extremely high levels of substantiation for theories supporting cultural inter-hemispheric diffusion. Anything less will not pose a threat to the prevailing traditional view that no contact across the oceans occurred. For the most part, the refusal to accept any idea that overseas contacts with Mesoamerica ever occurred has discouraged the airing of alternative explanations at university symposiums sponsored by departments of archaeology and anthropology, in professional journals, and especially in university publications. As discussed in the Introduction of this book, the majority of doctoral-level anthropology and archaeology graduates have gone on to teach the theories they learned as the basics of their field. As a result, most students of Mesoamerican studies are simply not of a mind to vary from the established theories they were taught at their universities.

Inflexibility

Cyrus Gordon, a distinguished scholar of Near Eastern studies, with more than 600 publications to his credit, once met Aleš Hrdlika, an influential dean of American archaeology. Gordon writes of Hrdlika's opposition to diffusionism and his unyielding position on this subject.

> His dogma was that Old World man entered pre-Columbian America by only one route: across the Bering Strait. Unless a young anthropologist subscribed to that view, it was virtually impossible for him to get a museum or university job in American anthropology or archaeology. This explains some of the inflexibility in that field down to the present.[1]

Today, however, Mesoamerican studies are constantly evolving. Ideas that held sway until the early 1950s, for example, have changed considerably. The great Mayanist, J. Eric S. Thompson, who was associated with the Carnegie Institution of Washington, dominated Maya studies for many years. Few, if any, dared contradict his theories. Even though he was one of the finest scholars in the field for his time, his illusions of a peaceful Maya culture, and especially his views on hieroglyphic writing, are now being rejected. Out of respect for him and his many great contributions to Maya studies, the decipherment of Maya texts was thwarted for many years. Thompson investigated calendar glyphs and made significant advancements in the field; however, he ignored any possible decipherment of hieroglyphic texts. He was actually of the opinion that it could never be accomplished. The suggestion by some early scholars that the individual components of a hieroglyph were phonetic was debunked by Thompson. He believed glyphs had only mysterious, mystical meanings that could not be interpreted by scholars.[2] He was wrong!

Independent Thinking

An unknown Russian author and researcher by the name of Yuri Knorosov wrote a paper entitled "Ancient Writing of Central America," which was published in an anthropological journal by the Academy of Sciences of the U.S.S.R. in 1952. Today Knorosov's research is recognized as having led to interpreting the Maya script.[3] He was not under the influence of current opinions of the time as pronounced by Thompson. Knorosov was an independent thinker and his work grew in isolation from the rest of the intellectual world of Maya studies. M. Coe noted that Knorosov's methodology would lead the way to the full decipherment.[4] For those interested in the subject, an excellent discussion of the history of interpreting Maya hieroglyphs may be found in Coe's *Breaking the Maya Code* (Thames and Hudson, 1992).

Scholars Are Not Infallible

A lesson we may all learn from Thompson's mistakes is that even the most respected individual in his field may espouse incorrect theories. As a highly recognized scholar, Thompson unknowingly impeded progress in epigraphic studies as he was determined to spread his personal views, considering everyone else's ideas on the subject of Maya hieroglyphs as ludicrous and fanciful. This greatly hurt Mesoamerican research and we cannot help wonder if this is exactly what is happening today with regard to the topic of cultural diffusion (transoceanic voyages from the Old World to the New World). After Knorosov's ground breaking research was made known in *The New York Times,* Thompson made light of Knorosov's work and attempted to not only discredit his logic but to destroy him as a person. Thompson went so far as to call Knorosov's decipherment "a Russian propaganda ploy."[5] Soon after this Russian's work was published, especially in additional languages, others took up the banner and recognized the validity of Knorosov's thesis. Thompson died in 1975 and since that time great strides have been taken by epigraphers who continually crack the Maya code.

Scholars who voice their opinion deserve applause. The outspoken Shanks, a prominent Near Eastern specialist, advised, "It is true that books on archaeology of Jerusalem, including my own, now contain a lot of misinformation. More bluntly, they are wrong. The lesson: The archaeological story is never finished."[6] The same is certainly true of Mesoamerican archaeology.

The Mesoamerican symbol system endured for hundreds of years from beginning to end. Therefore, iconographic components remained recognizable with limited variations in form, meaning, and content. The same may be said in the ancient Near East, yet somewhat to a lesser degree due to the diverse surrounding cultures. In other words, images and traditions from the past present a long persistent life span in Mesoamerica. In light of this view, apparent time gaps between the ancient Near East and Mesoamerica would seem to become narrower.

For most scholars, voyages from the Old World to Mesoamerica have not been scientifically determined or pinpointed. Was there more than one transoceanic crossing or many? Were these excursions before the Christian era or after? These are questions that need to be answered with further investigation and, perhaps, new discovery of tangible evidence. Also, what constitutes proof? Perhaps, as attempted here, it is a repetitious but diversified system of referents.

An assortment of data is presented here from non-Indians with beards to DNA studies, from a comparison of dying and resurrecting grain gods to themes of creation and re-creation, from symbolism of the fish and rebirth to the association of men with flowers, from the theme of the king as the World Tree to his close subordinate, the scribe; and from themes of nature, earth, and sky, to the great mountain/temple of creation. Specific information supports these ideas in many diverse and complex ways. We see a multitude of coinciding elements that should be considered potentially diffused cultural traits that span the continents.

Works of art in Mesoamerica and the ancient Middle East were often metaphorical images. They were to assist the lay person to better understand a concept containing multilayered meanings. This phenomenon runs like a golden thread through our study of traditions that are central to the cultures considered in this analogous discussion. To better assimilate these various concepts, comparison tables follow (corresponding to Chapters II through X) to show the intricacy of these plausibly shared principles and, hopefully, to stimulate a reappraisal of what has been said about cultural diffusion.

THE GRAIN GODS OF EGYPT AND MESOAMERICA

	EGYPT	MAYA IN MESOAMERICA
The Characters		
Grain God	Osiris	Hun Hunahpu
Son(s) of Grain God	Horus (loses a hand)	Hero Twins: Hunahpu (loses an arm) and Xbalanque
The Enemy	Seth, a lord of death (who wanted to be like the Sun)	Lords of Death and Vucub Caquix (who wanted to be the Sun of this Creation)
The Acts		
The killing of Grain God	By decapitation and dismemberment	By decapitation
Placement of Grain God's body after death	Body parts of Osiris placed in a tree	Head of Hun Hunahpu hung in a tree
Deceased Grain God has progeny	Through sperm, although offspring were sometimes born of spittle by Egyptian gods	Through spittle
Trials in Underworld	Deceased must face	Deceased must face
Destroying the enemy	Horus defeats Seth	Hero Twins defeat Lords of Death and Vucub Caquix
Germination	Body of Osiris sprouts grain	Head of Hun Hunahpu sprouts maize
Fish transformation	Deceased persons (a type of Osiris) are sometimes portrayed as fish	Hero Twins become fish after their ashes thrown in river
Sun and Moon transformation	The eyes of Horus represent the Sun and the Moon	Working in concert, one Hero Twin becomes the Sun, the other the Moon
A Lord of the Underworld	Osiris becomes Lord of the Underworld. He is reborn, but cannot leave the Underworld	Hun Hunahpu lives in Ballcourt of the Underworld. He is reborn, but can not leave the Underworld
Associations		
Living King	Pharaoh associated with Horus	King associated with Hero Twins
Deceased King	Pharaoh associated with Osiris	King associated with Hun Hunahpu
Chaos & Rebirth	Osiris reborn during five epagomenal days at end of year	Hun Hunahpu reborn during five epagomenal days at end of year
Sacrifice of Substitute King	During Sed Festival of renewal, king appears as reborn	Ritual sacrifices substitute for king, as well as victim in ballgame. King appears as reborn

CREATION AND RE-CREATION (A)

	Mesopotamia	Near East (Israel)
Creation Myths and the Monster	Tiamat split, the body parts became heaven and earth	
Council of Gods		God among assembly of gods in Psalms & elsewhere
Creation by "Word"		Creation took place through God's word
Meaning of New Year	Time of renewal comparable to day of creation	Time of renewal comparable to day of creation
Measuring Sacred Space		Boundaries measured at the time of creation
Processional Walk		King made processional walk on New Year's day around his domain
Cleansing Sacred Space	Area purified, evil removed	Area purified, evil removed
Fire Kindling		
The Creation Play	New Year *Akitu* festival time of performing creation play	Israelite New Year festival time of creation play where chaos defeated
Raising World Tree		
Ritual Rebirth	At New Year, king symbolically died and was reborn	

CREATION AND RE-CREATION (B)

	Egypt	Mesoamerica
Creation Myths and the Monster		Monster torn apart, pieces became all things on earth
Council of Gods		Council of gods as in *Popol Vuh* and Vase of Seven Gods
Creation by "Word"	Creation took place through God's word	In the *Popol Vuh*, the gods spoke and creation took place
Meaning of New Year	Time of renewal comparable to day of creation	Time of renewal comparable to day of creation
Measuring Sacred Space	Stretching the cord ceremony by Pharaoh symbolized an act of creation	Supernaturals measured earth and sky with cords at creation. Rituals recreated event
Processional Walk	Pharaoh walked the "Circuit of the Wall" at the Sed Festival	New Year processions designated areas of sacred space--world was reborn
Cleansing Sacred Space	Area purified, evil removed	Area purified, evil removed
Fire Kindling	New Fire kindled at Sed Festival by Pharaoh	Fire lit at New Year and at time of inaugural cememonies
The Creation Play	King shown defeating enemies (chaos) on Shabako stone--a re-creation ritual. Re-creation ceremonies necessary for world's continuance	Reiteration of *Popol Vuh* creation story performed. Re-creation ceremonies necessary for world's continuance
Raising World Tree	Raising the Djed-Pillar at Sed Festival	Raising of World Tree at New Year Festival
Ritual Rebirth	Pharaoh performed annual ritual playing role of the dying and resurrecting god	Aztec king performed ritual where he symbolically died and was reborn

THE FISH, TRANSITION, AND RELATED SYMBOLISM

	Near East (general)	Old World (Mediterranean and/or European)	Egypt	Mesoamerican
Fish Symbol of:				
Embryo/Fetus	X	X	0	X
Womb Area	0	X	0	X
Rebirth	X	X	X	X
Fertility	X	X	X	X
Transition of Soul	0	X	X	X
Fish Associated with:				
Mother Goddesses	0	X	0	X
Funerary Items	0	X	X	X
Men	X	X	X	X
Grain	0	?	X	X
Shells	0	X	0	X
Acts Performed:				
Catching Fish for Rebirth	0	0	X	X
Birth from Serpents	0	?	X	X

GENEALOGY & RELATED SYMB0LISM

	Near East (general)	Egypt	Mesoamerica
Descended from God(s)	"Adam, which was the son of God"	Pharaoh descended from his god	Palenque rulers descended from ancestral gods
Lineage Trees	Descendants referred to as shoots and branches		Descendants equated with flowers, fruit, and branches. Metaphorical "birth" from trees
Human Thigh Symbolic of Lineage		X	X
Wilted Flower Signified Death	X		X

THE KING & THE WORLD TREE

	Near East & Old World (general)	Egypt	Mesoamerica
THE KING			
	King was anointed son of God(s)	Pharaoh was literal son of god	Rulers descended from divine ancestors
	King was representative and messenger of god(s)	Pharaoh was representative and messenger of god(s)	King was conduit between gods and men
	Substitute sacrificed on behalf of king; king reborn	Substitute king sacrificed at Sed Festival; Pharaoh reborn	Substitute sacrificed on behalf of king; king reborn
	Sacrifice was without blemish in Israel		Sacrifice was without blemish among Aztec
		Pharaoh equated with sun as it is born each day	King equated with sun
	King considered gardener of all nature		Gardener king among Aztec
	Ruler associated with First Man		Maya king associated with Maize God (First Father)
	King represented *axis mundi*, center of world	Pharaoh represented *axis mundi*, center of world	King represented *axis mundi*, center of world
	King represented World Tree	King represented World Tree	King represented World Tree
THE TREE			
	Tree was axis of the World	*Djed* was central pillar of the sky	Tree was axis of the World
	Cutting down tree = death of old cycle		Cutting down tree = death of old cycle
	Raising a pole/tree = rebirth and life	Raising *Djed* = rebirth and life	Raising a pole/tree = rebirth and life
	Tree, bird, and guardian theme		Tree, bird, and guardian theme
		Tree accouterments worn by Pharaoh	Tree accouterments worn by King
	Tree equated with Milky Way and path of souls		Tree equated with Milky Way and path of souls

EGYPTIAN AND MESOAMERICAN SCRIBES

Egypt	Mesoamerica

Master of Writing
  Used Red & Black Ink
  Anointed Writing Boards
	Master of Writing
	  Used Red & Black Ink
	  Anointed Writing Boards

Master of Art	Master of Art
Master of Arithmetic	Master of Arithmetic
Master Surveyor	
Master of Astronomy	Master of Astronomy
One Who Prophesied	
One Who Used Priesthood Magic	
Master of Medicine	
Patron of Music	Patron of Music
	Patron of Dance
	Jeweler
Keeper of Books	Keeper of Books
Patron of History	Patron of History
A God of the Underworld	A God of the Underworld

Associated with:
  Baboon (moon or sun)
  Net (baboons used)
	Associated with:
	  Monkey (sun)
	  Net Headdress on Pawahtun

Human scribe wore kilt and pens behind ear. Highly esteemed	Human scribe wore kilt and pens behind ear. Highly esteemed

MOTHER GODDESS & RELATED SYMBOLISM

	Near East (general)	**Egypt**	**Mesoamerica**
Female Earth	X	0	X
U-shaped Element = Womb	X	X	X
Caves Associated with Womb & Birth	X	?	X
Womb of Sky Concept	X	X	X
Night Sky = Underworld	0	X	X
Goddess & Moon Association	X	X	X
Rabbit & Moon Association	X	X	X
Vase (Womb) Theme	X	X	X
Earthen Jar (Womb) to Bury Deceased	X	0	X
Goddess & Serpent Association	X	?	X
Net Patterns & Earth	X	X	X
The Feminine Tree	X	X	X

185

MOUNTAIN & TEMPLE SYMBOLISM (A)

	Mesopotamia	Near East (Israel)
Separation of Earth & Sky	Performed by Enlil, god of air and storm	Divided by the "firmament," with waters above (in the clouds) and waters below (on the earth)
Earth Cracked Open, Man Emerges	Performed by Enlil with pickax. Man grows like vegetation	0
Crack in Primordial Mound = Mountain of Creation	X	0
Temple and Mountain Symbolic of Primordial Mound of Creation	X	X
Serpent & Mountain Associated	?	Sculpted serpents on Solomon's Temple (scholars have suggested)
Mountain/Temple Place of Communication with Gods(s)	X	X
Waters of Creation Close to, or Coming from, Under the Temple	X	X

MOUNTAIN & TEMPLE SYMBOLISM (B)

	Egypt	Mesoamerica
Separation of Earth & Sky	Performed by Shu, god of air	Performed by Echecatl, god of wind, or Quetzalcoatl as a tree (among the Aztec), or by World Tree, via First Father the maize god (among the Maya)
Earth Cracked Open, Man Emerges	0	Performed by Chak, storm god, with lightning ax. Mankind & maize are born
Crack in Primordial Mound = Mountain of Creation	Dual mountains on the horizon, or two pylons	Two heaps of stones, cleft in mountain, two hills next to each other, or two temples (e.g., Templo Mayor)
Temple and Mountain Symbolic of Primordial Mound of Creation	X	X
Serpent & Mountain Associated	0	Snake Mountain theme throughout Mesoamerica
Mountain/Temple Place of Communication with Gods(s)	X	X
Waters of Creation Close to, or Coming from, Under the Temple	X	X

MISCELLANEOUS PARALLELS

	Mesopotamia	Near East (general)	Egypt	Mesoamerica
Nine Gods of the Underworld	X	0	X	X
Atlantean Figures Support Sky	?	X	X	X
Dog Guides the Dead	?	0	X	X
Deer & Sun	0	X	0	X
Felines and Sun	?	?	X	X
Felines Back to Back	0	0	X	X
Birth & Flowers Related	0	X	X	X
Day of the Dead	0	0	X	X
Bones = Seeds	?	X	?	X
Deceased As Stars	?	X	X	X
Goods for the Dead	?	X	X	X
Wheeled Funerary Objects	X	?	?	X
Incense Parallels	X	X	X	X
Sacred Banners	?	X	X	X
Standing/Sitting on Prisoners	?	X	X	X
Grasping Hair of Prisoners	0	0	X	X
Removal of Lower Jaw of Captive	0	0	X	X

Timeless Nature of Traditions

In the field of archaeology not everything that once existed is going to be found. We cannot date the origin of concepts portrayed in art by the media in which they are first discovered. Ideas expressed in stone, for example, may have had their precursors in wood and/or fabric and most assuredly in oral tradition. When reading of similar customs hundreds and even thousands of years apart, this reality should be considered because it cannot be known with certainty when such practices were indisputably established in a particular culture.

This approach may appear apologetic, nevertheless, it remains a fact. We might see it as unfortunate that in various archeological sites, Mesoamerican cultures did not leave written histories in stone describing their religious beliefs in Pre-Classic times for archaeologists to ponder. This is perhaps one of the greatest drawbacks in our academic institutions to understanding the philosophical nature of Mesoamerican thought before the common era. Whereas the Old World possesses extensive texts from very early times, Mesoamerica does not. Even when an efficient hieroglyphic writing system in Mesoamerica was used by the Maya, it was not the choice of other Mesoamerican cultures to express history or ideas in this manner. Thus, we have a quandary. Traditions that Mesoamerican cultures possessed enabled their descendants to share major portions of their ancestral roots, beliefs, and world view. These customs were passed from one generation to the next with some deviation, however, they held together remarkably intact over the centuries. This created a cultural continuity between old and new ways. Their traditions were not forgotten—indeed, they were ageless.

Ballcourts

Mention was made of the timeless nature of Mesoamerican practices such as the long history of building pyramids. There is also the Maya imagery of the Late-Classic *Popol Vuh* characters that was borrowed from their Pre-Classic predecessors in Izapa, and perhaps even further back to the Olmec (see Fig. II.22). Nothing, however, says it like the ever-present ballcourt. In 1995 a ballcourt was discovered at Paso de la Amada in Chiapas, Mexico, by a graduate student from the University of British Columbia. This is especially unique because the ballcourt dates back to 1700 B.C., which is the earliest ballcourt known to date. It was no small feat to construct it as it is twenty-three feet wide and eighty yards long—nearly the length of a modern-day football field. Radiocarbon dating of organic remains and artifacts found in conjunction with it indicate that it was utilized for about three centuries.[7] Imagine Pasadena's Rose Bowl in use for that length of time! Ballcourts were prolific throughout Mesoamerica, many sites having more than one court. Nevertheless, the real clincher is that the ballgame was a tradition in Mesoamerica for over 3,000 years. It is truly a prime example of the timeless nature of a belief system in pre-Columbian times.

Linguistics

The matter of linguistics has not been addressed in this study except for the mention of a few key words, which are pregnant with meaning and important in our understanding of iconographic messages. An example of these words include: *xok* [Yucatec Mayan] which can mean "shark," "waist," "hips," or "woman." The Huichol words *mu'ri iku'ri* and *iku'ri* mean "fish" and "corn" respectively; *chukah* means "capture" or "capture for birth"; *bak* means "heron," "captive," "child," or "bone"; *r-k'a'* [Tzotujil Mayan] means "hand" or "branch"; and *uech* means "face," "fruit," or "children." The interpretation of these words, of course, depends on the context in which they were used. Word play or punning is a feature that was utilized extensively by both Middle Eastern and Mesoamerican peoples. In fact, there were probably no people that loved word play more than the Egyptians and the Maya.[8] This too presents a strong connection to the study of linguistics in Mesoamerica.

Chiasmus

It would not be out of line here to examine a parallel literary style called chiasmus. Chiasms were used in the Middle East, known in texts written in Hebrew, Egyptian, Ugaritic, Akkadian, Sumerian, Hittite, and Greek.[9] The special feature of chiastic phrases is that the first line parallels the last, the second the penultimate, the third the antepenultimate, etc., coming to a central point and forming, when diagramed, an X, which derives from the Greek letter CHI that gives chiasmus its name.[10]

The *Popol Vuh* of the Quiché Maya contains phrases expressed in chiasmus as do prayers of the Lacandon Maya of Chiapas. McGee studied and lived among the Lacandon and finds that their use of chiasmus customarily ran ten lines, but some were as long as sixty to 100 lines.[11] With this very unique literary style one cannot help wonder why or how it came to be employed by both those of the ancient Near East and the Maya of the New World.

SUMMARY

Accepting the plausibility of early voyages to the Americas from other parts of the world does not belittle the talents or inventions of the indigenous people. No one knows to what extent any newcomers may have influenced cultural development. Independent duplication of traditions and inventions is not denied here, for many are a result of basic human needs both physical and psychological. But, the subject of parallels cannot be written off easily. Even though we may never be able to determine to what extent or how significant any foreign impact affected cultural development in Mesoamerica, it does not mean that cultural diffusion never took place.

Demarest, a highly respected Maya scholar at Vanderbilt University, employs an open mind when it comes to possible cultural contacts with Mesoamerica from across the sea. In an article in *The Atlantic Monthly* he is quoted as saying:

> Within orthodox academics there are a lot of people who simply dismiss the argument out of hand on the ground that the mechanics of overseas diffusion themselves are too difficult. But there are others—and I put myself in that group—who don't doubt there's been contact. I don't think that the transport problems are such that they prevented people from moving between continents.[12]

Not all scholars will be convinced that the parallels presented here are valid. In fact, many may even choose to attack the general hypothesis. Admittedly, not all comparisons stated in this work will prove to be relevant ties between the Old and New Worlds. However, many of them are so intricate, detailed, and multifarious in nature that they surely must be considered by scholars of this and future generations. Patterns of customs have been sought that appear to be linked. If some of these seemingly parallel traditions appear to the reader to be ambiguous, then alternative solutions should be reached to explain the apparent cultural continuities between Mesoamerica and the ancient Middle East. Continued research on these subjects will surely expand on the package of information presented.

As Remington remarks: "New discoveries . . . wreak havoc with old hypotheses."[13] Conventional ideas, as we saw with Eric Thompson's view of Maya hieroglyphics, are not always correct ones. It is true that accepting the hypothesis that Mesoamerica was influenced by ancient Middle Eastern traditions would disrupt the entire field of Mesoamerican research. Nevertheless, if there is truth in this premise then let it evolve and develop until these overlooked parallel connections become established fact or fancy, as the case may be. Mistaken conceptions and deductions must be replaced by new theories and interpretations as evidence surfaces if we are to proceed effectively to understand the past.

Perhaps pre-Columbian history will require a rewrite. That, however, is already being accomplished. With the decipherment of Maya hieroglyphics, our concept of the Maya world changed from "the peaceful Maya," to an understanding of their polities that conquered others for power and material gain, bringing their opponents' rulers to shame, humiliation, and eventual sacrifice. This major historical reconstruction will pale in comparison to the inclusion of foreign elements from the Middle East. As the great scholar Cyrus Gordon exclaimed, "The full story may take a long time to unfold, but the fact of global diffusion is here to stay."[14]

NOTES - Epilogue

1.   Gordon, "A Hebrew Inscription Authenticated," 76.
2.   Coe, *Breaing the Maya Code*, 141.
3.   Ibid., 145.
4.   Ibid., 151.
5.   Ibid., 141.
6.   Hershel Shanks, "Everything You Ever Knew About Jerusalem is Wrong," *Biblical Archaeology Review* 25/6 (1999), 20.
7.   *American Archaeology*, "Ballcourt Find Comes as a Pleasant Surprise" (Fall 1998), 7.
8.   Morenz, 183; Marcus, *Mesoamerican Writing Systems*, 38.
9.   Chiasmus was used by the Hebrews as may be viewed in many passages of the Old Testament, particularly in Psalms and the poetry of Job.
10. Information on the subject of chiasmus supplied by John Tvedtnes to Diane Wirth, April 9, 1999.
11. John McGee, "Place of Palenque in Lacandon Mythology," (paper presented at the IXth Texas Symposium, March 12, Austin: University of Texas, 1993).
12. Mark K. Stengel, "The Diffusionists Have Landed," *The Atlantic Monthly* 285/1 (2000), 47.
13. Judith Ann Remington, "Mesoamerican Archaeoastronomy: Parallax, Perspective, and Focus," in *Archaeoastronomy in the Americas*, ed. Ray A. Williamson, No. 22 (Los Altos, California: Ballena Press, 1981), 200-02.
14. Gordon, "A Hebrew Inscription Authenticated," 78.

BIBLIOGRAPHY

Adams, Richard E. W.
  1971   "The Ceramics of Altar de Sacrificios." *Papers of the Peabody Museum of Archaeology and Ethnology* 63/1. Cambridge, Massachusetts: Peabody Museum of Archaeology and Ethnology, Harvard University.
American Archaeology
  1998   "Ballcourt Find Comes as a Pleasant Surprise." (Fall): 7.
The Ancient Egyptian Book of the Dead
  1985   Translated by Raymond O. Faulkner, edited by Carol Andrews. Revised edition. New York: Macmillan Publishing Company.
Anderson, Robert D.
  1987   *Egypt in 1800: Napoleon's Description de L'Egypte.* London: Barrie and Jenkins.
Andrews, Carol
  1993   "Ancient Egyptian Funerary Amulets: Protection, Power and Patronage." Paper presented at The Annual American Research Center in Egypt Symposium, jointly sponsored by the Brooklyn Museum, December 4.
  1994   *Amulets of Ancient Egypt.* Great Britain: British Museum Press, and Austin: University of Texas Press.
Anthes, Rudolf
  1961   "Mythology in Ancient Egypt." In *Mythologies of the Ancient World*, edited by Samuel Noah Kramer. Garden City, New York: Doubleday.
Bach, Caleb
  1996   "Michael Coe: A Question for every Answer." *America Magazine* 18/1: 14-21.
Baldwin, John D.
  1872   *Ancient America.* New York: Harper and Brothers.
Bancroft, Hubert Howe
  1883   *The Native Races.* Vols. II & III. San Francisco: Bancroft & Co.
Baring, Anne, and Jules Cashford
  1991   *The Myth of the Goddess: Evolution of an Image.* New York: Viking Arkana through Penguin Books.
Barkay, Gabriel, and Amos Kloner
  1986   "Jerusalem Tombs from the Days of the First Temple." *Biblical Archaeology Review* 12/2: 22-39.
Bassie-Sweet, Karen
  1991   *From the Mouth of the Dark Cave.* Norman: University of Oklahoma Press.
Baudez, Claude-François
  1994   *Maya Sculpture of Copán: The Iconography.* Norman: University of Oklahoma.
Beals, Carleton
  1961   *Nomads and Empire Builders.* Philadelphia: Chilton.
Beidelman, T. O.
  1966   "Swazi Royal Ritual." *Africa* 36: 373-405.
Benitez, Fernando
  1975   *In the Magic Land of Peyote.* Austin: University of Texas Press.
Benson, Elizabeth P., and Beatriz de la Fuente, editors
  1996   *Olmec Art of Ancient Mexico.* National Gallery of Art, Washington. New York: Harry N. Abrams, Inc.
Berger, Pamela
  1985   *The Goddess Obscured.* Boston: Beacon Press.
Berjonneau, Gerald, and Jean-Louis Sonnery
  1985   *Rediscovered Masterpieces of Mesoamerica.* Boulogne, France: Edition Arts.
Berlin, Heinrich
  1993   "Nominal Glyphs of the Palenque Sarcophagus." *Texas Notes on Precolumbian Art, Writing, and Culture* 37. Translated by Khristaan D. Villela. Austin: The Center for the History and Art of Ancient American Culture, Art Department, University of Texas, 1-13.
Bernal, Ignacio
  1969   *The Olmec World.* Berkeley and Los Angeles: University of California Press.
Bernal-García, María Elena
  1988   "La Venta's Pyramid: The First Successful Representation of the Mesoamerican Sacred Mountain." Preliminary Paper for Spring 1988 Seminar at the Center for Latin American Studies. Cambridge: England.
Berrin, Kathleen, editor
  1988   *Feathered Serpents and Flowering Trees.* San Francisco: The Fine Arts Museums of San Francisco.
Biblical Archaeology Review
  2002   Vol. 28, No. 6, 21-22.
Bishop, Jerry E.
  1993   "Strands of Time: A Geneticist's Work on DNA Bears Fruit for Anthropologists." *Wall Street Journal* CCXXII/93 (November 10).
Black, Jeremy, and Anthony Green
  1992   *Gods, Demons and Symbols of Ancient Mesopotamia.* Austin: University of Texas Press.
Blackman, Aylward M.
  1924   "The Rite of Opening the Mouth in Ancient Egypt and Babylonia." *Journal of Egyptian Archaeology* 10/ Pt. I: 47-59.

Bleeker, C. J.
    1983   "Isis and Hathor: Two Ancient Egyptian Goddesses." In *The Book of the Goddess Past and Present*, edited by Carl Olson. New York: Crossroad, 29-48.

Boas, Franz
    1891   "Dissemination of Tales Among the Natives of North America." *Journal of American Folk Lore* 6: 13-20. Boggs, Stanley H.
    1973   "Salvadoran Varieties of Wheeled Figurines." *Contributions to Mesoamerican Anthropology*, Pub. No. 1. Miami: Institute of Maya Studies of the Museum of Science.

Borhegyi, Stephan F.
    1956   "El Incensario de 'Tres Asas' de Kaminaljuyu, Guatemala." *Antropológia e Historia de Guatemala*, 8(2).
    1970   "Wheels and Man." *Archaeology* 23 (January): 18-25.

Borowski, Elie
    1992   "Against All Odds." *Biblical Archaeology Review* 19/2: 46-53.

Bowen, Sharon, and Lloyd Anderson
    1994   "The Palenque Emblem Bird *Mat* and *Matawil*." In *U Mut Maya V*, edited by Carolyn and Tom Jones: Arcata, California: U Mut Maya, 37-69.

Boyland, Patrick
    1987   *Thoth: The Hermes of Egypt*. Chicago: Ares Publishers, Inc. Original edition. London, 1922.

Bradley, Douglas E., and Peter David Joralemon
    1992   *The Lords of Life: The Iconography of Power and Fertility in Preclassic Mesoamerica*. Indiana: The Snite Museum of Art, University of Notre Dame.

Brandon, S. G. F.
    1975   *Man and God in Art and Ritual*. New York: Charles Scribner's Sons.

Briffault, Robert
    1969   *The Mothers*. Vol. 2. New York: Johnson Reprint Corporation. Original edition, New York: Macmillan, 1927.

Brisko, Jo Ann
    1993   "Aztec Goddesses: A Historical Perspective." Master's thesis, San Jose: San Jose State University.

Broda, Johanna
    1987   "The Provenience of the Offerings: Tribute and Cosmovision." In *The Aztec Templo Mayor*, edited by Elizabeth Hill Boone. Washington, D.C.: Dumbarton Oaks Research Library and Collection.

Brotherston, Gordon
    1979   *The Image of the New World*. London: Thames and Hudson.

Bruce, Robert D.
    1967   "Jerarquia Maya Entre los Dioses Lacandones." *Anales de I.N.A.H.* Mexico: Instituto Nacional de Antropologia e Historia
    1975   *Lacandon Dream Symbolism*. Mexico, D.F.: Ediciones Euroamericanas Klaus Thiele.

Bruhns, Karen Olsen, and Tom Weller
    1973   *A Coloring Album of Ancient Mexico and Peru*. Berkeley: Saint Heironymous Press.

Brundage, Burr Cartwright
    1985   *The Jade Steps: A Ritual Life of the Aztecs*. Salt Lake City: University of Utah Press.

Budge, E. A. Wallis
    1961   *Osiris: The Egyptian Religion of Resurrection*. Two volumes in one. Reprint, New Hyde Park, New York: University Books. Original edition, London: British Museum, 1895.
    1967   *The Book of the Dead: The Papyrus of Ani*. New York: Dover Publications.
    1969   *The Gods of the Egyptians*. Vols. I & II. New York: Dover Publications. Original edition, London: Methuen & Co., 1904.
    1987   *The Mummy: A Handbook of Egyptian Funerary Archaeology*. London: KPI.
    1988   *From Fetish to God in Ancient Egypt*. Reprint, New York: Dover Publications. Original edition, London: Oxford University Press, 1934.
    1989   *The Egyptian Heaven and Hell*. Reprint, La Salle, Illinois: Open Court. Original edition, London, 1925.
    1991   *Tutankhamun: Amenism, Atenism and Egyptian Monotheism*. Reprint, New York: Dover Publications, Inc. Original edition, London: Martin Hopkinson, 1923.

Burland, Cottie A.
    1970   *The People of the Ancient Americas*. London: Paul Hamlyn.
    1973   *Montezuma: Lord of the Aztecs*. New York: G. P. Putnam's Sons.

Butterworth, E. A. S.
    1970   *The Tree at the Navel of the Earth*. Berlin: Walter de Gruter & Co.

Byland, Bruce E., and John M. D. Pohl
    1994   *In the Realm of 8 Deer*. Norman: University of Oklahoma.

Campbell, Joseph
    1976   *The Masks of God: Oriental Mythology*. Reprint, New York: Viking. Original edition, New York: Viking Penguin, Inc., 1959. Revised edition, 1969.
    1987   *The Masks of God: Primitive Mythology*. Reprint, New York: Penguin Books. Original edition, New York: Viking Press, 1964.
    1988   *Vol. II: The Way of the Seeded Earth, Part 1: The Sacrifice*. Historical Atlas of World Mythology. New York: Harper & Row, Pub.

Carlson, Robert S., and Martin Prechtel
    1991   "The Flowering of the Dead: an Interpretation of Highland Maya Culture." *MAN* 26: 23-42.

Carmack, Robert M.
    1981   *The Quiche Mayas of Utatlan*. Norman: University of Oklahoma Press.

Carmichael, Elizabeth, and Chloë Sayer
    1991   *The Skeleton at the Feast: The Day of the Dead in Mexico*. Austin: University of Texas Press.

Casson, Lionel
    1965   *Ancient Egypt*. New York: Time Life Books.

Cavendish, Richard, Editor
    1970   *Man, Myth and Magic* Vol. 2. Long Island, New York: Marshall Cavendish Corp.

Chase Coggins, Clemency
    1990   "The Birth of the Baktun at Tikal and Seibal." In *Vision and Revision in Maya Studies*, edited by Flora S. Clancy and Peter D. Harrison. Albuquerque: University of New Mexico Press, 77-98.

Chavero, Alfredo, editor
    1891   *Obras Historicas de Ixtlilxochitl* Vol. 1. Mexico.

Christenson, Allen
    1997   "Prehistory of the K'ichean People." In *Texas Notes on Precolumbian Art, Writing and Culture* 75. Austin: The Center for the History and Art of Ancient American Culture, Art Department, University of Texas, 1-75.

Ciaramella, Mary A.
    1994   "The Lady with the Snake Headdress." In *Seventh Palenque Round Table, 1989* Vol. IX, general editor Merle Greene-Robertson, volume editor, Virginia M. Fields. San Francisco: Pre-Columbian Art Research Institute, 201-09.

Cirlot, J. E.
    1971   *A Dictionary of Symbols*. Translated from the Spanish by Jake Sage. New York: Philosophical Library, Inc.

Clark, R. T. Rundle
    1959   *Myth and Symbol in Ancient Egypt*. New York: Thames and Hudson.

Coe, Michael D.
    1973   *The Maya Scribe and His World*. New York: Grolier Club.
    1975a   "Death and the Ancient Maya." In *Death and the Afterlife in Pre-Columbian America*, edited by E. P. Benson. Washington, D.C.: Dumbarton Oaks, 87-104.
    1975b   "Three Maya Figurines from Jaina Island." *Yale University Art Gallery Bulletin* 35. New Haven: Yale University, 24-25.
    1977   "Supernatural Patrons of Scribes and Artists." In *Social Process in Maya Prehistory*. Studies in honour of Sir Eric Thompson, edited by Norman Hammond. London: Academic Press, 327-47.
    1978   *Lords of the Underworld: Masterpieces of Classic Maya Ceramics*. Princeton: The Art Museum, Princeton University.
    1987   *The Maya*. 4th edition. New York: Thames & Hudson.
    1988   "Ideology of the Maya Tomb." In *Maya Iconography*, edited by Elizabeth P. Benson and Gillett G. Griffin. Princeton: Princeton University Press, 222-35.
    1989   "The Hero Twins: Myth and Image." In *The Maya Vase Book*, Vol. 1, by Justin Kerr. New York: Kerr Associates, 161-84.
    1992   *Breaking the Maya Code*. New York: Thames and Hudson.
    1993   *The Maya*. 5th edition. New York: Thames & Hudson.

Coe, Michael D., and Justin Kerr
    1982   *Old Gods and Young Heroes: The Pearlman Collection of Maya Ceramics*. Jerusalem: The Israel Museum.
    1998   *The Art of the Maya Scribe*. New York: Harry N. Abrams, Inc.

Coe, William R.
    1968   "In Search of the Mayan Past." In *The World Book Year Book*. Chicago: Field Enterprises Educational Corp.

Cohodas, Marvin
    1974   "The Iconography of the Panels of the Sun, Cross, and Foliated Cross at Palenque: Part II." In *Primera Mesa Redonda de Palenque, Part I*, edited by Merle Greene-Robertson. Monterey, California: Robert Louis Stevenson School, 95-108.
    1976   "The Iconography of the Panel of the Sun, Cross, and Foliated Cross at Palenque: Part III." In *The Art, Iconography and Dynastic History of Palenque*, edited by Merle Greene-Robertson. Pebble Beach, California: Pre-Columbian Art Research, Robert Louis Stevenson School, 156-76.
    1978   "Some Unusual Aspects of Cross Group Symbolism." In *Tercera Mesa Redonda de Palenque* Vol. IV, edited by Merle Greene-Robertson and Donnan Call Jeffers. Palenque, Chiapas, Mexico: Pre-Columbian Art Research, 215-32.

Collin, Dominique
    1987   *First Impressions: Cylinder Seals in the Ancient Near East*. Chicago: University of Chicago Press.

Cook, Roger
    1974   *The Tree of Life*. New York: Avon Books, A division of The Hearst Corporation.

Coto, Fray Th. de (O.F.M.)
    1983   *Vocabviario de la lengua Cakchquel v Guatemalteca, nueuamente hecho y recopilado con summo estudio, trauajo y erudicion*, edited by René Acuña. Mexico: Universidad Nacional Autonoma de Mexico.

Couch, N. C. Christopher
    1988   *Pre-Columbian Art From the Ernest Erickson Collection*. New York: American Museum of Natural History.

Coudert, Allison
    1987   "Horns." In Vol. 8 of *The Encyclopedia of Religion*, edited by Mircea Eliade. 16 vols. New York: Macmillan Publishing Company, 462-63.

Covarrubias, Miguel
    1971   *Indian Art of Mexico and Central America*. New York: Alfred A. Knopf.

Culianu, Ioan Petru
    1987   "Sky: The Heavens as Hierophany." In Vol. 13 of *The Encyclopedia of Religion*, edited by Mircea Eliade. 16 vols. New York: MacMillan Publishing Company, 343-45.

Dahood, Mitchell
    1968   *Psalms II: 51-100*. New York: The Anchor Bible, Doubleday.
    1970   *Psalms III: 101-150*. New York: The Anchor Bible, Doubleday.

D'Auria, Sue, Peter Lacovara, and Catharine H. Roehrig
1988   *Mummies & Magic: The Funerary Arts of Ancient Egypt.* Boston: Museum of Fine Arts.

Davies, Jon
1999   *Death, Burial and Rebirth in the Religions of Antiquity.* New York: Routledge.

Davis, Virginia Lee
1984   "Identifying Ancient Egyptian Constellations." *Archaeoastronomy* 9: 102-4.

Day, Jane Stevenson
1992a   *Aztec: The World of Moctezuma.* Niwot, Colorado: Denver Museum of Natural History and Roberts Rinehart Publishers.
1992b   "Treasures from the Templo Mayor." *Archaeology* 45/5: 42-47.

DeHorrack, J.
1878   "Louvre Papyrus No. 3284." *Bibliotheque Egyptologique.* XVII: 110-37.

de Landa, Diego
1978   *Yucatan Before and After the Conquest.* Translated with notes by William Gates. Reprint, New York: Dover Publications, Inc. Original edition, Baltimore, The Maya Society, 1937.

Derchain, P.
1965   "Le Papyrus Salt 825." *Memoires of the Academie Royale de Belgique*, 58. Belgium: Palais des Academies.

D'Harcourt, Raoul
1950   *Primitive Art of the Americas.* New York: Tudor Publishing Co.

Diehl, Richard A., and Michael Coe
1997   "Olmec Archaeology." In *The Olmec World in Ritual and Rulership.* Princeton: The Art Museum, Princeton University, 11-26

Dixon, E. James
1993   *Quest for the Origins of the First Americans.* Albuquerque: University of New Mexico.

Drucker, Philip, Robert Heizer, and Robert J. Squier
1959   *Excavations at La Venta, Tabasco, 1955*, Bulletin 170. Washington D.C.: Bureau of American Ethnology.

Durán, Fray Diego
1963   *Atlas de la historia de las Indias de Nueva España y Islas de Tierra Firme.* Mexico: Librería Anticuaria, G. M. Echaniz.
1964   *The Aztecs: The History of the Indians of New Spain.* Translated with notes by Doris Heyden and Fernando Horcasites. New York: Orion Press.
1984   *Historia de las Indias de Nueva España e Islas de la Tierra Firme.* 2 Vols., edited by Angel Maria Garibay K. Mexico: Editorial Porrúa. Original manuscripts entitled *Libro de los ritos y ceremonias en las fiestas de los dioses y celebracion de ellas*, 1576-79; *El calendario antiquo*, 1597; and *Historia de las Indias de Nueva España e islas de la tierra firme* 1580-81, National Library, Madrid.

Dütting, Dieter
1976   "The Great Goddess in Classic Maya Religious Belief." *Zeitschrift Fur Ethnologie* V/111: 42-146.
1978   "Birth, Inauguration and Death in the Inscriptions of Palenque, Chiapas, Mexico." In *Tercera Mesa Redonda de Palenque* Vol. IV, edited by Merle Greene-Robertson & Donnan Call Jeffers. Palenque, Chiapas, Mexico: Pre-Columbian Art Research, 183-214.
1985a   "On the Astronomical Background of Mayan Historical Events." In *Fifth Palenque Round Table, 1983* Vol. VII, general editor Merle Greene-Robertson, volume editor Virginia M. Fields. San Francisco: Pre-Columbian Art Research Institute, 261-74.
1985b   "Lunar Periods and the Quest for Rebirth in the Mayan Hieroglyphic Inscriptions." *Estudios de Cultura Maya* XVI: 113-43.
1991   "Aspects of Polyvalency in Maya Writing: Affixes T12, T229, and T110." In *Sixth Palenque Round Table, 1986* Vol. 8, general editor Merle Greene-Robertson, volume editor Virginia M. Fields. Norman: University of Oklahoma Press, 273-84.

Edmonson, Munro S.
1988   *The Book of the Year: Middle American Calendrical Systems.* Salt Lake City: University of Utah Press.

Egyptian Book of the Dead: The Book of Going Forth by Day
1994   Translation by Raymond Faulkner and Ogden Goelet, and edited by Eva von Dassow. San Francisco: Chronicle Books.

Ekholm, Gordon F.
1946   "Wheeled Toys in Mexico." *American Antiquity* 11/3: 222-28.

Ekholm, Susanna M.
1985   "The Lagartero Ceramic 'Pendants'." In *Fourth Palenque Round Table, 1980* Vol. VI, edited by Merle Greene-Robertson. San Francisco: Pre-Columbian Art Research Institute, 211-20.

Eliade, Mircea
1954   *The Myth of the Eternal Return: Or, Cosmos and History.* Bollingen Series, No. 46. Translated by Willard R. Trask. Princeton: Princeton University Press.
1958   *Rites and Symbols of Initiation: The Mysteries of Birth and Rebirth.* London: Harvill Press.
1959   *The Sacred and the Profane: The Nature of Religion.* Translated by Willard R. Trask. London: Harcourt, Brace, Jovanovich.
1961   *Images and Symbols: Studies in Religious Symbolism.* Translated by Philip Mairet. London: Harvill Press.
1963   *Myth and Reality.* Translated by Willard R. Trask. New York: Harper & Row.
1988   *Symbolism, the Sacred, and the Arts.* Edited by Diane Apostolos-Cappadona. New York: Crossroad.

Elk, Black
1967   *The Sacred Pipe*, recorded and edited by Joseph Epes Brown. University of Oklahoma Press, Norman.

Enuma Elish: The 7 Tablets of Creation Vol. I
1999   Translated and edited by L. W. King. Reprint, Escondido, California: The Book Tree. Original edition, London: Luzac and Co., 1902.

Fairman, H. W.
1958   "The Kingship Rituals of Egypt." In *Myth, Ritual, and Kingship*, edited by S. H. Hooke. Oxford: Claredon Press.

Farbridge, Maurice H.
1923   *Studies in Biblical and Semitic Symbolism.* Hartford, England: Stephen Austin and Sons., Ltd.

Fash, William
  1991a   *Scribes, Warriors and Kings: The City of Copan and the Ancient Maya.* New York: Thames and Hudson.
  1991b   "Lineage Patrons and Ancestor Worship Among the Classic Maya Nobility: The Case of Copan Structure 9N-82." In *Sixth Palenque Round Table, 1986* Vol. 8, general editor Merle Greene-Robertson, volume editor Virginia M. Fields. Norman: University of Oklahoma Press, 68-80.
Ferguson, Thomas Stuart
  1958   *One Fold and One Shepherd.* San Francisco: Books of California.
Fields, Virginia
  1991   "The Iconographic Heritage of the Maya Jester God." In *Sixth Palenque Round Table, 1986* Vol. 8, general editor Merle Greene-Robertson, volume editor Virginia M. Fields. Norman: University of Oklahoma Press, 167-74..
Foster, George
  1945   Sierra Popoluca Folklore and Beliefs. *University of California Publications on American Archaeology and Ethnology* 42/2: 177-250.
Foster, Lynn, and Linnea Wren
  1996   "World Creator and World Sustainer: God N at Chichén Itzá." In *Eighth Palenque Round Table, 1993* Vol. X, general editor Merle Greene-Robertson, volume editors. Martha J. Macri and Jan McHargue. San Francisco: The Pre-Columbian Art Research Institute, 259-70.
Fox, Hugh
  1976   *Gods of the Cataclysm.* New York: Harper & Row.
Francé, Raoul Heinrich
  1924   *Das Buch des Lebens.* Berlin. Franco, Jose-Luis
  1971   "Musical Instruments from Central Veracruz in Classic Times." In *Ancient Art of Veracruz*, edited by Olga Hammer. Los Angeles: Ethnic Art Council of Los Angeles, Los Angeles County Museum of Natural History, 18-22.
Frankfort, Henri
  1944   "A Note on the Lady of Birth." *Journal of Near Eastern Studies* 3: 198-200.
  1970   *The Art and Architecture of the Ancient Orient.* Baltimore: Penguin Books.
  1978   *Kingship and the Gods.* Chicago: University of Chicago Press. Original edition, 1948.
Frazer, James G.
  1942   *The Golden Bough.* New York: Macmillan Company.
Freidel, David A.
  1992   "Children of the First Father's Skull: Terminal Classic Warfare in the Northern Maya Lowlands and the Transformation of Kingship and Elite Hierarchies." In *Mesoamerican Elites*, edited by Diane Z. Chase and Arlen F. Chase. Norman: University of Oklahoma Press, 99-117.
Freidel, David, Linda Schele, and Joy Parker
  1993   *Maya Cosmos: Three Thousand Years on the Shaman's Path.* New York: William Morrow & Company, Inc.
Frost, Frank J.
  1993   "Voyages of the Imagination." *Archaeology* 46/2: 41-51.
Furst, Jill Leslie
  1977   "The Tree Birth Tradition in the Mixteca, Mexico." *Journal of Latin American Lore* 312: 183-226.
  1978   *Codex Vindobonenis Mexicanus 1:A commentary.* Albany: Institute for Mesoamerican Studies, State University of New York.
  1982   "Skeletonization in Mixtec Art: A re-evaluation." In *The Art and Iconography of Late Post-Classic Central Mexico*, edited by E. H. Boone. Washington, D.C.: Dumbarton Oaks, 207-25.
Furst, Jill, and Peter T. Furst
  1980   *Pre-Columbian Art of Mexico.* New York: Abberville Press.
Furst, Peter T.
  1973   "West Mexican Art: Secular or Sacred?" In *The Iconography of Middle American Sculpture*, edited by Dudley T. Easby, Jr. New York: The Metropolitan Museum of Art, 98-133.
  1975   "House of Darkness and House of Light: Sacred Functions of West Mexican Funerary Art." In *Death and the Afterlife in Pre-Columbian America*, edited by Elizabeth P. Benson. Washington, D.C.: Dumbarton Oaks Research Library, 33-68.
  1976   "Fertility, Vision Quest and Auto-sacrifice: Some Thoughts on Ritual Bloodletting among the Maya." In *The Art, Iconography, and Dynastic History of Palenque, Part III,* edited by Merle Green Robertson. Pebble Beach, California: Pre-Columbian Art Research, 181-93.
  1998   "Shamanic Symbolism, Transformation, and Deities in West Mexican Funerary Art." In *Ancient West Mexico: Art and Archaeology of the Unknown Past*, general editor Richard F. Townsend. New York: The Art Institute of Chicago, Thames and Hudson, 169-90.
Gardiner, Alan H.
  1982   *Egyptian Grammar*, (3rd. Ed). Oxford: Oxford University Press.
Gaster, Theodor H.
  1987   "Seasonal Ceremonies." In Vol. 13 of *The Encyclopedia of Religion*, edited by Mircea Eliade. New York: Macmillan Publishing Company, 148-51.
Gay, Carlo T. E.
  1973   "Olmec Hieroglyphic Writing." *Archaeology* 26/4: 278-88.
Gibson, Frances
  1974   *The Seafarers: Pre-Columbian Voyages to America.* Philadelphia: Dorrance & Co.
Gimbutas, Marija
  1989   *The Language of the Goddess.* San Francisco: Harper & Row.
Ginzberg, Louis
  1953   *The Legends of the Jews.* 7 Vols. Philadelphia: The Jewish Publications Society of America. Original Edition, 1909.

Girard, Rafael
  1962   *Los Mayas Eternos*. Mexico City: Antigüa Libereria Robredo.
  1966   *Los Mayas: Su civilizacion, su historia, sus vinculaciones continentales*. Mexico: Libro Mex. Editores.
  1972   *Le Popol Vuh*. Paris: Payot.
  1979   *Esotericism of the Popol Vuh*. Translated by Blair A. Moffett. Pasadena: Theosophical University Press.
Godfrey, Laurie R., and John Cole
  1979   "Biological Analogy, Diffusionism, and Archaeology." In *American Anthropologist* 81/3: 37-42.
Gohary, Jocelyn
  1992   *Akhenaten's Sed-festival at Karnak*. New York: Kegan Paul International.
Golan, Ariel
  1991   *Myth and Symbol: Symbolism in Prehistoric Religions*. Translated from the Russian by Rita Schneider-Teteruk. Jerusalem: Ariel Golan.
Goldsmith, Elizabeth E.
  1928   *Life Symbols*. New York: G. P. Putnam's Sons.
Gonen, Rivka
  1992   "The Late Bronze Age." In *The Archaeology of Ancient Israel*, edited by Amnon Ben-Tor, and translated by R. Greenberg. New Haven: Yale University Press, 211-57.
Goodenough, E. R.
  1964   *Jewish Symbols in the Greco-Roman Period*. New York: Pantheon.
  1988   *Jewish Symbols in the Greco-Roman Period*. Abridged edition, edited by Jacob Neusner. Princeton: Bollingen Series, Princeton University Press.
Gordon, Cyrus H.
  1971   *Before Columbus: Links Between the Old World and Ancient America*. New York: Crown Publishers.
  1974   *Riddles in History*. New York: Crown Publishers, Inc.
  1990   "A Hebrew Inscription Authenticated." In *By Study and Also by Faith* Vol. 1, edited by John M. Lundquist and Stephen D. Ricks. Salt Lake City: Deseret Book Company, and Provo, Utah: FARMS, 67-80.
Graulich, Michel
  1997   *Myths of Ancient Mexico*. Norman: University of Oklahoma Press.
Graves, Robert, and Raphael Patai
  1966   *Hebrew Myths: The Book of Genesis*. New York: McGraw Hill.
Gray, John
  1969   *Near Eastern Mythology*. New York: Hamlyn Publishing.
Greene-Robertson, Merle
  1991   *The Sculpture of Palenque, Vol. IV*. Princeton: Princeton University Press.
Greene-Robertson, Merle, Alfonso Morales, and David Stuart.
  1999   "Cross Group Project Discovers Tomb, Throne and Limestone Panel in Palenque." *Pre-Columbian Art Research Institute*, Newsletter No. 28, June 1.
Griffiths, J. Gwyn
  1960   *The Conflict of Horus and Seth*. Liverpool: Liverpool University Press.
  1970   *Plutarch's De Iside et Osiride*, translation and commentary. Cardiff, Wales: University of Wales Press.
  1980   *The Origins of Osiris and His Cult*. Supplement to no. XL. Leiden: E. J. Brill.
Grove, David C.
  1984   *Chalcatzingo: Excavations on the Olmec Frontier*. New York: Thames and Hudson.
Guernsey Kappelman, Julia
  1997   "Of Macaws and Men: Late Preclassic Cosmology and Political Ideology in Izapan-style Monuments." Ph.D. Diss. Austin: University of Texas.
Gutierrez, Mary Ellen
  1993   "Ballcourts: The Chasms of Creation." *Texas Notes on Precolumbian Art, Writing and Culture* 53. Austin: The Center for the History and Art of Ancient American Culture, Art Department, University of Texas, 1-3.
Hadingham, Evan
  1984   *Early Man and the Cosmos*. New York: Walker & Co.
Haran, Menahem
  1995   "Altar-ed States." *Bible Review* (February) 30-37, 48.
Harris, John
  1997   "Mayan Hieroglyphs Represented by Whole Human Bodies." *The Codex* 6/1, October. Philadelphia: University of Pennsylvania Museum of Archaeology and Anthropology.
Hart, George
  1986   *A Dictionary of Egyptian Gods and Goddesses*. London: Routledge & Kegan Paul.
  1990   *Egyptian Myths*. Austin: University of Texas.
Helck, H. W.
  1950   "Rp't auf dem Thron des Geb." *Orientalia* 19, cited in *Abraham in Egypt* by Hugh Nibley. Salt Lake City: Deseret Book Company, 1981: 46.
  1954   "Bemerkungen zum Ritual des Dramatischen Ramesseums-*papyrus*." *Orientalia* 23: 383-411.
Hellmuth, Nicholas M.
  1987   *Monster und Menschen in der Maya-Kunst*. Graz, Austria: Akademische Druck-u. Verlagsanstalt.
Henderson, Joseph L., and Maud Oakes
  1990   *The Wisdom of the Serpent*. Princeton: Princeton University Press.

Hestrin, Ruth
  1991   "Understanding Asherah." *Biblical Archaeology Review* 17/5: 50-59.
Heyden, Doris
  1975   "An Interpretation of the Cave Underneath the Pyramid of the Sun in Teotihuacan, Mexico." *American Antiquity* 40/2: 131-47.
  1981   "Caves, Gods, and Myths: World-View and Planning in Teotihuacan." In *Mesoamerican Sites and World-Views*, a Conference at Dumbarton Oaks, October 16 and 17, 1976, edited by Elizabeth P. Benson. Washington, D.C.: Dumbarton Oaks, 1-40.
  1983   *Mitologia y simbolismo de la flora en el Mexico prehispanico*. Mexico City: Universidad Nacional Autonoma de Mexico.
  1986   "Metaphors, Nahualtocaitl, and Other 'Disguised' Terms Among the Aztecs." In *Symbol and Meaning Beyond the Closed Community: Essays in Mesoamerican Ideas* Vol. 1, edited by Gary H. Gossen. Studies on Culture and Society. Albany: Institute for Mesoamerican Studies, University of Albany, 35-44.
  1987   "Mesoamerican Religions: Classic Cultures." In Vol. 9 of *The Encyclopedia of Religion*, edited by Mircea Eliade. New York: Macmillan Publishing Company, 409-19.
Highbarger, E. L.
  1940   *The Gates of Dreams*. Baltimore.
Hinnells, John R.
  1985   *Persian Mythology*. New York: Peter Bedrick Books.
Historia Tolteca-Chichimeca: Anales de Quauhtinchan
  1976   Edited by Paul Kirchoff, O. Gümes, and L. Reyes Gracia. Translated from Nahuatl into Spanish by Heinrich Berlin and Silvia Rendon. New edition. Mexico: Instituto Nacional de Antropologia e Historia
Histoyre du Mechique (Historia de Mexico)
  1965   In *Teogonia e Historia de los Mexicano*, edited by Angel Maria Garibay K., and translated by R. Rosales Munguia. Mexico: Editorial Porrúa, S.A., 91-116.
Hopfner, T.
  1941   *Plutarch über Isis u. Osiris*. Prague: I. Teil, Orientalisches Institute, Die Sage.
Hopkins, Nicholas A.
  1991   "Classic and Modern Relationship Terms and the 'Child of Mother' glyph (TI:606.23)." In *Sixth Palenque Round Table, 1986* Vol. 8, general editor Merle Greene-Robertson, volume editor Virginia M. Fields. Norman: University of Oklahoma Press, 255-65.
  Hornung, Erik
  1971   Politische Planung u. Realität im Alten Aegypten. *Saeculum* 22.
  1982   *Conceptions of God in Ancient Egypt: The One and the Many*. Translated by John Baines. Ithaca, New York: Cornell University Press.
  1990   *The Valley of the Kings: Horizon of Eternity*. Translated by David Warburton. New York: Timken Publishers, Inc.
  1992   *Idea Into Image*. Translated by Elizabeth Bredick. New York: Timken Publishers, Inc.
Houston, Stephen D.
  1993   *Hieroglyphs and History at Dos Pilas*. Austin: University of Texas Press.
  1996   "Symbolic Sweatbaths of the Maya: Architectural Meaning in the Cross Group at Palenque, Mexico." *Latin American Antiquity* 7/2: 132-51.
Houston, Stephen, and David Stuart
  1989   "The *Way* Glyph: Evidence for 'Co-essences' among the Classic Maya." *Research Reports on Ancient Maya Writing* 30. Washington, D.C.: Center for Maya Research.
  1996   "Of gods, glyphs and kings: divinity and rulership among the Classic Maya." *Antiquity* 70: 289-312.
Howey, M. Oldfield
  1989   *The Cat in Magic, Mythology, and Religion*. New York: Crescent Books.
Hristov, Romero H., and Santiago Genovés
  1998   "Viajes transatlánticos antes de Cólon." *Arqueologia Mexicana* VI/33: 48-53.
Hultkrantz, Ake
  1980   *The Religions of the American Indians*. Los Angeles: University of California Press.
Ions, Veronica
  1968   *Egyptian Mythology*. Middlesex: Hamlyn Publishing Group, Ltd.
Jacobsen, Thorkild
  1946   "Sumerian Mythology: A Review Article." *Journal of Near Eastern Studies* V: 134-38.
Jakeman, M. Wells
  1958   *Stela 5, Izapa, Chiapas, Mexico, a Major Archaeological Discovery of the New World*. Special Publication 2. Provo, Utah: The University Archaeological Society.
Jastrow, Morris
  1915   *The Civilization of Babylonia and Assyria*. Philadelphia: J. P. Lippincott Co.
Jett, Stephen C.
  1978   "Pre-Columbian Transoceanic Contacts." In *Ancient Native Americans*, edited by Jesse D. Jennings. San Francisco: W. H. Freeman and Company, 592-650.
  1996   "Comments on Covey's 'The Egypto-Libyan Presence in Precolumbian America'." In *Midwestern Epigraphic Journal* 10/1: 35-38.
Johnson, Buffie
  1990   *Lady of the Beasts*. New York: Harper Collins Publishers.
Jones, Carolyn, and Cheyenne Spetzler
  1992   "Where Have All the Fathers Gone? An Analysis of Site Q Altar 1." In *U Mut Maya IV*, edited by Tom and Carolyn Jones. Arcata, California: U Mut Maya, 104-16.

Jones, Tom
  1991   "Jaws II: Return of the Xoc." In *Sixth Palenque Round Table, 1986* Vol. 8, general editor Merle Greene-Robertson, volume editor Virginia M. Fields. Norman: University of Oklahoma Press, 246-54.
Josserand, J. Kathryn
  1991   "The Narrative Structure of Hieroglyphic Texts at Palenque." In *Sixth Palenque Round Table, 1986* Vol. 8, general editor Merle Greene-Robertson, volume editor Virginia M. Fields. Norman: University of Oklahoma Press, 12-31.
Junell, Cathy, and Brian Stross
  1994   "The Deer as Western Sun." In *U Mut Maya V*, edited by Carolyn and Tom Jones. Arcata, California: U Mut Maya, 239-46.
Justeson, John S.
  1989   "The Representational Conventions of Mayan Hieroglyphic Writing." In *Word and Image in Maya Culture*, edited by William F. Hanks and Don S. Rice. Salt Lake City: University of Utah Press, 25-38.
Kampen, Michael E.
  1972   *The Sculptures of El Tajin, Veracruz, Mexico.* Gainsville: University of Florida Press.
Kaplan, Jonathan
  2000   "Monument 65: A great emblematic depiction of throned rule and royal sacrifice at Late Preclassic Kaminaljuyu." *Ancient Mesoamerica* 11/2: 185-198.
Keel, Othmar
  1987   "The Peculiar Headrests for the Dead in First Temple Times." *Biblical Archaeology Review* 13/4: 50-53.
Kelley, David H.
  1976   *Deciphering the Maya Script.* Austin: University of Texas Press.
Kempinski, Aharon
  1992   "The Middle Bronze Age." In *The Archaeology of Ancient Israel*, edited by Amnon Ben-Tor, translated by R. Greenberg. New Haven: Yale University Press, 159-210.
Kerr, Justin
  1989   *The Maya Vase Book.* Vol. 1. New York: Kerr Associates.
  1990   *The Maya Vase Book.* Vol. 2. New York: Kerr Associates.
  1994   *The Maya Vase Book.* Vol. 4. New York: Kerr Associates.
Kidder, Alfred V., Jesse D. Jennings, and Edwin M. Shook
  1946   *Excavations at Kaminaljuyu, Guatemala.* Publication no. 561. Washington D.C.: Carnegie Institute of Washington.
Kingsborough (Edward King) Lord
  1848   "The Works of Ixtlilxochitl." In Vol. IX of *Antiquities of Mexico.* London: Henry G. Bohn, Pub.
Kitchen, K. A.
  1982   *Pharaoh Triumphant: The Life and Times of Ramesses II.* Ontario, Canada: Benben Publications. Klein, Cecelia F.
  1976   *The Face of the Earth.* New York: Garland Publishing, Inc.
  1987   "The Ideology of Autosacrifice at the Templo Mayor." In *The Aztec Templo Mayor*, edited by Elizabeth Hill Boone. Washington D.C.: Dumbarton Oaks, 293-370.
Knorozov, Yuri
  1982   *Maya Hieroglyphic Codices.* Translated from the Russian by Sophie D. Coe. Albany: Albany Institute for Mesoamerican Studies, State University of New York.
Koontz, Rex Ashley
  1992   "Cosmology and Natural Modeling Among Aboriginal American Peoples: Mesoamerica." Paper presented at the Second D. J. Sibley Conference on World Traditions of Culture and Art. Austin: University of Texas.
  1994   "The Iconography of El Tajin, Veracruz, Mexico." Ph.D. Diss. Austin: University of Texas.
Krauss, Rolf
  1997   "Astronomische Konzepte und Jenseitsvorstelungen in den pyramidentexten." *Aegyptologische Abhandlungen* 59. Wiesbaden: Harrassowitz.
Krickeberg, Walter, et al.
  1968   *Pre-Columbian American Religions.* Great Britain: George Weidenfeld and Nicolson, Ltd.
Kristensen, W. Brede
  1960   *The Meaning of Religion.* The Hague: Martinus Nijhoff.
Kroeber, A. L.
  1923   *Anthropology.* New York: Harcourt, Brace & Co.
Krupp, E. C.
  1983   *Echoes of the Ancient Skies: The Astronomy of Lost Civilizations.* New York: Harper & Row.
  1991   *Beyond the Blue Horizon: Myths and Legends of the Sun, Moon, Stars, and Planets.* New York: Harper Collins Publishers.
  1997   *Skywatchers, Shamans and Kings.* New York: John Wiley & Sons, Inc.
Kubler, George
  1962   *The Art and Architecture of Ancient America: The Mexican, Maya and Andean Peoples.* Baltimore: Pelican Press.
Kubler, George, and Charles Gibson
  1951   "The Tovar Calendar: An illustrated Mexican manuscript of ca. 1585." *Memoirs, Connecticut Academy of Arts and Sciences* 11.
Kurbjuhn, Kornelia
  1985   "Busts in Flowers: a Singular Theme in Jaina Figurines." In *Fourth Palenque Round Table 1980* Vol. VI, general editor Merle Greene-Robertson, volume editor Elizabeth P. Benson. San Francisco: Pre-Columbian Art Research Institute, 221-34.
Labbé, Armand J.
  1982   *Man and Cosmos in Prehispanic Mesoamerica.* Santa Ana, California: Bowers Museum Foundation.
Lafaye, Jaques
  1972   *Manuscrit Tovar: Origines et croyances des indiens du Mexique.* Graz, Austria: Akademische Druk-u. Verlagsanstalt.

Lambert, W. G.
    1968   "Myth and Ritual as Conceived by the Babylonians." *Journal of Semitic Studies* 13.

Lanzone, R. V.
    1881-85 *Dizionario di Mitologia Egisiz.* Vol. 2. Turin.

Laughton, Tim
    1998   "Izapa: A Preclassic Codex in Stone." *Indiana Journal of Hispanic Literatures* No. 13: 16-23.

Layard, Austen Henry
    1893   *The Monuments of Ninevah.* London.

LeFort, Genevieve
    1995   *Lady Alligator Foot Emerges From the Past: Maize God Iconography at Yomop.* Paris: Galerie Mermoz.

Leisegang, Hans
    1978   "The Mystery of the Serpent." In *The Mysteries: Papers from the Eranos Yearbooks* Vol. 2, edited by Joseph Campbell. Translated by Ralph Manheim, except for the paper by C. G. Jung which was translated by R. F. C. Hull. Princeton: Princeton University Press, Princeton: Princeton University Press, 194-160.

Leyenaar, Ted J., Gerald W. Van Bussel, and Gesine Weber
    1992   *Von Küste zu Küste: Prä-Kolumbische Skulpturen aus Meso-Amerika.* Germany: Verlag Weber & Weidemeyer Kassel.

Lichtheim, Miriam
    1973-80 *Ancient Egyptian Literature.* 3 vols. Berkeley: University of Calfiornia Press.

Lind, Michael, and Javier Urcid
    1983   "The Lords of Lambityeco and Their Nearest Neighbors." *Notas Americanas* 9: 78-111.

Lipp, Frank J.
    1991   *The Mixe of Oaxaca.* Austin: University of Texas Press.

Littauer, M. A., and J. H. Crouwel
    1979   *Wheeled Vehicles and Ridden Animals in the Ancient Near East.* Leiden: Brill.

Long, Bruce J.
    1987   "Underworld." In Vol. 15 of *The Encyclopedia of Religion*, edited by Mircea Eliade. 16 vols. New York: Macmillan Publishing Co., 126-34.

Looper, Matthew G.
    1991   "The Dances of the Classic Maya Deities *Chak* and *Hun Nal Ye*." Master's thesis, Art Department. Austin: University of Texas.

López Austin, Alfredo
    1987   "The Masked God of Fire." In *The Aztec Templo Mayor*, edited by Elizabeth Hill Boone. Washington, D.C.: Dumbarton Oaks, 257-92.

Lothrop, Samuel K.
    1952   "Metals from the Cenote of Sacrifice, Chichen Itza, Yucatan." *Memoirs of the Peabody Museum Memoirs of the Peabody Museum* 10/2. Cambridge, Massachusetts: Harvard University. Lounsbury, Floyd G.
    1985   "The Identities of the Mythological Figures in the Cross Group Inscriptions of Palenque." In *Fourth Palenque Round Table, 1980* Vol. VI, general editor Merle Greene-Robertson, volume editor Elizabeth P. Benson. San Francisco: Pre-Columbian Art Research Institute, 45-58.

Lumholtz, Carl
    1900   "Symbolism of the Huichol Indians." *Memoirs of the American Museum of Natural History* Vol. 1. New York: American Museum of Natural History, New York.

Lundquist, John M.
    1984   "The Common Temple Ideology of the Ancient Near East." In *The Temple in Antiquity* Vol. 9, edited by Truman Madsen. Provo, Utah: Religious Studies Center, Brigham Young University, 53-76.
    1993   *The Temple: Meeting Place of Heaven and Earth.* New York: Thames and Hudson.
    1994   "What is a Temple? A Preliminary Typology." In *Temples of the Ancient World: Ritual and Symbolism*, edited by Donald W. Perry. Salt Lake City: Deseret Book Co., and Provo, Utah: FARMS, 83-117.

Lurker, Manfred
    1980   *The Gods and Symbols of Ancient Egypt.* New York: Thames and Hudson.

MacLeod, Barbara
    1989   "The 819-Day-Count: A Soulful Mechanism." In *Word and Image in Maya Culture*, edited by William F. Hanks and Don S. Rice. Salt Lake City: University of Utah Press, 112-26.

MacLeod, Barbara, and Justin Kerr
    1994   *The Proceedings of the Maya Hieroglyphic Weekend, November 19-20, 1994.* Transcribed and edited by Phil Wanyerka. Cleveland: Cleveland State University.

Magelby, Kirk A.
    1979   "A Survey of Mesoamerican Bearded Figures." *F.A.R.M.S. Report*, MAG-79. Provo, Utah: F.A.R.M.S.

Makemson, M. W.
    1951   *The Book of the Jaguar Priest: A Translation of the Book of Chilam Balam of Tizimin, with Commentary.* New York: Henry Schuman.

Makenzie, Donald Alexander
    n.d.   *Myths of Pre-Columbian America.* London: Gresham Publishing Co. Ltd.

Marcus, Joyce
    1992a   "Royal Families, Royal Texts: Examples from the Zapotec and Maya." In *Mesoamerican Elites*, edited by Diane Z. Chase and Arlen F. Chase. Norman: University of Oklahoma Press, 221-41.
    1992b   *Mesoamerican Writing Systems: Propaganda, Myth, and History in Four Ancient Civilizations.* Princeton: Princeton University Press.

Mathews, Peter

    1980   "Notes on the Dynastic Sequence of Bonampak, Part 1." In *Third Palenque Round Table, 1978/Part 2* Vol. 5, edited by Merle Green Robertson. University of Texas Press, Austin, 60-73.

Matos Moctezuma, Eduardo

    1987a   "Symbolism of the Templo Mayor." In *The Aztec Templo Mayor*, edited by Elizabeth Hill Boone. Washington, D.C.: Dumbarton Oaks Research Library and Collection, 185-210.

    1987b   "The Templo Mayor of Tenochtitlan History and Interpretation." In *The Great Temple of Tenochtitlan: Center and Periphery in the Aztec World*, edited by Johanna Broda, David Carrasco, and Eduardo Matos Moctezuma. Berkeley: University of California Press, 15-60.

    1995   *Life and Death in the Templo Mayor*. Translated by Bernard R. and Thelma Ortiz Montellano. Niwot, Colorado: University Press of Colorado.

Maudslay, Alfred P.

    1889-02   *Archaeology: Biologia Centrali-Americana.* 5 vols. London: R. H. Porter and Dulau and Co.

McDonald, Andrew J.

    n.d.   "Izapa's Stela 5 in a Mesoamerica Setting" (unpublished manuscript).

McGee, John

    1993   "Place of Palenque in Lacandon Mythology." Paper presented at the IXth Texas Symposium, March 12. Austin: University of Texas.

McKeever Furst, Jill Leslie

    1995   *The Natural History of the Soul in Ancient Mexico*. New Haven: Yale University Press.

Mead, Margaret, and Nicolas Cales, Editors

    1953   *Primitive Heritage*. New York: Randon House.

Mercer, Samuel Alfred Brown

    1951   *The Pyramid Texts* Vol. 4. London: Longmans, Green.

Midrash Rabbah

    1961   Edited by H. Freedman and Maurice Simon. London: Socino Press. Original edition, 1939.

Milbrath, Susan

    1987   "Birth Images in Mixteca-Puebla Art." In *Role and Gender in Precolumbian Art and Architecture*, edited by Virginia E. Miller. Lanham: University Press of America.

Miller, Arthur G.

    1974   "The Iconography of the Painting in the Temple of the Diving God, Tulum, Quintana Roo, Mexico: The Twisted Cords." In *Mesoamerican Archaeology: New Approaches*, edited by Norman Hammon. London: Duckworth, 167-86.

    1991   "The Carved Stela in Tomb 5, Suchilquitongo, Oaxaca, Mexico." *Ancient Mesoamerica* 2/2: 215-24.

Miller, Jeffrey H.

    1974   "Notes on a Stelae Pair Probably from Calakmul, Campeche, Mexico." In *Primera Mesa Redonda de Palenque, Part I*, edited by Merle Greene-Robertson. Pebble Beach, California: Pre-Columbian Art Research, 149-61.

Miller, Mary Ellen

    1986   *The Art of Mesoamerica from Olmec to Aztec*. New York: Thames and Hudson.

    1999   *Maya Art and Architecture*. London: Thames and Hudson, Ltd.

Miller, Mary, and Karl Taube

    1993   *Gods and Symbols of Ancient Mexico and the Maya: An Illustrated Dictionary of Mesoamerican Religion*. New York: Thames & Hudson.

Millon, René

    1981   "Teotihuacan: City, State and Civilization." In *Supplement to the Handbook of Middle American Indians, Vol. I*, edited by Victoria R. Bricker and Jeremy A. Sabloff. Austin: University of Texas Press, 198-243.

Morell, Virginia

    1990   "Research News: Confusion in Earliest America." *Science* (27 April): 248.

    1998   "Genes May Link Ancient Eurasians, Native Americans." *The American Association for the Advancement of Science* 280/5363: 520.

Morenz, Siegfried

    1990   *Egyptian Religion*. Translated from the German by Anne E. Keep. Ithaca, New York: Cornell University Press. Original Edition, "Ägyptische Religion." *Religionsen der Menschheit* 8. Stuttgart: Kolhammer, 1960.

Moret, A.

    1913   *Mysteres Egyptiens*. Paris: A. Colin.

Mountjoy, Joseph B.

    1982   "An Interpretation of the Pictographs at La Pena Pintada, Jalisco, Mexico." *American Antiquity* 47(1): 110-126.

Moyer, David

    1994   "Temples, Tombs and the Egyptian Universe: an ARCE Brooklyn Museum Symposium Report." *KMT* 5/2: 61-64, 78-83.

Museum of Primitive Art

    1964   *A Maya Sculpture in Wood*. New York: Museum of Primitive Art.

Naville, Edouard

    1877   "Le dieu Thoth et les points cardinaux." *Zeitschrift fuer Aegyptische Sprache und Altertumskunde* 15: 28-31.

Neumann, Erich

    1974   *The Great Mother*. Translated by Ralph Manheim. Princeton: Princeton University Press.

Neurath, Marie

    1964   *They Lived Like This in Ancient Egypt*. Isotype Institute, Franklin Watts, Inc.

New Larousse Encyclopedia of Mythology
    1972   New York: Paul Hamlyn. Original edition, 1959.

Nibley, Hugh
    1951   "The Hierocentric State." *Western Political Quarterly* 4.
    1981   *Abraham in Egypt*. Salt Lake City: Deseret Book Company.
    1992   *Temple and Cosmos*. Salt Lake City: Deseret Book Company, and Provo, Utah: F.A.R.M.S.

Nicholson, Henry B.
    1971   "Religion in Prehispanic Central Mexico." In Vol. 10/1, *Handbook of Middle American Indians*, edited by Robert Wauchope. Austin: University of Texas Press, 396-446.

Nicholson, Henry B., and Rainer Berger
    1968   "Two Aztec Wood Idols." *Studies in Pre-Columbian Art and Archaeology* 5. Washington, D.C.: Dumbarton Oaks.

Nicholson, Irene
    1959   *Firefly in the Night*. London: Faber and Faber.
    1967   *Mexican and Central American Mythology*. New York: Paul Hamlyn.

Nielsen, Kjeld
    1991   "Ancient Aromas: Good and Bad." *Bible Review* (June): 26-33.

Niwiski, Andrzej
    1989   *Theban Funerary Papyri*. Freiburg, Switzerland: Universitäts-Verlag.

Norman, V. Garth
    1976   "Izapa Sculpture." Part 1: *Text. Papers of the New World Archaeological Foundation, No. 30*. Provo, Utah: New World Archaeological Foundation, Brigham Young University.

Nuttall, Zelia
    1901   "The Fundamental Principles of Old and New World Civilizations: A Comparative Research Based on a Study of the Ancient Mexican Religious, Sociological and Calendrical Systems," Vol. II. *Archaeological and Ethnological Papers of the Peabody Museum*. Cambridge, Massachusetts: Harvard University.

Oesterley, W. O. E.
    1933   "Early Hebrew Festival Rituals." In *Myth and Ritual*, edited by S. H. Hooke. London: Oxford University Press.

Olmec Art
    1997   *Arqueologia Mexicana*. Special Edition, Mexico.

Parabola
    1993   "Where You Want to Be: An Investigation of the *Popol Vuh*." XVIII/3. New York: Society for the Study of the Myth & Tradition.

Parsons, Lee Allen
    1969   "Bilbao, Guatemala: An Archaeological Study of the Pacific Coast Cotzumalhuapa Region Vol. 2." *Publications in Anthropology* 12. Milwaukee, Wisconsin: Milwaukee Public Museum.

Pasztory, Esther
    1997   *Teotihuacan: An Experiment in Living*. Norman: University of Oklahoma Press.

Patai, Raphael
    1978   *The Hebrew Goddess*. New York: A Discus Book, Avon Books.
    1983   *On Jewish Folklore*. Detroit: Wayne State University Press.
    1998   *The Children of Noah: Jewish Seafaring in Ancient Times*. Princeton: Princeton University Press.

Perry, John Weir
    1991   *Lord of the Four Quarters: The Mythology of Kingship*. New York: Paulist Press.

Peterson, Jeanette Favrot
    1990   *Precolumbian Flora and Fauna: Continuity of Plant and Animal Themes in Mesoamerican Art*. La Jolla, California: Mingei International.

Piankoff, Alexandre
    1942   *Le Livre du Jour et de la Nuit*. Cairo: Inst. Fr. d'Arch.
    1955   *The Shrines of Tut-Ank-Amon*. Bollingen Series XL/2. New York: Bollingen.

Pickands, Martin
    1980   "The 'First Father' Legend in Maya Mythology and Iconography." In *Third Palenque Round Table, 1978/Part 2* Vol. 5, edited by Merle Greene-Robertson. Austin: University of Texas Press, 124-37.

Piña Chan, Roman
    1960   *Mesoamerica*. Cordoba, Mexico: Instituto Nacional de Antropologia e Historia.

Pohl, Mary
    1981   "Ritual Continuity and Change in Mesoamerica: Reconstructing the Ancient Maya Cuch Ritual." *American Antiquity* 46: 513-29.

Pritchard, James B.
    1969   *Ancient Near Eastern Texts Relating to the Old Testament*. 3rd Edition. Princeton: Princeton University.

Proskouriakoff, Tatiana
    1963   "Historical Data in the Inscriptions of Yaxchilan, Part I." *Estudios de Cultura Maya* 3:149-67.
    1974   "Jades from the Cenote of Sacrifice, Chichen Itza." *Memoires of the Peabody Museum, Harvard University* 10/1.

Quenon, Michel, and Genevieve le Fort
    1997   "Rebirth and Resurrection in Maize God Iconography." In *The Maya Vase Book* Vol. 5, by Justin Kerr, edited by Barbara and Justin Kerr. New York: Kerr Associates, 884-99.

Quirarte, Jacinto
    1977   "Early Art Styles of Mesoamerican and Early Classic Maya Art." In *The Origins of Maya Civilization*, SAR, edited by Richard E. W. Adams. Albuquerque: University of New Mexico Press, 249-83.

Quirke, Stephen
    1992   *Ancient Egyptian Religion*. London: British Museum Press.

Recinos, Adrián, and Delia Goetz
    1974   *The Annals of the Cakchiquels*. Norman: University of Oklahoma.

Recinos, Adrián, Delia Goetz, and Sylvanus G. Morley
    1950   *Popol Vuh: The Sacred Book of the Ancient Quiché Maya*. Norman: University of Oklahoma Press.

Reeder, Greg
    1993   "Running the Heb Sed." *KMT* 4/4: 60-71.

Reents-Budet, Dorie
    1994   *Painting the Maya Universe: Royal Ceramics of the Classic Period*. Durham: Duke University Press.

Reilly, Kent
    1992   "Cosmology and Rulership at the Olmec Site of La Venta, 900-500 B.C." Paper presented at *Origins: Creation and Continuity: Mythology and History in Mesoamerica*. The Maya Meetings at Texas, March 12-13, 1992, VIIIth Texas Symposium. Austin: University of Texas.
    1995   "Art, Ritual, and Rulership in the Olmec World." In *The Olmec World: Ritual and Rulership*. Princeton: The Art Museum, Princeton University, 27-46.

Remington, Judith Ann
    1981   "Mesoamerican Archaeoastronomy: Parallax, Perspective, and Focus." In *Archaeoastronomy in the Americas*, edited by Ray A. Williamson. Ballena Press Anthropological Papers, No. 22. Los Altos, California: Ballena Press, 200-202.

Ritner, Robert
    1989   "Horus on the Crocodiles: A Juncture of Religion and Magic in Late Dynastic Egypt." In *Religion and Philosophy in Ancient Egypt*, Yale Egyptological Studies 3, edited by William K. Simpson. New Haven: Yale University, 106-08.
    1993   *The Mechanics of Ancient Egyptian Magical Practices*. Chicago: Oriental Institute.

Robicsek, Francis
    1981   *The Maya Book of the Dead: The Ceramic Codex*. Charlottesville, Virginia: University of Virginia Art Museum.

Robinson, Theodore H.
    1933   "Hebrew Myths." In *Myth and Ritual*, edited by S. H. Hooke. London: Oxford University Press.

Roe, Peter G.
    1982   *The Cosmic Zygote: Cosmology in the Amazon Basin*. New Brunswick, New Jersey: Rutgers University Press.

Rosenberg, R. A.
    1965   "Jesus, Isaac, and the 'Suffering Servant'." *Journal of Biblical Literature* 84: 381-88.

Roys, Ralph L.
    1940   "Personal names of the Maya of Yucatan." *Carnegie Institution of Washington* Pub. 523, Contrib. 31, Washington, D.C.: Carnegie Institution of Washington.

Saad, Zaki Y.
    1969   *The Excavations at Helwan*. Norman: University of Oklahoma Press.

Sadovszky, Otto J. von
    1995   *Fish Symbol and Myth*. ISTOR Books 6. Budapest: Akadémia Kiadó.

Sahagún, Bernardino de
    1946   *Historia General de las Cosas de Nueva Espana*. S. A. Mexico: Editorial Nueva Espana.
    1953-82   *Florentine Codex: General History of the Things of New Spain*. Edited and translated by Arthur J. O. Anderson and Charles E. Dibble. Monographs of the School of American Research, no. 14. 12 bks., 13 pts. Sante Fe, New Mexico; and Salt Lake City: University of Utah Press.

Sammons, Kay
    1995   "Rhetorical Functions of Parallelism in Sierra Populuca." Ph.D. Diss. Austin: University of Texas.

Santillana, Giorgio de, and Hertha von Dechend
    1977   *Hamlet's Mill*. Boston: David R. Godine.

Sarna, Nahum M.
    1966   *Understanding Genesis*. New York: McGraw Hill.

Saul, J.
    1989-93   "As it is Above, so shall it be Below." *Archaeoastronomy* XI: 104-07.

Sayer, Chloë
    1991   *The Skeleton at the Feast: The Day of the Dead in Mexico*. Austin: University of Texas Press.

Schauss, Hayyim
    1938   *The Jewish Festivals*. Translated by Samuel Jaffe. New York: Schocken Books.

Schele, Linda
    1988   "The Xibalba Shuffle: A Dance After Death." In *Maya Iconography*, edited by Elizabeth P. Benson and Gillett G. Griffin. Princeton: Princeton University Press, 294-317.
    1990   "House Names and Dedication Rituals at Palenque." In *Vision & Revision in Maya Studies*, edited by Flora S. Clancy and Peter D. Harrison. Albuquerque: University of New Mexico Press, 143-58.
    1991   *Workbook for the XVth Maya Hieroglyphic Workshop of Texas*. Department of Art and Art History and the Institute of Latin American Studies. Austin: The University of Texas.
    1992a   *Workbook for the XVIth Maya Hieroglyphic Workshop at Texas*. Department of Art and Art History and the Institute of Latin American Studies. Austin: The University of Texas.
    1992b   *The Proceedings of the Maya Hieroglyphic Workshop, March 14-15, 1992*. Transcribed and edited by Phil Wanyerka. Austin: University of Texas.

1996   "The Olmec Mountain and Tree of Creation in Mesoamerican Cosmology." In *The Olmec World: Ritual and Rulership*. Princeton: The Art Museum, Princeton University, 105-117.

n.d.   Lords of Tikal lecture tour, December 1992 - January 1993, in association with Far Horizons Tours.

Schele, Linda, and David Freidel

1990   *A Forest of Kings: The Untold Story of the Ancient Maya*. New York: William Morrow and Company, Inc.

1991   "The Courts of Creation: Ballcourts, Ballgames, and Portals to the Maya Otherworld." In *The Mesoamerican Ballgame*, edited by Vernon L. Scarborough and David R. Wilcox. Tucson: University of Arizona Press, 289-316.

Schele, Linda, and Nikolai Grube

1994   "Some Revisions to Tikal's Dynasty of Kings." *Texas Notes on Precolumbian Art, Writing, and Culture* 67. Austin: Center of the History and Art of Ancient American Culture of the Art Department, University of Texas, 1-9.

Schele, Linda, and Peter Mathews

1993   *Notebook for the XVIIth Maya Hieroglyphic Workshop at Texas*. Austin: University of Texas.

1998   *The Code of Kings: The Language of Seven Sacred Maya Temples and Tombs*. New York: Scribner.

Schele, Linda, and Mary Ellen Miller

1986   *The Blood of Kings: Dynasty and Ritual in Maya Art*. New York: George Braziller, Inc., in association with the Kimbell Art Museum, Fort Worth, Texas.

Schellhas, Paul

1904   "Comparative Studies in the Field of Maya Antiquities." In *Central American Antiquities, Calendar Systems, and History* Bulletin 28. Translated by Charles P. Bowditch. Washington, D.C.: Smithsonian Institution.

Scott, Oral E.

1942   *The Stars in Myth and Fact*. Caldwell, Idaho: Caxton Printers, Ltd.

Sedat, David W.

1992   "Preclassic Notation and the Development of Maya Writing." In *New Theories on the Ancient Maya*, edited by Elin C. Danien and Robert J. Sharer. Philadelphia: University Museum, University of Pennsylvania, 81-90.

Séjourné, Laurette

1956   *Burning Water*. New York: Vanguard Press.

Seler, Eduard

1902-03   *Codex Vaticanus B*. English edition by A. H. Keane. Berlin and London.

1904   "The Mexican Chronology," *Mexican and Central American Antiquities, Calendar Systems, and History* Bulletin 28. Translated by Charles P. Bowditch. Washington, D.C.: Smithsonian Institution.

Sellers, Jane B.

1992   *The Death of Gods in Ancient Egypt*. New York: Penguin.

Sethe, K.

1928   *Das 'Denkmal memphitischer Theologie', der Schabakostein des British Museum*, Pt. 1of *Dramatische Texte zur altäag Mysterienspielen*. Leipzig: J. C. Hinrichs.

Shanks, Hershel

1999   "Everything You Ever Knew About Jerusalem Is Wrong." *Biblical Archaeology Review* 25/6: 20-29.

Shook, Edwin M., and Elayne Marquis

1996   *Secrets in Stone: Yokes, Hachas and Palmas from Southern Mesoamerica*. Independence Square, Philadelphia: American Philosophical Society.

Sibbett Jr., Ed

1978   *Ancient Egyptian Design*. New York: Dover Publications, Inc.

Silverman, David P.

1991   "Divinity and Deities in Ancient Egypt." In *Religion in Ancient Egypt*, edited by Byron E. Shafer. Ithaca: Cornell University Press, 7- 87.

Sjöö, Monica, and Barbara Mor

1987   *The Great Cosmic Mother*. San Francisco: Harper & Row, Publishers.

Smith, Joseph Lindon

1956   *Tombs, Temples, and Ancient Art*. Norman: University of Oklahoma Press.

Smith, William and Samuel Cheetham

1968   *A Dictionary of Christian Antiquities* [reprint, 1875-80, London], Vol. 2. New York: Kraus.

Sorenson, John L.

1998   *Images of Ancient America*. Provo, Utah: Research Press.

Sorenson, John L., and Martin H. Raish

1996   Pre-Columbian Contacts with the Americas Across the Ocean: An Annotated Bibliography. 2 Vols. Provo, Utah: F.A.R.M.S.

Spalinger, Anthony

1995   "Some Remarks on the Epigomenal Days in Egypt." *Journal of Near Eastern Studies* 54/1: 33-47.

Spence, Lewis

1990   *Ancient Egyptian Myth and Legends*. New York: Dover Publications, Inc.

Spencer, A. J.

1991   *Death in Ancient Egypt*. Reprint, New York: Penguin Books. Original edition, New York: Pelican Books, 1982.

Spinden, Herbert J.

1975   *A Study of Maya Art*. New York: Dover.

Standard Dictionary of Folklore, Mythology and Legend Vol. 1.

1949   New York: Funk and Wagnalls Co.

Stanton, Doug

1997   "South of the Border, Upside-Down Mexico Way." *Outside Magazine* (February).

Stengel, Mark K.

2000   "The Diffusionists Have Landed." *The Atlantic Monthly* 285/1: 35-48.

Stross, Brian

1992   "Maize and Blood: Mesoamerican Symbolism on an Olmec Vase and a Maya Plate." *RES: Anthropology and Aesthetics* 22: 82-107.

1994a   "Maize and Fish." *RES: Anthropology and Aesthetics* 25: 10-35.

1994b   "Glyphs on Classic Maya Vessels: The Introductory Formula of the Primary Standard Sequence." In *Seventh Palenque Round Table, 1989* Vol. IX, general editor Merle Greene-Robertson, volume editor Virginia M. Fields. San Francisco: The Pre-Columbian Art Research Institute, 187-94.

Stuart, David.

1984   "Blood Symbolism in Maya Iconography." *RES: Anthropology and Aesthetics* 7/8: 6-20.

Sullivan, Thelma D.

1976   "The Mask of Itztlacolichqui." *Actas del XLI Congreso Internacional de Americanistas, Mexico*, 1974, 2: 252-62. Mexico.

Tarn, Nathaniel, and Martin Prechtel

1981   "Metaphors of relative elevation, position and ranking in Popol Vuh." *Estud. Cult. Maya* 13: 105-23.

Tate, Carolyn E.

1991   "The Period-Ending Stelae of Yaxchilan." In *Sixth Palenque Round Table, 1986* Vol. 8, general editor by Merle Greene-Robertson, volume editor Virginia M. Fields. Norman: University of Oklahoma Press, 102-209.

1992   *Yaxchilan: The Design of a Maya Ceremonial City.* Austin: University of Texas Press.

Taube, Karl A.

1985   "The Classic Maya Maize God: A Reappraisal." In *Fifth Palenque Round Table, 1983* Vol. VII, general editor Merle Greene-Robertson, volume edition Virginia M. Fields. San Francisco: The Pre-Columbian Art Research Institute, 171-83.

1986   "The Teotihuacan Cave of Origin: The iconography and architecture of emergence mythology in Mesoamerica and the American Southwest." *RES: Anthropology and Aesthetics* 12: 51-82.

1988a   "The Ancient Yucatec New Year Festival: The Liminal Period in Maya Ritual and Cosmology ," 1: Text. Ph.D. Diss. New Haven: Yale University.

1988b   "A Study of Classic Maya Scaffold Sacrifice." In *Maya Iconography*, edited by Elizabeth P. Benson and Gillett G. Griffin. Princeton: Princeton University Press, 331-51.

1992a   "The Iconography of Rain and Lightning in Ancient Maya Myth and Ritual." Paper presented at The Maya Meetings at Texas, "Origins: Creation and Continuity: Mythology and History in Mesoamerica," VIIIth Texas Symposium. Austin: University of Texas.

1992b   "The Major Gods of Ancient Yucatan." *Studies in Pre-Columbian Art & Archaeology* 32. Washington, D.C.: Dumbarton Oaks.

1992c   The Temple of Quetzalcoatl. *RES: Anthropology and Aesthetics* 21: 53-87.

1996a   "The Rainmakers: The Olmec and Their Contribution to Mesoamerican Belief and Ritual." In *The Olmec World: Ritual and Rulership*. Princeton: The Art Museum, Princeton University, 83-104.

1996b   The Olmec Maize God. *RES: Anthropology and Aesthetics* 29/30: 39-81.

Taylor, Dicey

1992   "Painted Ladies: Costumes for Women on Tepeu Ceramics." In *The Maya Vase Book* Vol. 3, by Justin Kerr. New York: Kerr Associates, 513-25.

Tedlock, Barbara

1982   *Time and the Highland Maya.* Revised edition. Albuquerque: University of New Mexico Press.

Tedlock, Dennis

1985   *Popol Vuh: The Definitive Edition of the Mayan Book of the Dawn of Life and the Glories of Gods and Kings.* New York: Simon and Schuster, Inc.

1992   "Myth, Math, and the Problem of Correlation in Mayan Books." In *The Sky in Mayan Literature*, edited by Anthony F. Aveni. New York: Oxford University Press, 247-273.

1996   *Popol Vuh: The Definitive Edition of the Mayan Book of the Dawn of Life and the Glories of Gods and Kings.* Revised edition. New York: Simon and Schuster, Inc.

Thompson, Gunnar

1989   *Nu Sun: Asian-American Voyages 500 B.C.* Fresno: Pioneer Publishing Co..

1992   *American Discovery.* Seattle: Argonauts Misty Isles Press.

Thompson, Henry O.

1967   "Tell el-Husn—Biblical Beth-shan." *Biblical Archaeologist* 30/4: 110-35.

Thompson, J. Eric S.

1937   *Mexico Before Cortez.* New York: Charles Scribners. Original edition, 1933.

1950   *Maya Hieroglyphic Writing.* Publication 589. Washington, D.C.: Carnegie Institution of Washington.

1954   *The Rise and Fall of Maya Civilization.* Norman: University of Oklahoma Press.

1962   *A Catalog of Maya Hieroglyphs.* Norman: University of Oklahoma Press.

1970   *Maya History and Religion.* Norman: University of Oklahoma Press.

1972   *A Commentary on the Dresden Codex.* Vol. 93. Philadelphia: American Philosophical Society.

Thureau-Dangin, François

1921   *Rituals Accadiens.* Paris: Leroux.

Tilley, Maureen

1992   "Typological Numbers: Taking a Count of the Bible." *Bible Review* (June). Tondrian, J.

1950   "Le tatouage sacre et la relig. de dionysiaque." *Aegyptus* 30: 57-66.

Tower Hollis, Susan
    1990   *The Ancient Egyptian "Tale of Two Brothers": The Oldest Fairytale in the World*. Norman: University of Oklahoma.
    1994-95   5 Egyptian Goddesses. *KMT* 5/4: 45-51, 82-85.

Townsend, Richard Fraser
    1979   "State and Cosmos in the Art of Tenochtitlan." *Studies in Pre-Columbian Art and Archaeology* 20. Washington, D.C.: Dumbarton Oaks.
    1987   "Coronation at Tenochtitlan." In *The Aztec Templo Mayor*, edited by Elizabeth Hill Boone, Washington, D.C.: Dumbarton Oaks, 371-410.

Tozzer, Alfred M.
    1941   "Landa's Relación de las Cosas de Yucatán." *Papers of the Peabody Museum of American Archaeology and Ethnology* 18. Cambridge, Massachusetts: Harvard University.

Turner, Wilson G.
    1980   *Maya Design*. New York: Dover.

Tvedtnes, John A.
    1983   "Burial as a Return to the Womb in Ancient Near Eastern Belief." *Newsletter and Proceedings of the Society for Early Historic Archaeology* 152. Provo, Utah: S.E.H.A., 5-7.

Umberger, Emily
    1987   "Events Commemorated by Date Plaques at the Templo Mayor: Further Thoughts on the Solar Metaphor." In *The Aztec Templo Mayor*, edited by Elizabeth Hill Boone. Washington, D.C.: Dumbarton Oaks, 411-50.

Urcid, Javier
    1993   "The Pacific Coast of Oaxaca and Guerrero." *Ancient Mesoamerica* 4/1: 141-66.

van Kirk, Jacques, and Parney Bassett-van Kirk
    1996   *Remarkable Remains of the Ancient Peoples of Guatemala*. Norman: University of Oklahoma Press.

van Zantwijk, R. A. M.
    1977   *Handel en Wandel van de Azteken De Sociale geschiedenis van voor-Spaans*. Assen/Amsterdam: Van Gorcum.

Vogt, Evon Z.
    1969   *Zinacantan: A Maya Community in the Highlands of Chiapas*. Cambridge, Massachusetts: The Belknap Press of Harvard University Press.
    1970   *Zinacantecos of Mexico*. 1st Edition, Holt, Rinehart, and Winston.

Wagner, Elizabeth
    2002   "Jade – theGreen Gold of the Maya." In *Maya: Divine Kings of the Rain Forest*, edited by Nicolai Grube. Cologne, Germany: Könemann Verlagsgesellschaft, mbh, 66-69.

Walker, Barbara G.
    1988   *The Woman's Dictionary of Symbols and Sacred Objects*. San Francisco: Harper and Row, Publishers.

Ward, W. H.
    1910   *Seal Cylinders of Western Asia*. Washington D.C.

Waters, Frank
    1950   *Masked Gods: Navaho and Pueblo Ceremonialism*. Chicago: Swallow Press, Inc.

Watterson, Barbara
    1998   *The House of Horus at Edfu: Ritual in an Ancient Egyptian Temple*. Stroud, Glousestershire: Tempus Publishing Limited.

Wertime, Richard A., and Angela M. H. Schuster
    1983   *Inanna: Queen of Heaven and Earth*. New York: Harper & Row, Publishers.
    1993   "Written in the Stars: Celestial Origin of Maya Creation." *Archaeology* 46/4: 26-32.

Widengren, Geo
    1951   *The King and the Tree of Life in Ancient Near Eastern Religion*. Wiesbaden, Germany: Uppsala Universitets Ärsskrift.

Wili, Walter
    1990   "The Orphic Mysteries and the Greek Spirit." In *The Mysteries: Papers from the Eranos Yearbooks* Vol. 2, edited by Joseph Campbell. Translated by Ralph Manheim, except for the paper by C. G. Jung which was translated by R. F. C. Hull. Princeton: Princeton University Press, 64-92.

Wilkinson, Richard H.
    1992   *Reading Egyptian Art: A Hieroglyphic Guide to Ancient Egyptian Painting and Sculpture*. New York: Thames and Hudson.
    1994   *Symbol & Magic in Egyptian Art*. New York: Thames and Hudson.

Winfield Capitaine, Fernando
    1990   *La Estella 1 de la Mojarra*. Mexico: Universidad Nacional Autonoma de Mexico.

Winters, Diane
    1991   "A Study of the Fish-in-Hand Glyph, T714: Part I." In *Sixth Palenque Round Table,1986* Vol. 8, edited by Merle Greene-Robertson and Virginia M. Fields. Norman: University of Oklahoma Press, 233-45.

Wirth, Diane
    1996   "The Seven Primordial Tribes: A Mesoamerican Tradition." *Ancient America Foundation Newsletter* 8: 1-8.
    1998   "Through Death Comes Life: The Dying and Resurrecting Grain Gods of Mesoamerica and Egypt." Paper presented at "The Aesthetics of Enchantment," a conference sponsored by The American Society of Phenomenology, Aesthetics & the Fine Arts, Harvard Divinity School, April 18-20, 1998. Cambridge, Massachusetts: Harvard University.

Wirth, Diane, and Brian Stross
    1997   "The 'le' Motif: Symbol of Lineage and Fertility Among the Olmec and Maya." In *U Mut Maya* VI, edited by Carolyn and Tom Jones. Bayside, California: U Mut Maya, 81-90.

Wise, Michael, Martin Abegg, Jr., and Edward Cook.
    1996   *The Dead Sea Scrolls: a New Translation*. San Francisco: Harper Collins.

Witt, R. E.

1997   *Isis in the Ancient World*. Baltimore, Maryland: John Hopkins University. Originally published in 1971 as *Isis in the Graeco-Roman World*, Ithaca, New York: Cornell University Press, 1971.

Wolkstein, Diane, and Samuel Noah Kramer

1983   *Inanna: Queen of Heaven and Earth*. New York: Harper & Row, Publishers.

Wosien, Marie Gabriele

1974   *Sacred Dance: Encounter with the Gods*. New York: Thames and Hudson.

von Wuthenau, Alexander

1965   *The Art of Terracotta Pottery in Pre-Columbian Central and South America*. New York: Crown Publishers.

1975   *Unexpected Faces in Ancient America*. New York: Crown Publishers.

Zehren, Erich

1962   *The Crescent and the Bull: a Survey of Archaeology in the Near East*. Translated from the German by James Cleugh. New York: Hawthorn Books, Inc.

Zingg, Robert M.

1982   *Los Huicholes: Una Tribu de Artistas*. 2 Vols. Translated by C. Paschero. Mexico: INI.

INDEX

208

ORDER FORM

for

PARALLELS: Mesoamerican and Ancient Middle Eastern Traditions

ISBN: 0-9602096-0-3
LCCN: 2003090603

by
Diane E. Wirth

Price:$17.95

1 Book . . . . .no discount
1 - 4 Books . . . . .20% off
5 - 9 Books . . . . .30% off
10 - 24 Books . . . . .40% off
25 - 49 Books . . . . .42% off
40 -74 Books . . . . .44% off
75 - 199 Books . . . . .48% off
200 or More Books . . . . .50% off

Sales Tax: Please add 6.25% for books sent to Utah addresses

Shipping & Handling: $2.50 for first book and $2.00 for each additional book.

Send Check to: Stonecliff Publishing
P.O. Box 911060
St. George, UT 84791-1060

Mail Book(s) to:

Name: _____

Address: _____

City: _____ **State:** _____ **Zip:** _____

E-Mail: stonecliffpub@aol.com